WORLDWIDE ISSUES IN GEOGRAPHY

Editor: Clive Hart

John Chaffey   Steve Crossley
Jane Entwistle   Nicholas Foskett
Rosalind Foskett

COLLINS EDUCATIONAL

Acknowledgements

The authors and publishers would like to thank the following for copyright information used in maps and diagrams.

Action Aid; Edward Arnold, *The Urban Environment* by I. Douglas (1983); Nick Baker, The Standard; Berkshire County Council; BSC Industry; Cambridge University Local Examinations; Croom Helm Ltd, *Where the Grass is Greener* by D. Smith; W.M. Dawson and Sons, *Studies in Industrial Geography – France* by J.H. Tuppen (1980); The Economist, *Britain's Urban Breakdown* (1982); Darwen Finlayson, *A History of Yorkshire* by W. Tate and F. Singleton; The Geographical Association, *Geography* Vol. 66: Fig. 6 Part 1, Fig. 1 Part 4; The Geographical Magazine, London; R.J.A. Goodland, 'Environmental Ranking of Amazonian Development Projects' in *Environmental Conservation* Vol. 7 (1980); The Guardian; Her Majesty's Stationery Office; Hong Kong Housing Authority; Methuen and Co., *Industrial Location and Planning in the United Kingdom* by D. Keeble (1976); Milton Keynes Development Corporation; New Internationalist; New Scientist; The Observer; Ordnance Survey; Oxfam; Oxford University Press; Penguin Books, *Oil and World Power* by P.R. Odell; Pergamon Press, *Cityport Industrialisation and Regional Development* ed. B. Hoyle; George Philip and Son Ltd, *Geographical Digest; Population Concern; Reuters;* Royal Geographical Society, *The Geographical Journal,* Vol. 149; Sage Publications Inc, 'Urban Britain: Beyond Containment' by R. Drewett, J. Goddard and N. Spence in *Urbanization and Counterurbanization* by B.J.L. Berry (1976); Sohio America, *Prudhoe Bay and Beyond;* State of the World Atlas; The Swanage Times; The Daily Telegraph; Times Newspapers Ltd; Timsway Holidays; Unicef; The University of Southampton; United States Department of the Interior, Bureau of Mines; VSO; Welsh Development Agency; John Wiley, *Regional Development in Western Europe* by H.D. Clout; World Bank, *World Development Report 1982* (OUP).

Photographs

Aero Camera Fig. 4.10; Aspect Picture Library p.14; Associated Press Fig. 7.21; Barnaby's Picture Library Fig. 2.9; James P. Blaird (c) 1983 National Geographic Society Fig. 5.77; Paul Brierley Fig. 5.11; British Steel Corporation Fig. 4.6; Dr Miriam Boyle Figs. 6.33, 6.34; Camerapix Hutchison Library Figs. 3.8, 3.22; Camera Press Figs. 4.32, 6.4; J. Allan Cash p. 35, Figs. 5.40, 5.41, 5.80, 5.82; Central Electricity Generating Board Fig. 6.39; Citroën Fig. 4.26; Danish Embassy Fig. 5.91; Danish Tourist Board p. 75; Earthscan Fig. 5.91; An Esso Photograph Fig. 4.9; Mary Evans Picture Library Fig. 2.17; Greenpeace Fig. 4.31; Robert Harding Picture Library Fig. 5.91; Hong Kong Housing Association Figs. 1.4, 1.5, 1.7; Frank Lane Picture Agency Fig. 7.8, 7.9, 7.14, 8.1; S.J. Lavender from *New Land for Old* (pub. Longman) Fig. 4.30; Mansell Collection Fig. 2.18; Milton Keynes Development Corporation Fig. 3.33; National Coal Board Fig. 6.31; Oxfam p. 1, Fig. 3.23; Panasonic UK Ltd Fig. 4.20; The Press Association Figs. 3.1a and b; Popperfoto Fig. 7.18; David Richardson Fig. 3.26; Rio Tinto Zinc Ltd Figs. 6.3, 6.5; Dr D.J. Spooner Fig. 6.30; Frank Spooner Figs. 4.2a, 6.38; Syndication International p. 149; Times Newspapers Ltd Figs. 2.5, 6.23; United States Steel Corporation Fig. 6.15; By courtesy of the West Sussex Gazette Figs. 8.4, 8.8; Derek Widdicombe Fig. 4.5.

First published 1985, Reprinted 1986 (twice), 1987 by Collins Educational, 8 Grafton Street. London W1X 3LA

ISBN 00 326557 9

Designed and produced by Snap Graphics Ltd.

Printed and bound in Great Britain by R. J. Acford

Contents

Introducing You To Worldwide Issues

Geography is a subject which studies the world and how its people treat it. Today, geographers are becoming more and more concerned about how we use the Earth. It is no longer possible for us to take our planet for granted in the hope that it will always fulfil our needs, whatever we do to it. More care and thought are needed about all the Earth's resources.

What are the Earth's resources? They are many and varied, and they include more than the familiar natural resources such as coal, oil and iron ore. People themselves are a vital resource and so are the natural environments which surround us. Few would argue over the conservation of particularly valuable landscapes because, when all is said and done, we regard them as worthwhile resources in their own right. Similarly, our major cities and towns are also important resources because they provide us with a built environment able to satisfy so many of our needs.

This book is about the ways in which we use the various environments in which we live and the varied resources at our disposal. It is a book about geographical questions and issues occurring in different places throughout the world. These issues are not necessarily global in scale — in fact, many of them concern the geography of particular places. For example, the building of an urban motorway in one British town is not a matter of global concern and yet many places all over the world have to face similar transport decisions. On the other hand, atmospheric pollution in one country leading to acid rain falling in another is a well-known issue that is regarded as a serious environmental matter on an international scale.

At this stage you may be asking, 'Why issues?' The reason is really quite straightforward and it concerns people, for it is they who play the most important role in deciding how, when, and where the world's resources will be used. In most respects it is people, and the decisions they make, that are at the centre of the active geography of everyday life. Two illustrations should help to make this clear.

Firstly, in Britain at the present time there is a lot of argument over the appearance of the countryside. This is because farmers are using their land in such a way as to change the character of the rural landscape. It is the decisions taken by farmers on what to grow and how to grow it that lead to changes in the way the countryside looks. Secondly, and on a larger scale, a government decision to go ahead and build the Channel tunnel is one that would have important repercussions for much of western Europe, and not least for the south-east region of this country. But could the British share of the cost be better spent on improving employment opportunities in the old industrial areas of the country? It is questions like this that are at the very core of geographical issues worldwide and at the centre of modern geography.

Behind the decisions taken by people are beliefs, opinions, attitudes and preferences. For different reasons, not everybody agrees with the development of nuclear power and it is the clash of opinions that has made nuclear power such a major issue in the 1980s. To help you understand the nature of beliefs and attitudes, study the picture strip below. This picture strip presents two opposing views on population and the use of natural resources. What attitudes towards people and resources do the two characters hold, and which of them appears to be protecting his interests the most? Who do you find yourself agreeing with?

(from the *New Internationalist*)

Broadly speaking, issues arise when separate individuals or groups of people cannot agree on how particular resources (whatever they may be) should be used. Not all issues, however, turn into major disputes. Geographers have a lively interest in many questions concerned with the environment and many of these will never reach crisis proportions. *Worldwide Issues* introduces you to a range of these issues and questions, and, from time to time throughout the book, you will be asked to think about where you stand on a particular matter. The map shows the worldwide locations of all the case studies used in the following chapters.

To the teacher

Worldwide Issues examines a range of case studies at a variety of scales. In all instances study may be enhanced by the use of conventional resources, such as atlases, while in a few cases specific items are required, e.g. an OS sheet in Chapter 5. Most of the issues covered in the book are either still very much 'alive' in themselves, or have close parallels elsewere in the world. The authors recommend augmenting the resources presented in the book with cuttings from readily available sources such as local and national newspapers and magazines.

Throughout the text, geographical terms which may be new to pupils are printed in capital letters; they may require additional explanation.

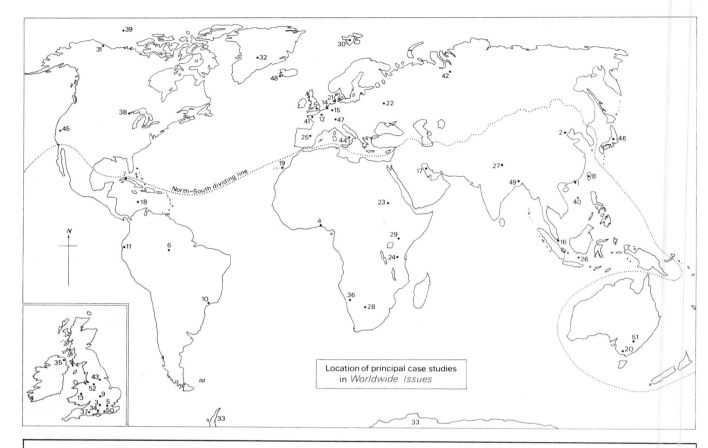

Location of principal case studies
in *Worldwide Issues*

Key

1	Hong Kong	18	Caribbean Sea	36	Arandis, Namibia
2	Peking, China	19	Lanzarote, Canary Islands	37	Dorset, UK
3	Berkshire, UK	20	Victoria, Australia	38	Minnesota, USA
4	Lagos, Nigeria	21	Sylt Island, West Germany	39	Beaufort Sea
5	London, UK	22	USSR	40	South China Sea
6	Amazonia, Brazil	23	Khartoum, Sudan	41	Brittany, France
7	Cuba	24	Tanzania	42	Urengoi, Siberia
8	Taiwan	25	Zaragoza, Spain	43	Selby, UK
9	The Midlands, UK	26	Indonesia	44	Avellino, Italy
10	São Paulo, Brazil	27	Nepal	45	California, USA
11	Guayaquil, Ecuador	28	Botswana	46	Honshu, Japan
12	Paris, France	29	Kenya	47	Airolo, Switzerland
13	Wales	30	Svalbard Island, Spitsbergen	48	Heimaey Island, Iceland
14	Rotterdam, Netherlands	31	Prudhoe Bay, Alaska	49	Bangladesh
15	The Ruhr, West Germany	32	Greenland	50	West Sussex, UK
16	Singapore, Malaysia	33	Antarctica	51	New South Wales, Australia
17	Persian Gulf	34	Hampshire, UK	52	Derbyshire, UK
		35	County Antrim, Northern Ireland		

Part I
People and the Quality of Life

In the first two chapters of *Worldwide Issues* the focus is on people. Chapter 1 is concerned with the size and distribution of the world's population and with the advantages and disadvantages that arise from the growing number of people in the world. However, not all population issues are caused by sheer numbers and all the problems are by no means confined to the less developed countries.

People create demands on all the Earth's resources, but there are major differences between the levels of resources at the disposal of individual nations. Economic well-being is a vital aspect of the quality of life in the more developed countries of the 'West', but it has often been bought at the expense of those nations which we now consider to be poor. Chapter 2 examines how the quality of life varies between different peoples and suggests that economic development is not necessarily the best way forward for everyone.

The quality of life — what makes it and who shapes it?

Chapter 1 PEOPLE

1.1 How Many People?

In 1982 there were approximately 4585 million people in the world. In 1940 there were about 2277 million and by 2020 there will probably be about 7678 million. The world can be compared with a classroom of people, Figure 1.1. This class has been given a list of the day's activities.

1 Sit at desks (20 desks in classroom).
2 Read *Worldwide Issues*. (10 copies in class.)
3 Play 5-a-side football.
4 Have lunch at school. (13 meat dishes and 13 puddings available.)
5 Girls go on a run. Boys play badminton on 2 courts.
6 8 go to woodwork lesson; 8 go to needlework lesson.
7 Move 18 stacks of chairs to the hall.
8 Go home. (3 people come in cars to give lifts home.)

▶ For each of the eight activities, what problems would arise as the students in Figure 1.1 attempt to carry them out? What does this suggest about the world, the space available (desks), the resources (books, food, cars), and the people themselves?

Figure 1.1   The 'classroom'

Figure 1.2   The 'classroom' 1970 and 1980: population growth

People — Hong Kong's greatest asset?

Hong Kong had a population of 5 233 000 in 1982. Since 1945 the population has increased rapidly and from 1970 to 1980 it increased by 30%. Figure 1.2 shows an increase of 30% in a classroom.

▶
1 How many pupils were there in the class in 1970?
2 How many pupils were there in the class in 1980?
3 How many extras were there in the class by 1980?
4 In 1970, Hong Kong could be divided into about 400 000 'classes' like the one shown on the left in Figure 1.2. By 1980 how many extra people were there in Hong Kong?

The population has grown because there have been more births than deaths each year. Also many immigrants, especially from China and Vietnam, have come to live in Hong Kong. Hong Kong has 1060 km² of land and most of the land is steep, infertile hillsides. Food and other crops can only be grown in the narrow valleys and on the alluvial areas where the majority of homes are also built.

Population density

Although the population has increased, the area of the land has remained the same. The density of population can be calculated by dividing population by area.

$$\text{DENSITY} = \frac{\text{POPULATION}}{\text{AREA}}$$

▶ Calculate the population density of Hong Kong in 1982.

The map of Hong Kong, Figure 1.3, shows that most people live in Kowloon, Tsuen Wan and Hong Kong Island. In this part of Hong Kong, the population density is 25 400/km² while in the 'New Territories' it is only 554/km². There is still lowland available in the New Territories but people are only just beginning to move there. The ring of high hills between the main built-up area and the rural New Territories has tended to stop people moving into the area.

The people's needs

For the people of Hong Kong to live, the land must provide them with their basic requirements, not only for food, but also for facilities. The greater the population, the more the land must provide. Each person in the main area of Hong Kong has 40 m² of land — about the size of your classroom.

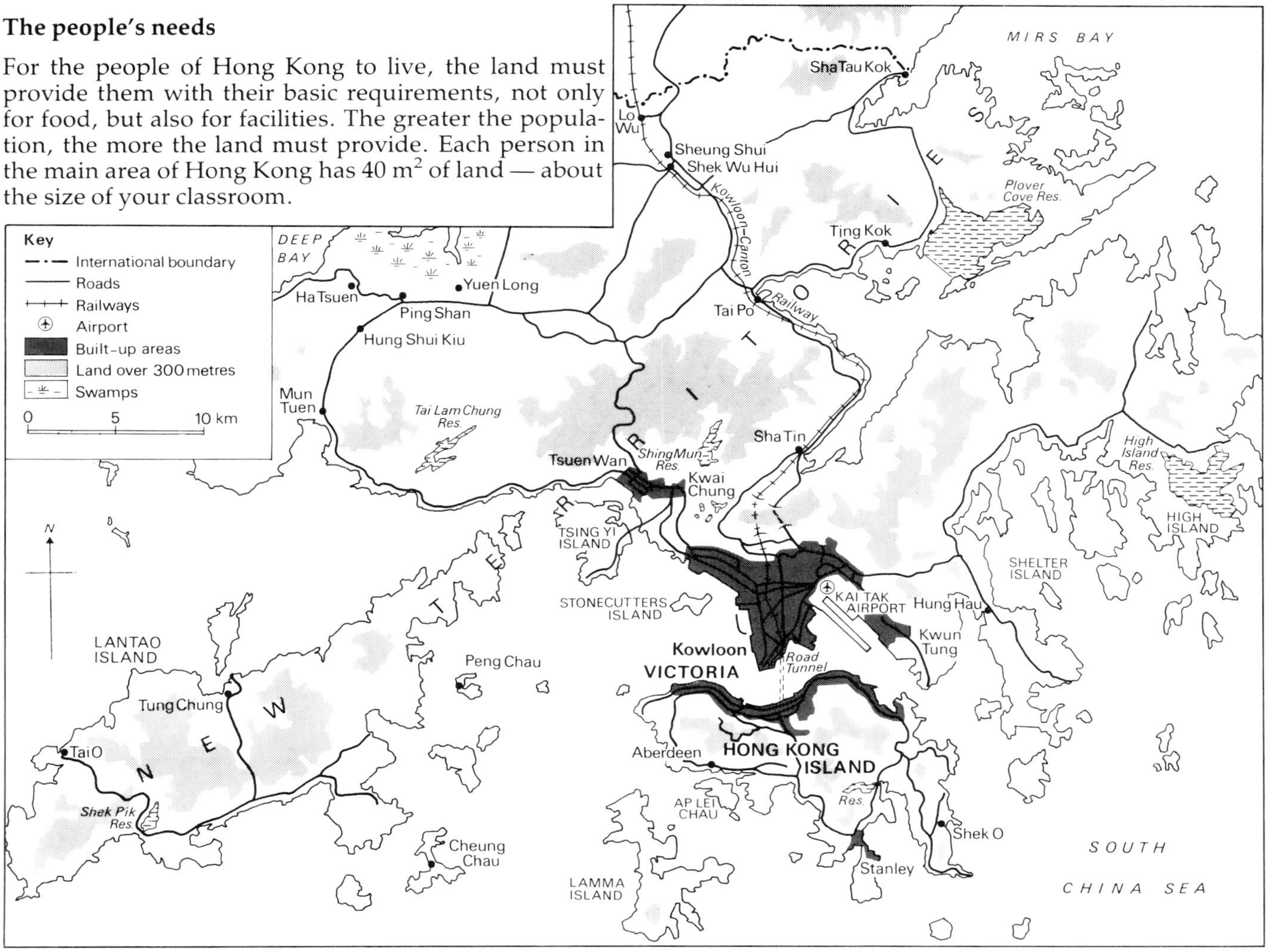

Figure 1.3   Map of Hong Kong and surrounding areas

▶ 1 Make a list of the buildings and open spaces which the following people use or visit each week:
   i) you, ii) your father, iii) your mother, iv) an old lady.
   2 Using your list and Figure 1.3, make a second list of what the land must be used for in Hong Kong.

▶ 3 What are the conditions like in Figures 1.4 and 1.5?
   4 How is your home different from those shown in Figures 1.4 and 1.5?
   5 Do you think there are **too many** people living in built-up Hong Kong? Explain your answer.

Figure 1.4   Interior of estate flat, Hong Kong

Figure 1.5   Shek Kip Mei Estate, Kowloon

Spreading the people

In order to give people more space, new towns have been built in the New Territories. Old market towns have also been expanded. Figure 1.6 shows a plan of the new town of Sha Tin. 500 000 people are being resettled and will live, shop, work and play there.

▶ 1 What is the land used for in Figure 1.7?
2 What was lost when Sha Tin was built on this land?
3 What has the land been used for in Sha Tin (Figure 1.6)?
4 In what ways would people find Sha Tin different from their previous homes?

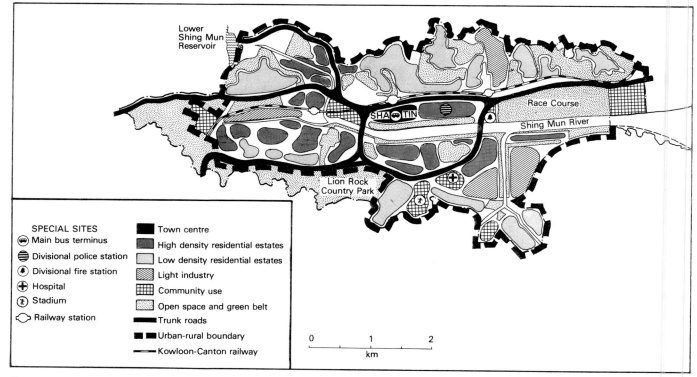

Figure 1.6   Sha Tin new town: general land use

Figure 1.7   The Upper Sha Tin Valley

▶ 5 Divide the following statements into two columns. Label one column 'The Advantages of Many People' and the other column 'The Disadvantages of Many People'.
  i Agricultural land built on for new towns.
  ii Food imports increase.
  iii Insufficient land for extensive grazing (i.e. cattle, sheep) so pigs and poultry are reared indoors for food.
  iv Plenty of friends and neighbours.
  v Large labour force — keeps wages lower.
  vi High property prices.
  vii Busy streets.
  viii Home on the 5th floor of a block of flats.
  ix Difficult to provide enough water.
  x 312 100 squatters (not in proper houses) in 1980 in the urban areas of Hong Kong.
  xi 4 beds in hospital for every 1000 people. (8 beds in Britain for every 1000 people.)
  xii Shortage of open space and other facilities.
  xii Demolition of 15 year old building to build a higher one.
  xiv New 13-storey sports stadium opened in 1980.
6 The title of this section was 'People — Hong Kong's greatest asset?' On balance, do you think that the large number of people in a small area is an asset (advantage) or not? Give reasons for your answer.

A growing concern

The leaflet shown in Figure 1.8 was issued by a group called Population Concern.

▶ 1 By looking at the diagrams, the dates and the descriptions, explain what the 'concern' is about.
2 What problems does Population Concern believe the world faces today?
3 What does Population Concern believe each person in the world needs?
4 Describe your own idea of a 'decent environment to live in'.

At the beginning of the 16th century, although there were many births each year, there were also many deaths. Many babies died before they were one year old and few adults lived to be more than 60. During the Black Death (1348 – 1349), there had been more deaths than births, but the general trend was for the number of births to exceed the number of deaths. The population was balanced or stable and by the year 1800, 'the conquest of disease' had begun. The death rate for adults fell and people began to live longer. Also, more babies were born alive and survived. The scales in Figure 1.9 show the situation today.

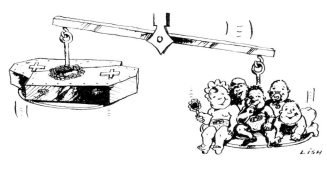

Figure 1.9   Births and deaths in 1980

Population change

The diagram (Figure 1.10), called the Demographic Transition Model, shows how population changes over time. The gap between the birth rate and the death rate shows the amount of change.

Figure 1.10   Demographic transition model

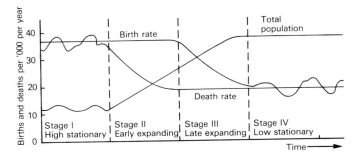

Figure 1.8   Population concern

Every beat of your heart a baby is born... and the world becomes a little smaller.

That is to say about 70 million more people – more than the combined populations of the U.K, Sweden and Denmark – are added to the population of the world every year. A delay of just one generation in stabilizing world population will result in approximately 3,000,000,000 additional people – all individuals needing food, shelter, clean water, work, education, medical care, as well as a decent environment to live in.

A D 1800 – 1000 million people
It took from 'the beginning' until around 1800 for the human population to reach its first 1000 million. Around that time the modern world was born in a cloud of steam and smoke and to the clang of the Industrial Revolution. The first trade unions were formed, railways spanned the continents and the conquest of disease had begun.

A D 1900 – 1650 million people
At the dawn of the 20th Century there were 1650 million mouths to feed. The first motor car was seen and the first aeroplane made a 12 second flight. Modern technology began to spread and man's average life span was slowly increasing. world population gathered a momentum unprecedented in human history.

 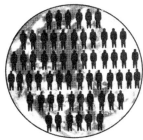

A D 1976 – 4,000 million people
Today world population has exceeded 4000 million and is fast approaching 5000 million. The impact of the modern rise in world population and the rapid use of non-renewable and limited resources has changed the physical face of the earth. This change has required the use of resources that would support a hundred thousand Roman Empires.
Some of the fundamental problems of today's world are:
The rapid growth in population in the less developed countries.
The rapid growth of consumption in the industrialized countries.
The lack of family planning information and services – at least half the world's couples are unable to plan their families.

A D 2000 – 6,000 million people
Only a disaster of appalling magnitude could now prevent the population of the world from reaching 6000 million by the end of the century.
If the world attained replacement fertility (2 children per woman) by the year 2,000 and stayed there – a very optimistic assumption – world population could be expected eventually to stabilize about 60 years later at 8½ thousand million. If replacement fertility is delayed to the year 2,020-25 world population could be expected eventually to stabilize at about 11 thousand million.

Area	Birth Rate per '000	Death Rate per '000	Population in '000s	Population Doubles in
More developed countries	15	10	1.2m	116 years
Less developed countries (excl China)	38	14	2.4m	33 years
China	22	7	1m	48 years

Figure 1.11 Population differences

World growth today

Figure 1.11 lists the birth rate and the death rate for three areas of the world. For every 1000 people in the more developed world in 1982, there were 15 births and 10 deaths. Thus there was a net gain of five people in every 1000 in 1982. There were 1.2 million groups of 1000 people. Therefore by 1983 there were 6 million (5 × 1.2) extra people in the more developed world.

Towards stability

To balance the scales and reach the low stationary stage of the model, the birth rate must change. A low birth rate is needed to match the low death rate. The chart (Figure 1.12) suggests ways in which this could be done.

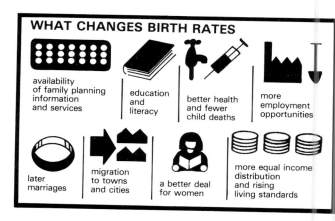

Figure 1.12 Changing the birth rate

One child policy in China

Peking (Reuter) – China has warned its 1,000 million people that if every couple continued to have two children instead of one, its population would not stop growing until it reached 1.8 billion in the year 2025.

All national newspapers carried a report yesterday from the National Family Planning Committee explaining the pressing economic reasons behind the Government's strict one-couple, one-child birth control regulations.

It said the policy under which people are criticized and fined for having more than one child and how more than two is made virtually illegal was the only way for the world's most populous nation to stabilize its size at around 1.2 billion by the end of the century.

In a separate official report, the English-language weekly *Beijing Review* conceded that the tough birth control measures had resulted in rare cases of the killing of baby girls by couples who wanted sons instead.

It said this was distressing and blamed it on "feudal ideas nurtured by a feudal system thousands of years old" – in other words, Confucianism, the state religion which taught male superiority and still shapes the thinking of most Chinese.

"For many centuries the concept of men being superior to women remained deep-rooted in people's minds", the magazine stated.

The Times, 31 January 1983

Chinese resist 'one child only' policy

By GRAHAM EARNSHAW in Peking

A CHINESE peasant grasped a double-headed axe and confronted three birth control officials, shouting: "If you force me to have a vasectomy, I'll kill all of you."

It was a small incident which ended in the peasant paying a large fine, and probably a vasectomy.

But it highlighted the increasing problems the Chinese Government is having in pushing its one-child a family policy.

From the national viewpoint, China clearly has to control the growth of its population, which last year officially passed the 1,000 million mark.

Forced abortion

But the effects of the current policy, from forced abortion and sterilisation to female infanticide, are extremely worrying.

The one-child-only policy has been generally successful in the cities, but the peasants, who make up 80 per cent of China's population are proving to be very stubborn.

The peasants want a lot of children to help work the fields and to look after them in old age. And they prefer boys to girls to the extent that they are willing to kill their daughters to make sure their one child is male.

The official newspaper SOUTHERN DAILY, published in Canton, recently confirmed what many people have suspected for a while: that China is officially following a policy of forced abortions and sterilisations to keep the birth rate down.

One sign of the fears raised by the birth control policy was a rumour in central China that the current smallpox inoculation campaign was really a pretext to sterilise children.

Daily Telegraph, 30 May 1983

Figure 1.13 Chinese family planning policy

One child per couple – China 1979

In 1975 the average family in China had three children. Had this average been allowed to continue, it is estimated that China's population in 2075 would equal the total world population of 1980. Instead, the Chinese aim to have a stable population (zero population growth) by AD 2000. The number of births will then equal the number of deaths.

The newspaper extracts in Figure 1.13 explain the situation in China today.

▶ 1   What must happen to balance the scales in Figure 1.9

2   In the Demographic Transition Model what made the gap between births and deaths widen in stage II?

3   What difference is there between stages II and IV in the model?

4   From Figure 1.11 calculate the extra people that can be expected in each area of the world today. An example is given in the section 'World growth today'.

5   In which group of countries is the highest number of extra people being added?

6   Read the newspaper extracts in Figure 1.13, and answer the following questions:

    i   What has been done in China to reduce the birth rate?

    ii   How would you feel if a 'one child per couple' rule were introduced in this country?

    iii   How have the Chinese reacted?

    iv   What will happen in 20 years time if each couple has one child, but if many of the baby girls that are born are killed?

    v   What would you advise the Chinese to do to solve the problem of their growing population?

    vi   A seven year old Chinese girl and her classmates at school sing this little rhyme:

> 'My mummy only had me,
> we don't want brothers and sisters,
> we are happy,
> all the house rejoices.'

      Why do you think she was taught this song?

    vii   In what other ways does the Chinese government try to influence people's decisions on family size? (See Figure 1.14).

WHY HAVE ONLY ONE CHILD?

For you with one child:
Free education for your one child.
Allowances to help bring up your one child.
Priority housing.
Pension benefits.

For those with two children:
No free education.
No allowances.
No pension benefits.
Payment of a fine to the state from earnings.

To help you:
Women must be 20 years old before they marry.
Men must be 22 years old before they marry.
Couples must have permission to marry.
Couples must have permission to have a child.
All hospitals have family planning officers.
Family planning help is available at work.
Redundant country people are to be encouraged to move to the towns.

REMEMBER: One child means happiness.

Figure 1.14   Government propaganda for the 'one child' policy

1.2 Changing the Pattern

Throughout the world people often move and therefore change the pattern of population distribution. Some people (nomads) move constantly. They probably live in temporary dwellings and keep few belongings. Other people move when they find a new job or retire. Both these movements are called 'free migrations' because the people want to move: they are free to choose what to do and where to go. 'Forced migrations' are when people are told to move by a government or because of persecution by other members of society. People who move from their original country to start a new home in another one are called immigrants. They very often bring traditions, customs and religious practices from their old country.

Where shall we live?

In Britain, people are free to live wherever they like. Firms can choose where to locate their premises and their workforce usually lives close by. Since World War II, people have tended to move out of the large cities into the surrounding New Towns. Figure 1.15 shows the areas with the highest population increases. The reason for the increase was not more births, but migration: people moved into these areas from other places. To cater for these extra people, houses and shopping centres, schools, hospitals and other services must be provided.

In April 1980, the Secretary of State for the Environment asked central Berkshire to specify land for 8000 new houses to be built during the 1980s. Central Berkshire lies to the west of London and many firms have chosen to locate or relocate in the area. One place where many new high technology industries are being set up is the 'Winnersh Triangle'. It lies between the M4, and A329(M) and near the M3. Figure 1.16 shows central Berkshire. The government wanted houses built so that people could move, with their firms, into this part of the country.

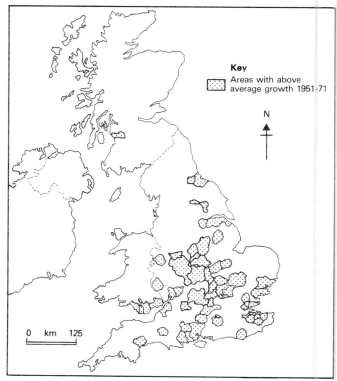

Figure 1.15   *Areas of population growth in England, Scotland and Wales*

The problems

Much of the land in central Berkshire is not available for building and Figure 1.17 mentions some of the types of land that cannot be used. Figure 1.16 shows the land that could be built upon but even these areas pose problems for development. The County Council does not want towns and villages to become joined together. Also, any new housing development must have adequate roads and services (water, shops, schools etc.) once it is built. In addition, the new houses should not suffer from motorway noise and pollution.

Figure 1.16 *Central Berkshire: land for development*

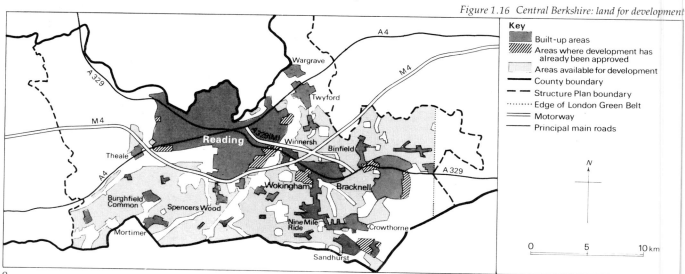

1	Green Belt
2	Land used by the government (e.g. army sites)
3	Land of special interest or beauty
4	Land for mineral workings (e.g. gravel pits)
5	Land liable to flooding
6	Public recreation land (e.g. playing field, parks, historic houses)
7	Common land
8	Top grade agricultural land

Figure 1.17   Land not to be used for building

The decision

Berkshire County Council suggested five alternative plans and then invited the public to attend meetings and to comment on them. Winnersh, one of the areas affected, is shown in Figure 1.18. The plans would allow for 700 to 1700 homes to be built in this area.

▶ 1 Look carefully at Figure 1.18 and decide where you would build 700 houses in Winnersh. Explain your choice. (One hectare [ha] of land would be needed to provide for services and 25 homes. There are 100 ha of land in each kilometre square on the map. 625 homes would fill one quarter of a kilometre square; they do not all need to be in one place.)

2 What other facilities apart from homes would be needed for this extra population of about 2800 people?

3 What criticisms do you think the people of Winnersh would have of your proposals to build 700 homes there?

After the public had commented, the Council decided where the housing land would be made available. It did not choose any of the original alternatives, but produced a new proposal. Winnersh, in fact, will now provide land for only 150 houses, but other small villages will have between 100 and 400 new homes. In addition, north-east Bracknell will provide land for 4000 of the required houses. Figure 1.19 shows the area where these houses will be built.

▶ 1 Bracknell is a new town. It was specially built to provide new homes, jobs and services for people moving into Berkshire. Why do you think so many of the new houses will be built here? Look at Figure 1.16 to help you.

2 Look at Figure 1.19 and make a list of the features of the landscape that you feel should not be altered by the housing development (i.e. land that should not be built on.) Refer to figure 1.17 as well.

3 Imagine that you are now one of the residents of the new estate in this part of Bracknell. Describe how new housing will change this area.

4 Who do you think has had the most influence on the decision over where to build these houses? Why do you think this?

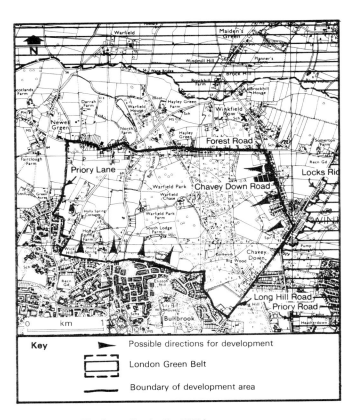

Figure 1.19   North-east Bracknell – 4000 homes

Key

▶ Possible directions for development

⬚ London Green Belt

— Boundary of development area

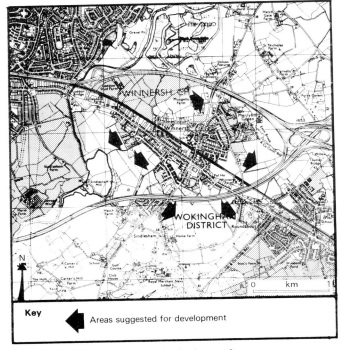

Key

◀ Areas suggested for development

Figure 1.18   Winnersh – an area for development?

Leave at once

January 31 1983 was a critical date for many people in Nigeria. Before the ECOWAS Treaty (Economic Community of West African States) was signed, people were allowed to move freely without travel papers from one country to another in West Africa. Many people went into Nigeria seeking jobs. On 17 January it was announced that anyone now in Nigeria must have satisfactory papers otherwise they would be classed as illegal immigrants and forced to leave. All illegal unskilled aliens (foreigners) had to leave by 31 January 1983. They had 14 days to leave. Skilled alien workers had an extra month.

It was estimated that there were 2 million 'illegal' aliens in Nigeria. Half of these were Ghanaians. Others were from Benin, Togo, Chad and other West African countries. Most of these immigrants had jobs and stayed in Nigeria until the deadline date.

How could they depart?

'Up to six people were feared drowned in the port of Lagos when thousands of illegal Ghanaian immigrants stormed on board two ships which were taking them home yesterday.

But thousands of others were still on their way. These are the lucky ones, for there are some who are destitute and have not been able to afford the high prices charged by lorry, bus and taxi owners. Either they will try to hide here or they will attempt to walk across bush paths into the countries of their origin.

To escape from Nigeria the fleeing 'illegals' have used scheduled airline services, the three ships sent for the Ghanaians, and flotillas of canoes piled high with people and luggage. Overland they have gone by taxi, lorry and bus, motor cycle and scooter.

Some of the 'illegals' will try to stay. Ghanaians have tried to entice village girls to marry them so that they could legally stay.'
The Times 2 February 1983

'International relief organisations spoke of at least 100 people dying of hunger and thirst during their overland trek from Nigeria to Ghana.' *The Times* 3 April 1983

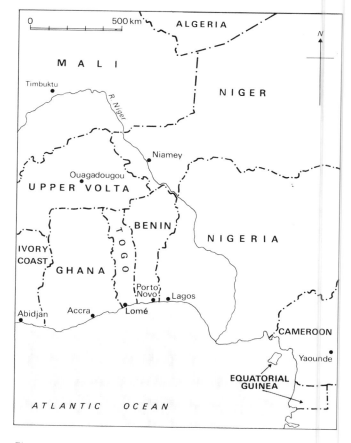

Figure 1.20   From Nigeria to Ghana

With what effects?

On the people:
The immigrants leaving Nigeria left behind them the life that they were used to. Many returned to the country which they chose to leave. Figure 1.21 shows what they left in Nigeria and what they went back to in Ghana.

Figure 1.21   The effect on the people

On the country returned to:

1 Benin feared that it would be swamped by refugees. 500000 settled in Benin: 200000 were Beninese and 300 000 were Ghanaians. The government worried about health and security. Ghanaians had not been vaccinated and their sanitary conditions gave rise to fears of epidemics. Bread, water and medicines were distributed. Many Ghanaians did not wish to return home and some supported themselves by banditry.

   Benin is one of the world's 25 least developed countries. It already had a very weak economy and could not support more people. There were already 3.5 million people in Benin and another 500 000 were very difficult to support. A 'national reception and movements committee' was set up to deal with the immigrants.

2 The returning 800000 Ghanaians became refugees in their own country. They needed food and shelter. Their belongings were mostly left in Nigeria. They had little money and no jobs. The Ghanaian authorities tried to send the people back to their original villages so that relations and friends could help to look after them and where they could perhaps share homes and begin to 'till the soil'. However, they had no tools, no clothes, bedding or furniture and they needed cooking equipment. After their journey many of them were unwell and needed medical treatment. In the villages in northern Ghana, food and water were already in short supply. The children needed to go to school. The Ghanaian government had very little money and could not provide for these people. There were not enough jobs in the towns or the villages. The returning Ghanaians faced mistrust and even hostility at home. Traditional rulers (tribal chiefs) were not prepared to make farmland available. The refugees posed a very difficult political situation for the Ghanaian leader, Flight Lieutenant Jerry Rawlings.

On the country expelling them:

'The order to quit has created a scarcity of essential commodities on the Nigerian market. Departing aliens have virtually purchased all the commodities on their home-bound journey – because of the scarcity of such goods in their own countries. As a result, they have forced prices of these goods up. A packet of Lipton Tea containing 25 bags formerly sold for 60K (Kobo) now sells for 80K.
   As if buying up of goods were not enough, some of the aliens resorted to arson as they left for home.' *Daily Times of Nigeria* 6 February 1983

'The expulsion order with its possibility of jobs for Nigerians has obvious appeal. . . .
   The expulsions have also hurt some Nigerians who have been harassed by people who mistook them for aliens.' *The Times* 2 February 1983

'Criticism inside Nigeria began to mount – described as 'Un-Islamic'. Government should make preparations to receive Nigerians who might be expelled in retaliation.'
'Nigerian leaders warned that Ghanaian, Ugandan and Liberian leaders had been overthrown after expelling aliens.' *The Times* 3 February 1983

'Nigerians arrest 100 illegal aliens.'
'Some building sites lost 60 per cent of their workforce through the expulsion.' *The Times* 10 February 1983

On the world:

Several African governments appealed to the Nigerians to take a humanitarian approach to the illegal immigrants and give them enough time to leave in an organised manner.

The Danish Red Cross flew to Accra to airlift 100 expelled Ghanaians from Nigeria.

The EEC sent 5000 tonnes of food aid to help the refugees from Nigeria. The United Nations Children Fund (UNICEF) delivered 25 tonnes of medical supplies to Ghana, 7 tonnes to Togo and 9 tonnes to Benin. UNICEF appealed for funds to boost the permanent community health and other programmes in rural Ghana.

1 Use an atlas map to find the distance from Central Nigeria to the Ghanaian Border:
   i) by land,   ii) by land and sea.
2 Read 'How could they depart' and make a list of the different ways by which the aliens left Nigeria. Which method would you have chosen and why? What problems would you have faced?
3 Use the information in 'With what effects and complete the following table:

Effect on	Good effects	Bad effects	Other
People			
Country returned to			

4 Do you think Nigeria benefitted from expelling the aliens? Give the reasons for your answer. It may help if you think about how the following groups were affected:
   i the Nigerian people,
   ii the Nigerian Government,
   iii the Nigerian leader,
   iv the Nigerians whom the Ghanaians worked for.
5 In what ways did the rest of the world try to help the Ghanaians who were being expelled from Nigeria? What other actions could have been taken?
6 What other international expulsions have you heard of?

Where is home?

'One aspect of race relations is hardly ever discussed —the problems of the second generation of immigrant families.

This second generation are those born and educated in Britain, but they are children of Indian, African, Chinese or other ethnic groups. I, Robin, was born in St Mary's Paddington (the same hospital as Prince William) in 1960, grew up in Dollis Hill in the London suburbs and was educated at St Marylebone Grammar School and Christ Church College, Canterbury: but my parents were born in India.

My father came from the bustling city of Calcutta, and my mother grew up in Kerala. (See Figure 1.22.) They came to England in the fifties to study, met in London and married. They acquired British nationality and settled down to a British way of life. My sister and I are thus members of the second generation. The disadvantages start from the moment we sit at our first school desks. Teachers ask us how a typical menu is prepared, or how we dispose of our dead. But when I first went to school I hardly knew I was Indian at all.

Naturally we do not want to cut ourselves off from our culture. It provides one very important half of us, which complements and is complemented by our British nationality. Neither do we want to upset our parents by forgetting our Indian-ness. However, we would like to be thought of as Indians born and bred in this country and able to draw on two experiences, of the Indian and the British Cultures.'

Adapted from, *Sunday Telegraph Magazine* article 'A Problem of Place as well as Race', Robin Dutt 2 January 1983

Figure 1.22   *My parents' homes?*

In Britain today there are about 719 000 people who are Indian. They themselves describe their ethnic origin as 'Indian' but 220 000 of them were born in the United Kingdom. Even more of them are British Passport holders. Many of them may never have been to India but they look 'Indian' and therefore many people assume that they are not British and that they are only interested in Indian life. In reality, they probably know far more about Britain than they do about India and they want to be part of the British society.

Figure 1.23 gives some information about the Indian population in Britain in 1981. Often people of the same ethnic origin live near one another and they choose certain British cities for their homes. Many non-Indian British people choose to live near their family and friends while others do not want to 'move to the north' or to leave their home town. The Indian population often chooses to live in our bigger conurbations or

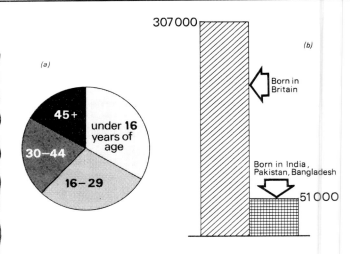

Figure 1.23 a   *Indian population in Britain in 1981, by age*
　　　　　　 b   *Birthplace of Indians, Pakistanis and Bangladeshis under 16, living in Britain in 1981*

cities such as London, Birmingham, Manchester, Leeds and Leicester. Many of these cities have traditional industries which used the skills of the original immigrants. The textile industries of Manchester, Leeds and Leicester are good examples. There is an established textile industry in India and many Indians leave jobs in the textile trade to come to Britain. Naturally they then look for a job in the same trade when they arrive here.

Leicester is my home

In Leicester, a city of 254 000 people, there are 48 000 Indians. All of them have decided to make Britain their home. Those who were not actually born here have made many sacrifices to come here. They have left their family and friends and the home and culture that they knew. In Britain they find many different attitudes and ways of doing things. However, many of them have been born in Leicester. Figure 1.24 shows the number of babies born in Leicester to mothers from India, Pakistan, Bangladesh and other areas of the New Commonwealth. Each year, of all the babies born in Leicester, about one in every three had a mother of New Commonwealth origin. Their families have their own religious beliefs in just the same way as the Roman Catholics, Anglicans, Jews and other groups. They have shops which sell the food they are used to, and they keep some of their Indian traditions and culture. But they attend British schools and learn English. They are British. Their home is Leicester.

Figure 1.24   *Babies born in Leicester*

Year	Total Live Births	Mother Born in New Commonwealth	% of Babies Born to New Commonwealth Mothers
1977	3843	1245	32
1978	3874	1263	33
1979	4247	1357	32
1980	4664	1535	33
1981	4527	1449	32

James from England

James was born in the United States of America. His parents were born in England but worked in America during World War II. His ethnic origin was European. James returned to England with his family after the war and went to school in Birmingham. He had to decide before he was 21 whether he wanted a British or an American passport. He chose an American passport and after three years at a British University went on to further study in America. He married an English girl who had also gone to America. Then, as America was at war in Vietnam, it was likely he would be asked to fight for the USA. He, like many Americans, moved to Canada to avoid joining the army. He now works and lives with his family in Canada but has an American passport. Where is his 'home'?

1 What is a 'second generation immigrant'?
2 In what ways does Robin seem very British?
3 In what ways is Robin Indian?
4 What problems does Robin face?
5 What passport do you think Robin would like to hold?
6 Calculate the proportion of Indians both born in Britain and still living here today. (220 000 ÷ 719 000 × 100%).
7 Use Figure 1.23 to help you describe the Indian populations in Britain in 1981.
8 Why do many Indians choose to live in a city such as Leicester?
9 Read 'James from England' and explain where you think his home is. Where should he live? Why?
10 Where should Robin live? Why? Compare your answer with that for Question 9.

1.3 Feeding the People

I'm still hungry
This child is too weak to eat. He is one of the victims of the 1984 drought in Ethiopia. To bring him back to health he needs small, regular feeds given by nasal tube

Have you had enough?

Many people in the world do not have enough food and cannot obtain a proper balanced diet. If they do not have enough food they are called under-nourished. If they do not have a balanced diet they are called malnourished (badly nourished). Sometimes people do not eat enough protein and so their bodies and minds cannot grow properly. They are also likely to die from common diseases such as measles because their body cannot fight the infection. If they do not eat enough vitamins or minerals they may become blind (vitamin A deficiency) or develop rickets (calcium deficiency). A balanced diet consists of proteins, carbohydrates, fats, vitamins and minerals. The table below shows which foods give us most protein, carbohydrate and fat. Cheese also provides many minerals.

Protein	Carbohydrates	Fats
Cheese	Rice	Butter
Meat	Bread	Margarine
Fish	Pasta	Cooking oil
Milk	Potatoes	
Eggs	Sugar	
Beans	Cake	
Lentils	Biscuits	

In order to lead an active life, people must have enough calories in their diet. When people diet they consume fewer calories and so use up some of their body fat and become slimmer. However, if they do not have much body fat, they will become very thin and will eventually die of starvation. The amount of food a person needs depends on the way in which they spend their day. The table below shows the varying number of calories used by an adult in one hour according to activity.

Activity	Calories
Sleep	70
Writing/Sitting	85
Housework/Playing	200
Sports	320

A baby needs about 820 calories a day whereas a 16 year old male needs 3500 calories per day. The world must produce 2300 calories per person per day to provide for everyone; this is the same as 227 kg of grain per person per year. The world actually produces 1300 million tonnes of grain per year which is enough for 6000 million people.

Why do you think that the grain produced by the world cannot feed the world?
Use the cartoon for some ideas (Figure 1.25).

Figure 1.25   Using the world's grain

Why are some people malnourished?

- They do not grow enough food for themselves. The seeds they can afford do not produce much grain or fruit. They do not have enough land on which to grow all the food they need.
- The land no longer produces good crops because it has been over used. They cannot afford fertilizers to improve the land. Because the crops do not grow, the land is left bare and any good soil is blown or washed away (eroded).
- Their food is damaged by drought, flood, rats, or bad storage.
- They grow food (tea, coffee, cocoa) to sell abroad and do not have enough land left for their own crops. Food is sold, but for little money because too many people take a share of the income from sales to the industrial countries.
- They cannot buy food easily at a market or shop. Often certain foods are just not available or they may be too expensive.
- There is not enough meat. Meat bought one day is bad by the next because of the hot weather and lack of refrigeration. Often meat can only be bought in the towns (perhaps a long walk away) and then it may only be available on certain days.

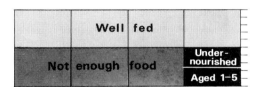

Figure 1.26 The food go-round

▶ 1 From Figure 1.26, calculate the percentage of people who:
   i are well fed,
   ii do not have enough food,
   iii are starving,
   iv are starving and aged between 1 and 5 years.
2 Make a list of the number of hours you spent yesterday doing the types of activity listed in the activity/calories table. Work out how many calories you used. (For example, if you slept all day you used 70 calories per hour sleeping × 24 hours in a day = 1680 calories.)
3 Draw a poster to inform the public about one way in which they are wasting the world's grain. (See Figure 1.25.) Also show on the poster why you think the world's grain should not be wasted.
4 You have been chosen by the people of your village to represent them at a meeting in the local town. At this meeting suggestions are to be made as to how more crops can be grown to feed the people. You will have to stand and give a short speech at the meeting. Choose three reasons why people are malnourished and explain how you think the problem can be solved if the government or foreign countries will help. Give your speech the heading 'What can be done to grow more food'. You may be asked to read your speech to the town meeting (the class).

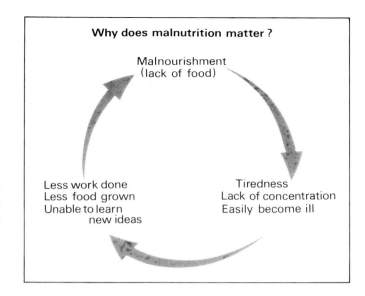

▶ 1 Sometimes the circle above is described as 'poverty, disease and illiteracy'. Draw the circle and put these titles next to the correct part of the diagram.
2 Explain why it is very difficult for people without enough food to improve their position.
3 Make a list of different ways in which malnourished people could be provided with adequate food. Read through this section again for ideas.

What to do with £½ million?

You are the lucky winner of the first ever all-Britain charity draw. Your postman brings hundreds of letters from people you do not know. All of them want to share some of your £½ million — and you must let them. You can keep £10000 for yourself, but the other £490000 must be sent to help the 'world's poor'. You can choose any five projects to receive this money which will be equally divided so each will receive £98000. (Oxfam in 1983–4 received a total of £23952000 so they and other large charities will find your gift generous but will be quite used to dealing with these amounts.)

▶ 1 Before making your decision, read the extracts from newspapers and journals that have been sent to you. Some of the points raised may help you in deciding which five projects to donate your money to.
2 When you have made your decision, write a paragraph to explain how you chose your five projects.
3 Now write another paragraph to explain why you did not choose the others.
4 How would you spend your own £10000? Give the reasons for your decision.
5 Write a paragraph to explain how you think you would spend the £10000 if you lived in a less developed country of the world.

Extracts from newspapers and journals sent for you to read.

'Which comes first, the chicken or the egg? For Save The Children there's no doubt about the answer to this age-old conundrum. If we provide an egg for a hungry child we only feed him for today — if we help his family to set up their own barndoor chickens he, and his brothers and sisters, will have a steady supply of all-important protein.'
The World's Children, June 1983

'Villagers in Abora Patoako in Ghana have increased their own food supplies because a VSO agriculturist has given them advice and training. Eritrean refugees have been trained by a VSO unit and can now build their own schools and health centres. Nepali weavers have been able to sell their own goods to more people and at markets further away because of advice from a VSO volunteer. Aid is effective if channelled in the right direction.' Extract of abridged letter from VSO Director, *The Times*, 24 April 1983

'Three things make self-help difficult in less developed nations. One is illiteracy. A second is lack of expertise — teachers, doctors, vets, engineers and so on are all needed. The third is poor transport which isolates communities and makes the exchange of ideas and goods difficult.' Modified from Save the Children pamphlet

Project 1.   VSO advertisment

No wonder the poor world only comes third.

Sending material relief to the poor and hungry is a crying necessity.
No one can deny it.
But it is a relief. Not a cure.
For as long as the poor world remains ill-equipped to help itself it will always be dependent.
It will stay hopelessly handicapped.
It will always come third.
One charity, Voluntary Service Overseas, approaches the problem in a different (but complementary) way.
We send people.
Skilled people, professional people, useful people – from all walks of life.
Each volunteer spends two years with a third world community, freely sharing his or her skill, as well as the prevailing standard of living.
One result is only to be expected.
The community receives a benefit which will endure for generations.
But there is another effect, less looked for, but invariably true.
The teacher returns deeply, richly taught.
If *you* would like to know more about volunteering, please return the coupon and we'll send you details.
If you're not free to go yourself, but you would like to help, then please send as much as you can afford.
We might live in a different world.
But we're all in the same race.

VSO

VOLUNTARY SERVICE OVERSEAS

Why not?

- Send me details about: Volunteering (my skill area is _____) □ VSO membership □
- I enclose a donation of £5 □ £10 □ £15 □ £ ___ (If applic. Access/Visa No _____)

Name _____
Address _____
_____
DM/C/23/1

Post to: Voluntary Service Overseas, 9 Belgrave Square, London SW1X 8PW. (S.A.E. appreciated.) Charity no. 313757.

Project 2.   Action Aid advertisement

Mwende is 8. She now has the chance of a brighter future. You.

Mwende Kamana lives in a small rural village in Kenya. Her father is dead. And her mother tills the dry, meagre soil in a struggle to feed her 8 children. She desperately wants Mwende to go to school, and to have the chance of a better life. You can give her that chance. Through ActionAid's Child Sponsorship Programme.

As an ActionAid sponsor you give direct, continuing help to an individual child in a poor community. Sponsors give £7.92 a month – **every penny of which is spent overseas to benefit the children in their communities.** It's not much – the cost of a newspaper or a small loaf of bread a day. But it's all that's needed for ActionAid to provide a child with an education and practical training for a more self-reliant future.

When you sponsor a child in need you'll know his or her name. You'll have a photograph to keep. And you'll receive regular news of his or her well-being and of the essential work being done to improve life for the whole community. Moreover, you'll know you are helping a child, a family and an entire village toward a more secure and productive future.

So please, cut out the coupon below and post it today. Your help will make a world of difference to a child like Mwende. Isn't that worth £7.92 per month?
ActionAid, 208 Upper Street, London N1 1RZ.

You can give another child that chance...
Send to: The Rt. Hon. Christopher Chataway, Hon. Treasurer, ActionAid, Dept. x x x , c/o Midland Bank plc, Box 1EC, 52 Oxford Street, London W1A 1EG.
□ Please send me details of one child who needs my help. I enclose £7.92/£95* as my first month's/year's contribution.
(*Delete as applicable)
□ I cannot sponsor a child immediately but enclose a gift of £200 □ £100 □ £50 □ £25 □ £5 □ £
□ Please send me further details on sponsorship.
(*Tick appropriate box.*)
Important: All cheques and postal orders should be made payable to ActionAid. Thank you.

Name
Address

Postcode
Telephone:
ActionLine ☎ For further information on sponsorship phone 01-226 9460, anytime today.

ActionAid
Change a child's world... Become a Sponsor

Project 3.   Uganda — baby health plan
In Uganda, many children die in babyhood, not solely because food is scarce, but because, due to superstition and tribal custom, they are not given all the food they need. Instead of issuing the correct food to every child, which would soon exhaust available funds, mothers with sick children are chosen from as many villages as possible. They are taught how to feed their children on suitable foods and also how to grow crops. When they return to their villages with now healthy children, they are expected to teach other mothers how to help themselves.

Project 4. Yemen—3000 killed: 400000 homeless

The earthquake struck at 11 a.m. when the able-bodied men and boys were working in the fields; women, very young children, and the elderly were crushed to death inside their homes. Oxfam distributed plastic tent material, corrugated iron sheeting, blankets and water packs. Other agencies provided hoes and seeds so that food production could be started as quickly as possible. Oxfam and two other agencies from abroad combined to produce a video tape and a demonstration house to show earthquake-resistant building techniques.

Project 5. Oxfam advertisement

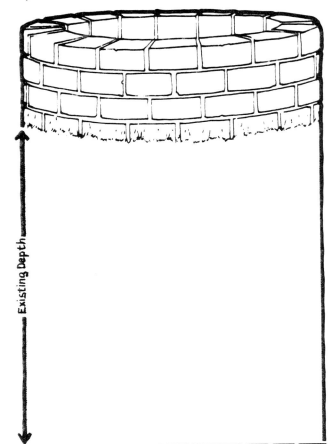

GIVE A VILLAGE MORE TO DRINK.

Three out of every five people in the Third World still run the risk of disease, even death, through lack of clean water.

Deepening one well by 60ft. could transform the health of a village.

But every day counts. And so does every pound. We need your help.

I'd like to help. I enclose £5   £10   £20   £_____

Name _____

Address _____

_____ Post Code _____

Send to: Guy Stringer, Oxfam, Room
FREEPOST, OXFORD OX2 7BR.
(No stamp required)

Project 6. UNICEF advertisement

As many as 1,700 Third World children have died during the last 60 minutes.

Most had not reached their first birthday. They were victims of disease, malnutrition, war and even lack of education.

This is not news; it has happened for years and years.

UNICEF (the United Nations Children's Fund) knows that 20,000 children can be saved, cheaply and simply, every day.

But we need money, from donations and more especially covenants (we get an extra 43% back from the taxman).

With that we can then supply developing countries with medicines, clean water and health and hygiene training to help children to survive.

There's a reason for giving money and help every two seconds, and the clock is still ticking.

A child dies every two seconds. Here's a chance to stop it.

I am interested in   taking out a covenant. Please send   me a leaflet.
I enclose a donation   of £
Post coupon to   address below.

Name _____

Address _____

UNICEF
Doing children a World of good.

UK Committee for UNICEF, Room 173P, 55 Lincoln's Inn Fields, London WC2A 3NB.
Or to the UK Committee for UNICEF, Room 173P, 69 Cross Street, Sale, Cheshire M33 1HE. Tel: 01-405 5592 or 061-973 4957.
Cheques made payable to UNICEF. Please send S.A.E. if receipt required.

Project 7. Surplus EEC Food

The EEC continues to produce more of some foods than the people of Europe need. If money can be found to transport this food to the poorer countries of the world, then this surplus can be distributed as aid to less developed nations.

Project 8. Nigeria – new capital at Abuja

In order to provide a better administration and government for the people of Nigeria, it is necessary to build a new capital city. New buildings will be provided as offices for government ministers, as well as new homes for them. A complex of meeting rooms, hotels, theatres and cultural centres will be built to ensure that Nigeria presents an impressive city to all foreign visitors.

Project 9. Major development of new power station in India

Many large firms and governments have been persuaded to give grants for the building of the new power station. In return, the firms will be given the work of constructing the power station and the governments have been promised that equipment will be bought from their country.

Project 10. All-weather road in Tanzania

Britain is to provide £40 million for the first all-weather road in southern Tanzania. It will run from Makambako to Songea. Many people will then be able to reach the market towns. This will help those with goods to sell.

Project 11. Putting an end to exploitation

Workers on tea plantations or coffee estates are often paid very low wages so that the plantation owners (often the large firms) can make as much profit as possible when they sell in Britain. Anyone buying shares in one of these companies could table a motion and speak at a general meeting of shareholders and put their opinions to the board. The board might then be influenced to modify its practices.

Please, Sir, can we have some more?

One of the most urgent problems is how to increase food production in the less-developed world. It would be a big mistake for the EEC to continue sending its food surpluses. Obviously this is necessary when there are disasters, but it is better to use our money to encourage farmers on the spot. Another problem is the belief that government-to-government aid is the best way of helping the world's poor. Now the British government and others are looking at ways of pumping aid into projects to help the 'poorest of the poor', and not to encourage impressive building of power stations and such like. Many developing countries are largely dependent upon foreign aid. If it is 'tied' it may have to be spent on goods supplied from the country giving the aid. Buying expensive machinery and trying to become 'Westernized' is not appropriate when jobs not machines are needed for the poor.

Western advisers have suggested two ways of producing more food in the world. They are 'the Green Revolution' and 'mechanisation' (using machines). Figures 1.27 and 1.28 show what changes these suggestions have made.

Figure 1.27   The Green Revolution (from the *New Internationalist*)

Figure 1.28   Farming small (from the *New Internationalist*)

Yes, certainly, help yourself

In Figure 1.29 a different approach is taken. The poor of the developing countries and their own governments are encouraged to make the changes.

Can we help too?

Figure 1.30 suggests ways in which we must change in order to help the developing world.

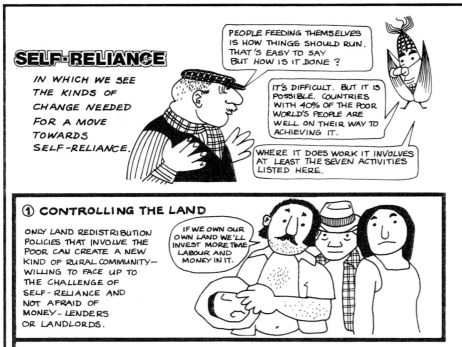

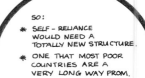

Figure 1.29   Self-reliance (from the *New Internationalist*)

1 Look at the two sets of cartoons, Figures 1.27 and 1.28. What changes do the Western advisers suggest?
2 Why does the Green Revolution not help the poor in the developing world? Figure 1.28.
3 How can a small peasant farm produce more than a mechanised large farm? Figure 1.28.
4 What changes would the peasants choose? Figure 1.27.
5 Figure 1.29 suggests 7 ways of improving conditions for the poor. Explain in your own words what you think the government of a developing country could do to help the poor.
6 Draw a poster to show one way in which the Western world can help the hungry. Figure 1.30.
7 You are an agricultural scientist in the West. Make a list of the good things that science has done to help agriculture.

Figure 1.30   What can we do? (from the *New Internationalist*)

Key Points: People

- People do not have equal amounts of living space or equal access to resources. Nevertheless, people need shelter, food, work and recreation in the areas in which they live.

- High population density has both advantages and disadvantages, but when cities expand it is usually at the expense of agricultural land.

- Few countries today can cope easily with a rapidly increasing population; new attitudes toward the size of families may be one way of easing the situation.

- While migrations of people may ease the pressure of population in some areas, few large-scale migrations occur without causing problems for the migrants themselves, for the country they leave and for the country they move to.

- Poverty and natural disasters do not fully account for the level of malnourishment in the world today. Political considerations and other factors are just as likely to be involved.

- Many attitudes need to change if the world's poor are to improve their standard of living.

Chapter 2 DEVELOPMENT

2.1 What is Development?

Inequality at home

Development studies often look only at the poorer people living in the developing countries of the world. They ignore the fact that many rich people also live in these developing countries and that rich countries continue to develop further. In a 'rich' country such as the United Kingdom, there are also poor people. Development is about who has what, where and how.

The United Kingdom has always had some areas which enjoy a higher standard of living than others. Figure 2.1 shows variations in QUALITY OF LIFE in the United Kingdom. The map takes four factors into account: unemployment, overcrowding, infant mortality and the quality of housing. These factors have been chosen because they give a fairly accurate guide to the social and economic health of a region. For example, taking all four factors into account, people living in Northern Ireland have a poorer quality of life when compared to people living in southern England.

▶ Write a short description of the variations in the quality of life as shown by Figure 2.1 Use an atlas to find out the names of specific places and areas and mention them in your description. Suggest reasons why some areas are better off than others.

Some areas in the United Kingdom are, therefore, more developed than others. This simply means that some areas are economically and socially more healthy. Often an area has social problems, e.g. poor housing and overcrowding, because it is not very healthy economically. Where industry is declining, unemployment will rise, people will move out of the area and so will wealth.

Figure 2.2 shows the pattern of economic health for different regions in the United Kingdom. Unemployment is a key economic indicator and migration is a sign of the success or failure of the job market.

Those regions which could be described as economically healthy are those which have an unemployment rate below average and which are attracting migrants.

▶ From Figure 2.2, work out the average rate of unemployment for all regions. On a copy of the map, colour in those regions which have an unemployment rate below average and which are attracting population. In the key, label these regions: 'Developed Regions'. Colour in the other regions and label these: 'Developing Regions'. Do you live in a developed or a developing region?

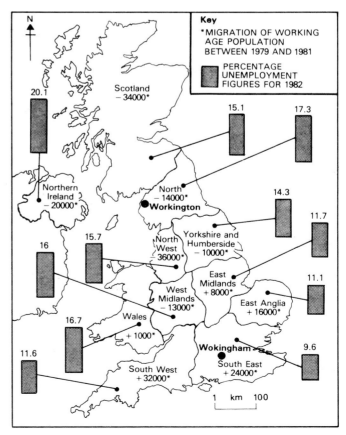

Figure 2.1 Variations in the quality of life in the United Kingdom

Figure 2.2 Unemployment and migration in the United Kingdom

IN Boomtown Wokingham they have a message for firms eager to set up shop in the heart of the M4 computer corridor: please go somewhere else. Pressure on space is such that companies are actually turned away.

Just 256 miles north, in work-starved Workington it's the army recruitment office that's turning people away. Even this traditional escape route for youngsters eager to avoid the dole queue has a six-to-12 months waiting list.

Wokingham is in the vanguard of the new information revolution which is changing the face of Britain just as much as the industrial revolution did 150 years ago. Then, Workington prospered as the steel industry mushroomed, while Berkshire was an impoverished agricultural county.

Today steel making in Workington has been savaged by the recession; coal has come and gone; and the new industries haven't taken their place. The unemployment statistics tell all: Wokingham has 7% on the dole, Workington 17.8%. The contrast among school leavers is even more staggering: only 5% of those who left Wokingham schools this summer are not either in a job or on youth training: the Workington figure is 41.5%.

WORKINGTON is everything that Wokingham isn't – a one-industry town for over a century, miles from major markets and isolated, trapped between the sea and the Lake District. Widespread steel redundancies over the last three years have devastated the town. Some 3,000 steel jobs have gone. There is precious little sign of high technology marching into Workington – not a single entry in the local Yellow Pages for a computer business, nor any sign of a software house or specialist computer shop in the area.

Wokingham has at least 25 electronics companies, ranging from Hewlett-Packard with over 1,000 employees to small software companies with half a dozen employees. The whole of Wokingham appears to be switched on to high technology. Over half the jobs advertised in a local employment agency require some computing skills. Schools are busy churning out computer-literate children.

As the level of computer awareness grows – whether home grown or through the importing of bright and talented graduates – so more firms, not all making computers, are attracted to the area.

IN WORKINGTON, the schools doggedly face up to the fact that the vast majority of the youngsters leave with little prospect of work. One local head reports that morale is surprisingly good, though last year just 6.6% of the school's leavers found jobs. Computing skills are taught, though the head recognises that 'there aren't many computing jobs in the area'.

On a cold and wet Monday morning, almost the busiest place in town is the local unemployment benefits office, while in nearby JR's American Pool Parlour, unemployed youngsters pass the time on the pool table.

The optimism in the south is understandable. Even if someone lacks any skills in Wokingham, they can usually be found a job within a month if they're prepared to travel. Few of Wokingham's unemployed are long term (57% have been unemployed for less than six months) while the vacancies are spread evenly across the economy, with a strong service sector showing.

One of the by-products of the influx of high growth electronics or software companies has been the increasing affluence of the Wokingham area.

This is most visible in house prices, which are not far off London levels. A three-bedroomed terrace house can go for £35,000 according to one local agent. For a similar property in Workington, £15,000 is judged a fair price.

Adapted from *The Sunday Times*,
18 December 1983

Figure 2.3   A tale of two towns

Workington and Wokingham are two towns in England with similar names but which are different in practically every other way. The location of these towns is shown on Figure 2.2. The information in Figures 2.3 and 2.4 gives a detailed picture of the economic health and quality of life in both towns.

▶ 1 Write down a definition of the term 'the quality of life'.
2 The quality of life index used in Figure 2.1 was based on unemployment, overcrowding, infant mortality and quality of housing. Make a list of other things which could be used to measure economic or social health.
3 Carefully study Figures 2.3 to 2.6. Summarise the main differences between Workington and Wokingham. Make a list of the reasons why Wokingham is booming and attracting industry and why Workington is not.
4 Imagine that the government is worried that the gap between the rich South and poor North is widening and that this might lead to serious social problems. You have been asked by the government to prepare a report outlining the facts about the variations in wealth and quality of life in the United Kingdom. (Use any of the information in this section but try to find some of your own information as well.)

WORKINGTON, Cumbria	WOKINGHAM, Berkshire
POPULATION: 27 000 and falling INDUSTRIES: steel, paper, vehicles	POPULATION 24 000 and rising INDUSTRIES: services, electronics, software, light engineering
UNEMPLOYMENT: 17.8% DISTANCE FROM LONDON: 326 miles	UNEMPLOYMENT: 7.3% DISTANCE FROM LONDON: 32 miles
COMMUNICATIONS: By road – A66, A595, A596. Rail – W coast main line connection at Carlisle (34 miles); link to Barrow. Nearest major airport – Newcastle (93 miles)	COMMUNICATIONS: By road – M4 (5 miles), M40, M3, M25. Rail – London-Bristol connection at Reading (8 miles); link to Gatwick Airport. Nearest major airport – Heathrow (22 miles)
REGIONAL AID: development area status allowing 15% grants on new plant and machinery; enterprise zone status allowing business 10-year holiday from rates	REGIONAL AID: none

Figure 2.4   Workington and Wokingham: the contrasts

Figure 2.5   A derelict part of Derwent Road, Workington

Switzerland	16440	Guinea	290
West Germany	13590	China	290
Sweden	13520	Tanzania	280
Denmark	12950	Sierra Leone	280
Norway	12650	Sri Lanka	270
Belgium	12180	Haiti	270
France	11730	India	240
Netherlands	11470	Mozambique	230
United States	11360	Malawi	230
Austria	10230	Zaire	220
Canada	10130	Burkino Faso	210
Japan	9890	Rwanda	200
Australia	9820	Burundi	200
Finland	9720	Mali	190
United Kingdom	7920	Burma	170
East Germany	7180	Nepal	140
New Zealand	7090	Ethiopia	140
Italy	6480	Bangladesh	130
Czechoslovakia	5820	Chad	120
Spain	5400	Bhutan	80

Figure 2.6   A prosperous suburb – Croft Road, Wokingham

Figure 2.7   The world's richest and poorest nations (GNP per capita US $)

Inequality abroad

Just as rich and poor people exist in the United Kingdom, so they exist in the world as a whole. The difference is one of scale. Millions more people are involved and THE DEVELOPMENT GAP between rich and poor is even greater.

It is difficult to measure inequality on a world scale because information is often inaccurate. Collecting information in rich, developed countries such as the United Kingdom is quite easy. We can afford the cost of a population census and virtually everyone can read and write, so this makes filling in the forms simple. Poorer, developing countries find it much more difficult to collect information. Poverty, rapid population growth and illiteracy all make information gathering a difficult business. Therefore, comparisons between developed and developing countries must be made with care.

Figure 2.7 shows the world's twenty richest and twenty poorest countries measured by Gross National Product (GNP) per capita. GNP measures the total domestic and foreign output of a country and is therefore a measure of a country's economic wealth.

▶ Use an atlas to find out where these countries are. On an outline map of the world mark on the location of each country. Use one colour for rich countries and a different colour for poor countries.
  Write a paragraph describing where rich and poor countries are found in the world. Which continents are rich and which are poor?

So far, we have only looked at a country's development in terms of economic wealth. GNP per capita is only a rough guide to development; a country's wealth alone does not guarantee that a country is developed. For example, Saudi Arabia is a very rich oil producing state in the Middle East and its large exports of oil ensure that the economic wealth of the country is great (GNP per capita in 1980 was US $11 260). This makes Saudi Arabia as rich as the United States in overall economic terms. However, the wealth in Saudi Arabia is concentrated in the hands of a few people. Also, only 16% of the population can read and write and life expectancy is 54 years. In the United States, 99% of the population are literate and life expectancy is 74 years. Therefore, although the two countries are equally wealthy, the United States is more developed in other ways.

▶ Study the three maps shown in Figure 2.8 (over). They show different aspects of development, one economic and two social.
  Draw out a table with three sections:

Most developed countries	Partly developed countries	Least developed countries

Using an atlas to help you, list the countries which fit into each section of the table. The most developed countries will score highly on all three development indicators. The least developed countries will have low scores on all three of the development indicators. Those countries which are partly developed will have average scores, or a mixture of scores.

In today's world, there is a huge gap between developed and developing countries. The developed countries are economically and socially in good health compared with countries in the developing world. There are many reasons why the development gap exists:

● Most developing countries are poor and the lack of money hinders their attempts at development. The average GNP per capita for the world's 20

25

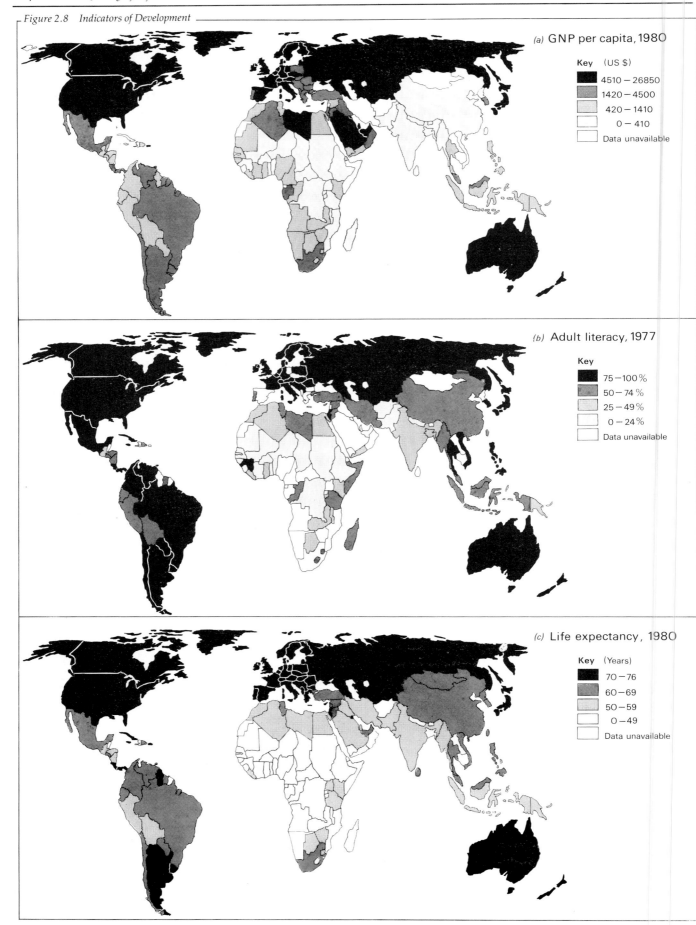

Figure 2.8   Indicators of Development

(a) GNP per capita, 1980

Key   (US $)

4510 – 26850
1420 – 4500
420 – 1410
0 – 410
Data unavailable

(b) Adult literacy, 1977

Key

75 – 100 %
50 – 74 %
25 – 49 %
0 – 24 %
Data unavailable

(c) Life expectancy, 1980

Key   (Years)

70 – 76
60 – 69
50 – 59
0 – 49
Data unavailable

poorest countries in 1980 was US $209 compared with an average of US $10278 for the world's 20 richest countries. There is simply more money available in the developed countries.

● Industrial activity is very limited in developing countries. Exports are frequently restricted to a limited range of primary products. For example, in Zambia copper accounts for 91% of all exports, in Ethiopia coffee accounts for 79% and in Bolivia tin accounts for 58%. World prices for these products have fallen in recent years making it very difficult to pay for imports with export earnings. Developed countries are not dependent upon one or two products and are affected less by price changes.

● Heavy dependence on foreign aid has led to the build-up of increasing debts in developing countries. A recent estimate put Brazil's foreign debt at US $93 billion and Mexico's at US $89 billion. Most of this money is owed to banks in North America and Western Europe. No one is really sure how these vast sums of money will be paid back. However, the burden of these debts is likely to keep poor countries poor for a very long time.

● Certain factors affect some developing countries but not others, e.g. political instability and wars which discourage investment and swallow up what little money does exist; poor natural resources which result in costly imports of fuel and minerals; and high population growth rates which increase pressure on the land and lead to unplanned urbanisation.

▶ 1 Write a paragraph to explain the term 'the development gap'.

2 The maps in Figure 2.8 show three indicators of development. Make a list of other items which could be used to measure development at the world scale.

3 Study the photographs shown in Figure 2.9. Write a paragraph describing the differences between the two photographs. Write a second paragraph suggesting how the lives of the people living in the two areas might be different.

4 Make a detailed study of one developing country. Gather information from an atlas, the library, encyclopedias, newspapers and other sources. In the study, include sections on the country's people, its farming and industry, and its development problems. The study should contain maps, diagrams, facts and figures, as well as written sections.

Figure 2.9   American suburb

. . . and Brazilian shanty town: two sides of development

2.2 Who Benefits?

Environment and development

Development involves change. Any attempt to raise the standard of living of people in the poor countries of the developing world involves changing the natural environment. The increasing need for food, fuel and shelter puts pressure on the environment and the outcome may include overgrazing, overfishing, loss of forest and grassland, and soil erosion. Construction of roads, dams, airports, irrigation systems, power and industrial plants can all create environmental difficulties as well.

It has been said that 'poverty is the worst form of pollution'. Under conditions of poverty, the environment often shows the effects of long years of mismanagement (overgrazing, soil erosion, water pollution, etc). Not only the quality of life but life itself is endangered, for it is difficult for these effects to be reversed. Other problems arise when ECONOMIC DEVELOPMENT is used to improve the quality of life. For example, agricultural improvement may involve constructing irrigation and drainage systems, clearing forests and using fertilisers and pesticides — all of which can cause damage to the natural environment. Industrial growth often results in the release of pollutants, especially into the air and sea.

▶ The United Kingdom is a highly developed country and many changes have been made to the natural environment through, for example, mechanised farming, the industrialisation of large areas, and the building of a dense communications system linking our towns and cities. Make a list of the environmental problems which such developments have brought.

In the past, development programmes have put economic concerns before environmental ones. The aim has been to produce more wealth in order to improve the country's economic position. However, a country does not develop just by getting richer. The environment must be protected as well, for it is the environment which is the source of much wealth.

Conflict between economic development programmes and environmental conservation has been common in many developing countries in recent years. In the past 20 years, many development projects have been threatening the tropical rain-forest of Amazonia in Brazil.

▶ Find a map of South America in an atlas. Using an outline map of South America draw on the boundary of Brazil. Mark on the position of the River Amazon and its main tributaries. Shade in the area covered by tropical rain-forest.

As Figure 2.10 shows, most of the world's tropical rain-forest occurs in about a dozen countries only. Most is in the area drained by the River Amazon and its tributaries. Brazil contains more of this type of vegetation than any other country. Tropical rain-forest is special for a number of reasons:

Country/Region	Area of Tropical Rain-Forest (km^2)
Brazil	2 800 000
Peru	500 000
Colombia	400 000
Venezuela	300 000
Guyanas☆	300 000
Bolivia	162 000
Ecuador	100 000
Africa (mainly Zaire and Gabon)	1 600 000
South-eastern Asia (mainly Malaysia and Indonesia)	900 000
World total	7 062 000

☆Includes Guyana, French Guiana and Surinam

Figure 2.10   Location of the world's tropical rain-forest

● It contains a great variety of plant and animal life — the greatest variety of any area on earth.
● It produces a great deal of the world's oxygen on which we depend for life. The forest vegetation 'breathes' in the carbon dioxide which we exhale. It is, therefore, part of the planet's life-support system.
● It is the home of the Amerindians, a traditional people who live in harmony with the forest by practising small-scale farming.

The Amazon rain-forest area of Brazil has been looked upon as an area where endless 'development' could take place. This could create wealth for Brazil, helping the whole country to develop. Some of the development projects which have been started in Amazonia are outlined in Figure 2.11. They have all brought serious environmental problems to the area.

Alternative approaches to development do exist for an area such as Amazonia. Tree-crop farming (e.g. rubber, palm oil and coconuts) is less damaging to the forest environment than cattle ranching or rice farming because it does not involve clearing vast areas of forest. In the past 50 years, 25 million ha (hectares) of tree-crop plantations have been established throughout the tropics. Environmental damage has been minimal.

The floodplain areas of Amazonia which are seasonally flooded are known as *varzea*. These areas are well suited to rice farming but they have been neglected in the past because new roads have linked upland areas, making them more accessible, and rice farming has developed here instead. More river transport instead of road transport would encourage rice farming in the *varzea* areas.

Mining could be one of the best forms of development for the Amazonian environment. Aluminium, tin, manganese, iron, kaolin, gold and diamonds are all found in the area. Mines take up quite small areas of land and forest destruction is limited. At the same time they bring jobs and the economic return is very high. Exploration, however, is difficult although satellite technology is now being used.

On a planet with a large population and a high demand for resources, environmental management will be of increasing importance.

Development Project	Project Description	Environmental Problems
1 Cattle ranching	Land and labour are cheap in Amazonia while the price of beef is high. This has encouraged farmers to clear vast areas of forest, convert it to pasture and collect large profits.	The land, stripped of its protective forest cover, soon becomes exhausted and must be abandoned. Serious soil erosion occurs and animal and plant life is lost. Farmers then move on to destroy a fresh area of forest.
2 Rice farming	Rice is the most widely planted crop in Amazonia. Forest is cleared and the rice takes the large amount of water it needs from the heavy rainfall. Most recent rice farming has been started in upland areas of Amazonia.	Rice is responsible for more deforestation than any other crop. The rainfed rice yields are very poor and get worse as soils lose their nutrients quickly. Farmers are quick to move to fresh areas of forest.
3 Plantation forestry	Original forest with its great variety of trees is destroyed and cleared to be replaced by a few species of trees which are grown for paper pulp.	Less damaging than cattle ranching or rice farming but a great deal of undocumented forest has been lost in Amazonia. Plant and animal life dependent on the original forest is also lost.
4 Roads	The vast size of Amazonia has made transport an important factor in development. In the early 1970s the Trans-Amazonian Highway Project involved the building of a highway across Amazonia from the Andes in the West, to the Atlantic Ocean in East.	The development of roads has opened up large areas of forest to cattle ranching and rice farming. Forest has been lost in order to provide a route for the roads themselves. The roads are expensive to construct and maintain, and they have made Brazil more dependent on imported oil.

Figure 2.11   Development projects in Amazonia

1 Write down a short explanation of the term 'economic development'.
2 Look at Figure 2.10 again. Now look in an atlas at the map which shows world vegetation regions. Compare the area of tropical rain-forest in West Africa and South-East Asia with South America. On a world map shade in the three main areas of tropical rain-forest.
3 Study Figure 2.11. Write a summary of the development projects which have been introduced into Amazonia and the environmental problems they have created.
4 Try to make up a check list of items for which any Amazonian development project should score well, e.g. a project should create jobs for local people.

Development successes

There are many sides to development. To some people development means economic growth brought about by more industry, better agriculture and increased exports. To others, development is about the things which affect the quality of everyday life — health, education and basic needs. Development is a mixture of both quantity and quality and takes place wherever common sense and good ideas have changed people's lives for the better.

In recent decades the developing countries of the world have changed dramatically. Thirty years ago most developing countries were economically poor and the quality of life was also poor. Today, the development gap between rich and poor nations still exists, as you have seen, but some progress has been made in poorer countries. DEVELOPMENT SUCCESS has been most noticeable in social rather than economic affairs. More children are now at school, fewer people are illiterate, more people have access to doctors and nurses and to clean, safe water.

Study Figure 2.12 which shows changes in death rates for Africa and Europe between 1960 and 1980.
Work out and record the change in death rates for both continents between 1960 and 1980. What reasons can you think of that might explain these changes? What do these changes tell us about development?

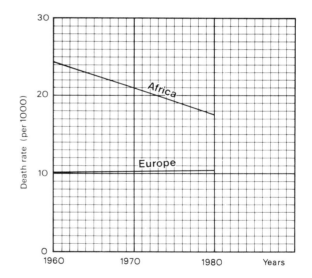

Figure 2.12   Changes in death rate in Africa and Europe

Developing countries have found it difficult to achieve the same sort of economic success that richer nations have had. However, the advances the poorer countries have made in health matters have been very impressive. More doctors and nurses, more hospitals, more medicines, and more health education have helped to control many diseases, such as malaria and smallpox, which were killing millions until recently. Life expectancy is now much longer in developing countries and although it is still far behind the richer countries, the rate of improvement is faster.

► Study Figure 2.13 which shows life expectancy in the United Kingdom and African Commonwealth countries for three separate dates.

Work out the average life expectancy for the African countries in 1960, 1970 and 1980. Draw a graph to show changes in life expectancy for the United Kingdom and the African countries (use the average figure) from 1960 to 1980.

What do these changes tell us about development?

Country	1960	1970	1980
United Kingdom	70	72	73
Ghana	36	41	49
Kenya	42	47	55
Lesotho	38	43	51
Malawi	35	38	44
Nigeria	33	38	39
Sierra Leone	36	41	47
Tanzania	37	42	52
Uganda	42	47	54
Zambia	38	43	49
Zimbabwe	44	49	55

Figure 2.13   Changes in life expectancy (in years) in selected African Commonwealth countries

There is no one path to development. Many countries are involved in trying out different paths taking into account their own circumstances. As natural environments, people, history, and economic opportunities differ, so will the different approaches to development adopted by countries. Figures 2.14 and 2.15 give two contrasting accounts of success in development.

► 1 Write down what you understand by the term 'development success'.
2 Study Figures 2.14 and 2.15 carefully. Use an atlas to find out where Taiwan and Cuba are located. Draw two sketch maps to show their locations.
3 Read the first paragraph of this section again. Which country appears to be more concerned with the quality of life in development? Which country is more concerned with economic growth in development?
4 Write a paragraph to explain how the development paths of Taiwan and Cuba are different. Which one do you think is the better?

Figure 2.14   Taiwan's 'economic miracle'

Taiwan is one of the most densely populated countries in the world. The land itself is about 75% mountainous, with some of the tallest peaks in the region. The only significant natural resources the island has are some deposits of coal, natural gas and water power, good weather and fertile soil.

In 1949 Taiwan became a refuge for the defeated Nationalist Government of Chiang Kai-Shek who arrived with millions of Chinese from the mainland. At the time it was thought Taiwan would soon be taken over by the new Communist government in Peking.

From this position has emerged one of the strongest of the newly-industrialised countries of Asia. Since the early 1950s Taiwan has maintained a real economic growth rate of over 8% per annum, one of the highest in the world. Even more significantly, the benefits of economic growth appear to have been evenly spread throughout Taiwanese society. Government figures indicate that the gap in income between the richest and poorest parts of the population has narrowed since the 1950s.

The question remains as to how Taiwan achieved its economic miracle against initially desperate odds. The answer is twofold. First, it had the support, after the Korean War broke out, of the USA. In the 1950s and 1960s the USA poured economic aid averaging $100 million a year into building up the country. Second, Taiwan itself was ready for development. The Nationalists, immediately after World War Two, regained control over Taiwan from Japan which had held it as a colony from 1895. The efficient Japanese had established an extensive communications system, reorganised agriculture so as to make it the most important export industry and left the foundations of many modern industries.

On this basis the exiled Nationalist government in 1949 began a series of reforms starting with a sweeping redistribution of land, reducing the power of landlords and giving tenant farmers a new start. The government also launched a series of plans which aimed first at reducing dependence on imports. In the 1960s Taiwan worked to expand export industries such as textiles and light electronics. By the early 1970s a modest plan for establishing heavy industries (steel, ship-building and petro-chemicals) was transforming the country beyond recognition.

adapted from *New Internationalist*, No. 80, October 1979

Figure 2.15   Cuba's 'harmony of development'

A visitor strolling through central Havana might be forgiven for wondering what economic success could possibly mean in Cuba. Cuba's greatest city has none of the bustle of Brazil's São Paulo or South Korea's Seoul. Private cars are few in number, commercial activity appears to be small, the atmosphere is calm.

Success has brought no boom to Havana, for booms are not what Cuba's revolution is about. When they took power in 1959 revolutionary leaders such as Fidel Castro and Che Guevara made it clear they hoped for rapid industrial development but they always gave priority to the development of social well-being. As a result, Havana today exhibits none of the ills of other major Third World cities. No crippled beggars stretch hands out to passers-by. Almost every dwelling, however humble, enjoys plumbing and electric light. At the workplace and in the neighbourhood a wide range of social, recreational and educational activities is available to every citizen.

Harmony of development is now the keynote and the emphasis more recently has been firmly placed on the countryside – yet another reason for the calm of Havana. In the Carribean, where massive bills for food imports are common, Cuba stands out as an example of the region's agricultural potential. The country has a big and growing dairy industry and nearly all the nation's basic foodstuffs are home-grown. A deep-sea fishing fleet earns more than $100 million a year from export earnings as well as helping the national diet. The citrus plantations provide a similar return. Fertiliser and cement plants have been built to service the needs of agriculture.

Many of Cuba's creations have provided other Third World countries with examples of development paths. The health and education systems, for example, have allowed the government to export thousands of teachers and doctors to other countries, particularly to African countries. Cuba is importing thousands of young Africans (mainly from Angola, Mozambique, Namibia and Ethiopia) to study in its unique 'schools in the countryside'. The students in these boarding schools work in neighbouring fields for about three hours a day. The labour that they do helps to meet the cost of their education and the results achieved in such schools have proved to be much better than in schools of the traditional type.

adapted from *New Internationalist*, No. 80, October 1979

2.3 North and South

History and development

Today's pattern of development is well-known. The countries of North America, Europe, Australasia and Japan are highly developed. They have great economic wealth and provide a high standard of living for their populations. By contrast, the countries of Central and South America, Africa and Asia are less developed. Many of these countries are poor and the standard of living is low. However, it should be remembered that this is a modern pattern. In the past, levels of development were very different in various parts of the world. Development is not just something affecting countries today. Throughout history parts of the world have been more widely developed than others.

▶ Study Figure 2.16 which shows some of the areas of the world that were highly developed between 3000BC and AD1500.
Make a list of the eleven centres of development shown on the map. Write down next to each one the name of the country, or countries, located there today.
How many of the countries that you have listed are developed countries?

The areas shown in Figure 2.16 were centres of civilisation and economic development at different times throughout history. Agriculture and industry were well developed, important scientific discoveries were made and great cities were built. Most of these centres of development were located in areas associated today with developing countries. The great cities and advanced agriculture and industry have now disappeared. It is interesting that up to AD1500 there were no centres of development in today's developed regions of North America and Australasia.

However, thoughout the Middle Ages Europe was undergoing change. By the end of the fifteenth century, Europe had made rapid advances in science and technology, using and building on many of the ideas from the ancient civilisations. Trade increased noticeably and a search began to seize, control and make use of the resources in the rest of the world. Europeans started to explore and expand beyond their known world and they began to conquer new lands and rule the people they found in them.

Land and gold were in demand above anything else. The Spanish and Portuguese were the first Europeans to venture out in search of these 'prizes' in the fifteenth and sixteenth centuries. Spanish explorers 'discovered' Central and South America and their reserves of gold and silver. These metals were important because they represented wealth and could be turned into gold and silver coins for trade. As these nations' trade increased, the demand for coins increased and so even more gold and silver were needed. The Spanish conquest of Central and South America which followed was a violent and cruel episode involving the murder of peoples on a massive scale.

Armies led by Cortés destroyed the highly developed Aztec society of Mexico and armies led by Pisarro destroyed the Inca civilisation in Peru. The gold and silver of their temples were shipped to Spain and the Spaniards claimed that these people were savages who needed to be civilised. The truth was that these were huge well-organised empires. Agriculture was more advanced than in Europe: crops such as maize, tobacco, potatoes and tomatoes, which did not exist in Europe at the time, were being grown. Arts and crafts were highly developed – especially cloth-making and jewellery and building and road-making were also very advanced. The Aztecs and Incas did not use money, and the vast quantities of gold and silver were for decoration and art only.

Figure 2.16   Developed areas, 3000 BC to AD 1500

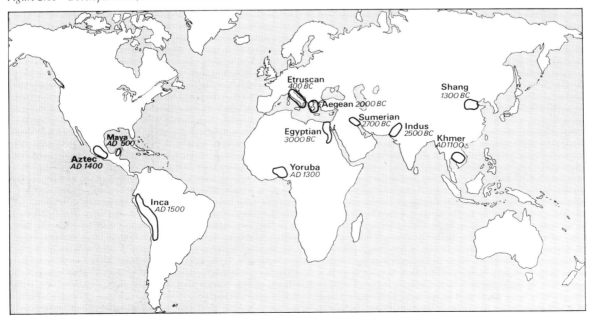

▶ Study Figures 2.17 and 2.18 which give an impression of life in Aztec and Inca society.
What evidence is there in the pictures that the Aztec and Inca societies were advanced? Make a list of as many things as possible.

▶ 1 Write a paragraph to explain the word 'colonies'.
2 Read through this section again. Write a summary of the impact of European contact on the Aztecs and Incas.
3 Study Figure 2.16. Choose one of the centres of development shown on the map. Using the school or local library, try to find out more about one of these highly developed societies. Why were they developed? What have they passed on to modern society? Why did they decline and disappear?

The Aztec and Inca peoples could not withstand the armies of the Spaniards. Firearms did not exist in South America until the Spaniards arrived, but even these would not have been enough to defeat the Aztec and Inca Empires. The Spaniards also brought with them diseases such as smallpox, measles and chicken pox, against which the local people had no resistance. Eventually, the people were enslaved to work in the mines and on the farms of Spaniards who settled in the area, but conditions were so harsh that they died in their thousands. The population of South America dropped drastically. It has been estimated that in AD1500 there were between 70 and 90 million Aztecs and Incas. By 1650 there were about 3.5 million.

The recent history of Africa and Asia is surprisingly similar to that of Central and South America. Other European nations such as Britain, France and the Netherlands followed the example of Spain and Portugal. Land was seized, resistance was crushed and COLONIES were set up across three continents. Some of these countries became colonies of exploitation, that is European countries used them as a source of cheap raw materials and as a market for their manufactured goods. Others became colonies of settlement where Europeans lived and established governments. This system of exploiters and exploited worked very much in favour of the developed countries of Europe and later of North America, Australasia and Japan. The modern pattern of richer and poorer nations has, therefore, developed over the past 500 years.

Figure 2.18   The Inca city of Cuzco in Peru, shortly after the conquest (the biggest building is the temple)

Figure 2.17   Reconstruction of an Aztec market scene – about AD 1500, before the Spanish conquest of Mexico

The Brandt Report

The Brandt Report (full title — 'North-South: A Programme for Survival') was published in 1980. It was produced by the Independent Commission on International Development and took its name from its chairman, the former Chancellor of West Germany, Willy Brandt. It was encouraged by the United Nations and the World Bank to study global problems and to suggest solutions to them. The Brandt Report is important because of the programme it put forward, and because of the influence it has had on governments since it was published.

The report did the following:

- Divided the world into a richer, developed 'North' and a poorer, developing 'South'.
- Gave a summary of world economic conditions in the late 1970s/early 1980s.
- Outlined recommendations for immediate action within the period 1980–85 to deal with what it saw as the world's most pressing problems.
- Outlined recommendations for action in the long term over the next 20 years.
- Suggested that world leaders should meet to discuss its findings.
- Suggested that a new international financial institution, the World Development Fund, be set up.

of the North as well as the countries of the South. To solve some of these pressing problems, the Brandt Report put forward an Emergency Programme for 1980–85 which is summarised in Figure 2.20. Twenty-two world leaders attended the Cancun Summit in Mexico, in October 1981, to discuss the Brandt Report and its recommendations. No agreement was reached and the richer countries of the North seemed unable to make the sacrifices necessary to speed up development and improve the quality of life in countries of the South. Now, in 1985, the poorer developing countries are still facing problems of poverty, famine and resource use as serious as those faced five years ago. So little had been done by governments by 1983 that the Brandt Commission produced a follow-up report (called 'Common Crisis — North-South: Cooperation for World Recovery') in which it stressed the need for action and outlined further proposals. It remains to be seen how great the common crisis must become before any real action is taken.

> 1 Write a paragraph to explain what is meant by the term 'North-South'.
> 2 Summarise the main recommendations of the Brandt Report. Explain why so little has been done by governments about the recommendations of the report.

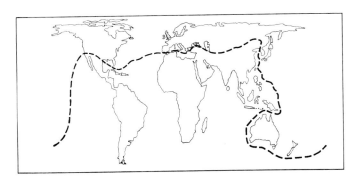

Figure 2.19   The North-South map

> 1 Study Figure 2.19 which shows the North-South division which the Brandt Report used. Make a list of some of the well-known countries in the North. Make another list for the South. Why are Australia and New Zealand included with the North although they are located south of the equator?
> 2 The map of the world which was used in the Brandt Report is known as a Peters' Projection. Compare it with a world map in your atlas which uses the more common Mercator Projection. Write a brief description of the differences between the two projections. Which countries appear to be i) over-represented, and ii) under-represented by each of the projections?

The people who drew up the Brandt Report were concerned that the world faced a number of pressing issues in NORTH-SOUTH relations. Poverty, famine, rapid use of non-renewable resources and unfair trade should all concern people in both the richer countries

Figure 2.20   An emergency programme: 1980–85

A large-scale transfer of resources to developing countries

By rich countries giving loans to the poorest countries which are interest-free and can be repaid over long periods.

By allowing countries with large debts, e.g. Mexico and Brazil, to spread repayments over longer periods.

An international energy strategy

This must aim to ensure regular supplies of oil. There should be stricter conservation of energy resources. Price rises for oil and other fuels should be gradual. Alternative and renewable energy sources, e.g. hydro-electric power, should be developed.

A global food programme

This would aim to increase food production especially in the South.

A system for long-term international food security needs developing. A grain reserve could be used for poor countries when cereal prices rise.

Major reforms in the international economic system

Steps towards an international monetary and financial system in which the South has a larger say. Increased efforts to improve developing countries' conditions of trade.

Key Points: Development

- The quality of life varies in different parts of the United Kingdom. Some regions are economically and socially healthier than others.

- The countries of the world can be divided into two groups: the richer developed countries and the poorer developing countries. The development gap between them is widening.

- Projects designed to create economic development in poorer countries sometimes create environmental problems. Conflicts of interest often exist between developers and conservationists.

- Despite widespread poverty, famine and disease in some developing countries, development success is being achieved by many poorer countries. Development involves social as well as economic affairs.

- Today's pattern of richer and poorer nations has developed over the last 500 years. In the past, the pattern of development was different and centres of economic development could be found in Central and South America, Africa and Asia.

- The Brandt Report has outlined the problems which the modern world faces and has put forward a programme for dealing with these problems. So far little has been achieved.

Part II
Managing Built Environments

In this part of *Worldwide Issues,* the emphasis is on urbanisation and industrialisation. Urban and industrial areas are our main built environments. They have been constructed by people for people, and this explains why some of the ideas raised in Part I are raised again here, especially those concerning the quality of life in urban areas.

Once towns and cities are established, they set in motion a number of events which it is difficult to change or stop. All over the world, cities attract people, often through their reputation for having 'streets paved with gold'. The reality, of course, is quite different and large urban areas give rise to many problems. Nevertheless, new towns continue to be built and old ones expanded. The urban environment seems to have a magnetic quality that just cannot be resisted.

Industry is a form of economic activity on which we all depend, but, just like the urban areas in which it is most often located, industry is subject to major changes from time to time. Most of these changes lead to an alteration in both the location of industry and the supply of jobs. Attracting new industry to old areas, and the creation of lasting jobs in new industries, has become a major issue in all the countries of the developed world. Finally, while industry can have a beneficial impact on the economic and social environment – by creating or sustaining employment, for example – it can also have an undesirable impact on the natural environment, through various forms of pollution.

Industry and housing — both built, but better kept apart?

Chapter 3 URBAN ENVIRONMENTS

3.1 Cities at Breaking Point

Britain's urban breakdown

In the spring and summer of 1981, several of Britain's biggest cities were hit by riots. The people involved were mostly young, unemployed and black. Their anger and violence were directed towards property and the police. Scenes such as the ones shown in Figure 3.1 were typical of the disturbances. The riots were the worst in Britain for more than a hundred years.

The first riots started in April in the Brixton area of London. In one weekend:
- 82 people were arrested.
- 279 police officers were injured.
- 45 members of the public were injured.
- 56 police vehicles were damaged or destroyed.
- 61 private vehicles were damaged or destroyed.
- 145 buildings were damaged, 28 of them by fire.

In July, fresh rioting broke out at Southall in London, Toxteth in Liverpool and Moss Side in Manchester. The damage to property and injury to people were again serious. The rioting in Toxteth was particularly bad.

Why did the riots take place? Why were these particular cities affected by riots?

Figure 3.1a   Moments of confrontation: the Brixton riots

Figure 3.1b   Moments of confusion: the Liverpool riots

Each riot had its own local causes but some factors were common to all the riots:

- Economic recession grew worse at the end of the 1970s and affected young people badly. In 1981 almost 20% of those aged between 16 and 24 were unemployed. Unemployment amongst young black people was even higher.
- Immigration into Britain during the more prosperous years of the 1950s and 1960s attracted a large number of black people from the countries of the old empire. They took jobs that British-born people preferred not to do and settled in the outworn urban areas where British-born people preferred not to live. Great Britain's population of 49 million in 1951 included about 75 000 black people (0.2% of the total population). In 1981, of a total population of 54 million, there were just over 2 million black people (about 4% of the total population).
- Racial prejudice excluded the black immigrants, and their British-born black children, from the better jobs and homes. Verbal and physical abuse of black people built up their anger and frustration.
- Street crime, especially crime involving personal violence, increased in the urban areas. The stop and search methods of the police focussed mainly on young black people. This offended black people.
- All of the riots happened in INNER CITY AREAS where the older housing is located, close to the centre of large cities. Inner city areas have been declining for many years. Jobs and people have been moving out of these areas. Figure 3.2 shows how population has fallen between the last two population censuses in Liverpool, Manchester and Inner London.

City	Population in 1971	Population in 1981	% Population change between 1971 and 1981
Liverpool	603 000	510 000	−15.4
Manchester	542 000	449 000	−17.2
Inner London	3 033 000	2 490 000	−17.9

Figure 3.2   Population change in the inner city

▶ On an outline map of Britain mark on the position of London, Manchester and Liverpool. Mark on the following cities which have populations of more than 250 000 each and which have large inner city areas: Belfast, Birmingham, Bradford, Bristol, Cardiff, Coventry, Edinburgh, Glasgow, Hull, Leeds, Leicester, Nottingham, Sheffield, Stoke-on-Trent and Wolverhampton.

7% of the British population live in inner city areas (about 3.8 million people). The quality of life in these areas is poor and problems include: poor housing, declining industries, poverty, poor services, heavy concentrations of young and old people, falling populations, high unemployment, high levels of vandalism and crime, and a poor physical environment.

▶ Read the newspaper extract (Figure 3.3). It gives an idea of living conditions for some people in Hackney, an inner city area of London. Imagine you are one of the people mentioned in the newspaper extract. Write a letter to your friend who lives in another town describing living conditions in Hackney.

On Mathias House estate children play on the concrete roadways, amid windblown rubbish, dumped mattresses and wrecked cars. The stairwell is scattered with broken glass, decorated with obscene graffiti, and stinking of urine.

Sarah Jones lives with her seven children on an upper floor: three years ago she was abandoned by her husband with £1 753 of rent and fuel debts, for which the courts held her, as co-tenant, responsible. Her electricity was cut off for two years, but after her toddlers burned themselves on candles and a paraffin heater, she illegally reconnected herself.

In the inner city you meet such cases at every turn. Ten-year-old Arvind Calane is shortly to begin secondary school. He lives with his Indian parents and baby brother in a single room 10 feet by 12 feet (rent = £12 per week). They share a bathroom with four other households. One weekly tubful of hot water is all they can afford for bathing: father first, mother and baby next, Arvind last. Arvind's bed is a mattress, laid down at night in the only space left among the furniture.

The Sunday Times, August 1983

Figure 3.3   Living in the inner city: Hackney, London

It was in these inner city areas, against this background of poverty and neglect, that the 1981 riots took place. Figure 3.4 shows what was happening at the time of the 1981 population census in London, Manchester and Liverpool where the worst riots occurred in the months that followed. In each of those districts there were high concentrations of young people, of black people and of unemployed people.

Social Statistic	Brixton	Inner London	Moss Side	Greater Manchester	Toxteth	Merseyside
% Population aged under 24	43.9	35.5	53.3	37.5	42.6	38.2
% Men unemployed	17.4	12.8	27.1	12.6	33.8	17.8
% People in households with NCWP☆ head	43.3	18.8	40.0	3.9	11.2	1.0

☆ Born in New Commonwealth or Pakistan, i.e. mainly black. Most Liverpool blacks are British-born

Figure 3.4   Young and idle in the riot zones, 1981

▶ 1 Write down a definition of an 'inner city area'.
2 Study Figure 3.1 a and b. Imagine you were a newspaper reporter on the scene when the riots were taking place. Write a short newspaper article describing what happened.
3 Study Figure 3.2. Calculate the total number of people that left Liverpool, Manchester and Inner London between 1971 and 1981. Was it a large exodus? Compare this number with the total population of the town where you live.
4 The government appointed a judge, Lord Scarman, to investigate the riots. They asked him to produce a report with recommendations for changes in the inner city areas. Write a short report in which you list the changes you would make in order to improve the quality of life in inner city areas. Use Figure 3.5 to help you with this task.

Figure 3.5 What they said about the riots

Africa's fastest growing city

Lagos, Nigeria's capital, is Africa's fastest growing city. Half the population is under 15 years of age and every day more people pour in from the surrounding countryside. They come in search of work and housing in the 'big city'.

▶ Find Nigeria, and its capital city Lagos, on a map in your atlas. Draw a sketch map of West Africa to show the position of Nigeria. Mark on the location of Lagos.

Nigeria is a developing country and its population is growing rapidly. Figure 3.6 shows how population has been growing in Nigeria in recent years and how it is likely to grow in the near future. An increasing number of these people are living in towns and cities. In 1980, 20% of Nigeria's total population was living in towns and cities — this was about 17 million people. Of these, 4 million people (nearly 5% of the total population of Nigeria) were living in Lagos.

Year	Population of Nigeria	Population of Lagos
1970	66 000 000	1 000 000
1980	85 000 000	4 000 000
1990☆	119 000 000	7 000 000
2000☆	169 000 000	10 000 000

☆ Estimates

Figure 3.6 Population growth in Nigeria and its capital, Lagos

▶ Using the information in Figure 3.6 draw two graphs to show the growth of population in Nigeria and Lagos. Write a short paragraph to describe what the graphs show.

Towns and cities of all sizes are growing in Nigeria. In 1970, there were 24 urban areas with populations over 100 000 and 2 urban areas with populations over 500 000. By 1980, there were 27 urban areas with populations over 100 000 and 9 urban areas with populations over 500 000. However, the most rapid URBAN GROWTH has been in Lagos which is growing so quickly that it is not possible to collect accurate population figures.

Why is Lagos growing so rapidly and what are the effects of rapid urban growth?

One reason why Lagos is growing more quickly than other urban areas is because it is already the largest city. As Nigeria's capital, its main port, its main industrial centre, and main centre for communications with other countries, it draws people in from surrounding towns and countryside. The larger the city, the greater are the attractions, and in addition to this in-migration of people, there is a large natural increase in population. In 1980, for every 1000 people in Nigeria, 50 were born and 17 died, an increase of 33 people for every 1000 in the populaton. The increase in Britain in 1980 was 2 per 1000. As Figure 3.7 shows, the city expands as a result of these differences in the flow of people.

The effects of urban growth are all too easily noticed in Lagos:

● Traffic jams and crowded public transport.
● The growth of slums.
● Not enough jobs for the increasing population.
● Power cuts and water shortages.

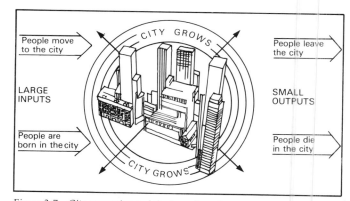

Figure 3.7 City expansion and the flow of people

A journalist wrote about Lagos:
'Not so long ago the United Nations called Lagos the dirtiest capital in the world. Since then, only feeble attempts have been made to clean up Africa's fastest growing city. It now chokes on bad housing and traffic jams. Whole streets are littered with compost, broken bottles, pieces of furniture, empty cans. The stench is intolerable during the dry season and worse when it rains. Then, over half the streets are flooded. But the city-dwellers have learnt to live with it all. Street

parties — owambes —are still held in the evenings. The children don't escape though. About a seventh of all babies die before their first birthday. Infant mortality is usually due to respiratory and infectious diseases. Food stalls are sometimes sited near rubbishdumps. . . .'

Housing conditions in Lagos are very bad for poor people: 86% of the population have no internal water in their houses, 60% of houses have no modern lavatory, 82% of houses have no public refuse disposal and 75% of all families in Lagos live in one room. Things are not much better in the rest of Nigeria. Of the 17 million people who live in towns and cities, nearly 4 million are living below the official poverty line.

What is happening today in Lagos is happening to a greater or lesser degree in cities throughout the developing world. Massive RURAL-TO-URBAN MIGRATION is adding its weight to population growth rates previously unknown in human history.

1 Write down a definition for 'urban growth'.
2 Look back through the information in this section. Make a list of the effects of urban growth in developing countries.
3 Study Figure 3.8. Using evidence from the photographs, describe the differences in the environment of richer and poorer parts of Lagos. Do cities in developed countries, such as Britain, show similar differences?
4 Study Figure 3.9 which lists Nigerian urban areas with more than 100000 people. Make a copy of Figure 3.10 which shows the location of these urban areas. Divide the urban areas into three or four groups (e.g. all the urban areas with populations between 100000 and 200000 could form one group.) Using a different symbol for each group of urban areas, place the appropriate symbol on each urban centre shown on your map. What other problems, besides urban growth, does Nigeria suffer from? The Nigerian government is planning to build a new capital at Abuja. Why do you think this may be a good idea? Should a developing country spend its limited resources on such a project?

Figure 3.8   The rich and poor faces of Lagos

No.	Urban Area	Population ('000s)
1	Lagos	4000
2	Ibadan	847
3	Ogbomosho	432
4	Kano	399
5	Oshogbo	282
6	Ilorin	282
7	Abeokuta	253
8	Port Harcourt	242
9	Zaria	224
10	Ilesha	224
11	Onitsha	220
12	Iwo	214
13	Ado-Ekiti	213
14	Kaduna	202
15	Mushin	197
16	Maiduguri	189
17	Enugu	187
18	Ede	182
19	Aba	177
20	Ife	176
21	Ila	155
22	Oyo	152
23	Ikerre-Ekiti	145
24	Benin City	136
25	Iseyin	115
26	Katsina	109
27	Calabar	103

Figure 3.9   Urban areas in Nigeria

The super cities

The twentieth century has seen a dramatic change in the way we live. By the year 2000, for the first time in human history, the majority of mankind will live in towns and cities. Some cities have grown with great speed with populations numbering many millions.

At the beginning of this century there were only six MILLIONAIRE CITIES (cities with more than one million inhabitants) in the world. These were found either in Europe or North America. By 1960, there were 25 millionaire cities spread over five continents.

▶ Figure 3.12 shows the location of millionaire cities in 1960. Using an atlas to help you, find out where each of the following cities is located on the map: London, Mexico City, New York, Peking, Tokyo, Cairo, Chicago, Detroit, Buenos Aires, Paris, Berlin, Jakarta, Osaka, Moscow, Leningrad, São Paulo, Baltimore, Calcutta, Canton, Bombay, Rio de Janeiro, Munich, Shanghai, Philadelphia, Los Angeles.

By 1980, the number of millionaire cities had increased to 64 spread over six continents – 39 new millionaire cities in just 20 years! These cities already had large populations in 1960 but the figures give some idea of how rapidly cities were growing, especially large cities. The spread of cities across each continent has also changed.

▶ Figure 3.13 shows the location of millionaire cities in 1980. Count up the number of cities in each continent and record your answer on a copy of the table shown in Figure 3.11. Write a paragraph to explain the changes which the table shows.

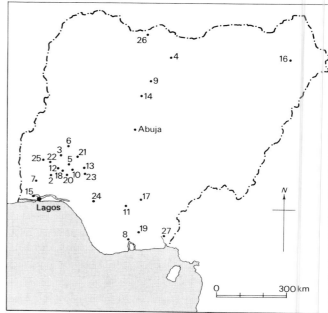

Figure 3.10   The location of urban areas in Nigeria

Some of the world's millionaire cities are very large indeed. For example, Mexico City is thought to have a population somewhere between 10 and 15 million. With so many people and with so many of the population unable to read or write, it is difficult to calculate an exact figure. There are 20 cities in the world which have a population of over 5 million each — these are the world's 'super cities'. Eight of these super cities are located in developed countries, e.g. Paris in France (nearly 10 million people) and Moscow in the USSR (just over 8 million people). Most of the super cities are located in developing countries, e.g. São Paulo in Brazil (nearly 9 million people) and Calcutta in India (just over 7 million people). Together these 20 cities contain nearly 200 million people and they are still growing. By the year 2000 many of the millionaire cities will also have populations of more than 5 million.

Continent	1960	1980
North America	7	
South America	3	
Africa	1	
Europe	6	
Asia	8	
Australasia	0	
Total	25	

Figure 3.11   The spread of millionaire cities

▶ 1 Write down a definition of a 'millionaire city'.
2 Study the information in the table in Figure 3.14. This shows the population growth rates in some of the world's largest cities between 1970 and 1985. On a world map draw vertical bars to show the growth rate of each city. You will need to position the base of the bar where the city is located. You will also need to work out a scale for the bars.
3 Describe the pattern shown on the finished map. What differences exist between cities in developed and developing countries? Why do some cities have much larger growth rates than others?

*Figure 3.12 Millionaire cities in 1960
(using standard metropolitan areas)*

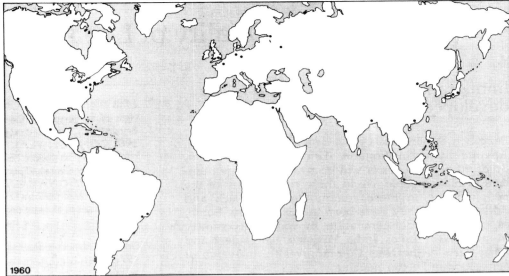

*Figure 3.13 Millionaire cities in 1980
(using standard metropolitan areas)*

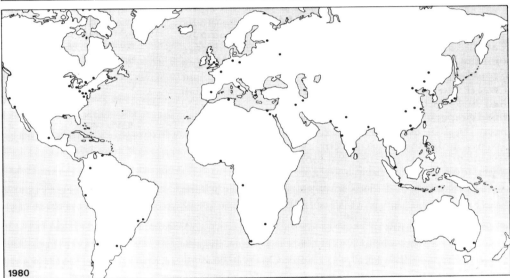

City	% Growth Rate 1970 – 1985
Los Angeles	63
New York	15
Mexico City	113
Bogota	146
Lima	121
Buenos Aires	39
São Paulo	115
Rio de Janeiro	68
London	6
Lagos	186
Moscow	13
Baghdad	145
Tehran	132
Karachi	163
Bombay	109
Calcutta	75
Bangkok	137
Bandung	242
Peking	71
Shanghai	43
Seoul	124
Tokyo	69
Osaka	55

Figure 3.14 Population growth in the world's major cities

3.2 The Quality of Life in Cities

Immigrants and the city – the developed world

People in Britain talk a great deal about IMMIGRATION. Anyone living in London, Leicester, Birmingham, Bradford or Manchester will be aware that large numbers of black people live in these cities. Many of the people living in these communities are black and British, that is they were born in this country. Some, especially the older generation, moved to this country from the West Indies, India, Pakistan, Bangladesh and other parts of the New Commonwealth, in search of better jobs and better housing.

We sometimes talk about immigration as though it were something new. Immigrants have been coming to Britain for a long time. For example Mohammed Zaman, an Asian, owns a house in Bradford. Before him the house had been lived in since 1945 by Matilda Rosenberg, a Jew; Michael Murphy, an Irishman, had lived in the house between 1921 and 1945; John Tindall had lived in the house between 1896 and 1921. Only the last person was born in Britain. The house had been lived in by immigrants for more than 60 years. Today, only the most recent newcomers, such as Asians and West Indians, are looked upon as immigrants; Jews and Irish people are not.

Most of the recent black immigrants came to Britain in the 1950s, 1960s and 1970s. Many of them came to escape the poverty of Britain's ex-colonies. In Britain there was the chance of a better job and a better house. In 1951 there were about 75 000 black people in Britain out of a total population of 49 million. By 1981 the total black population had reached 2 million out of a total population of 54 million. At first the new immigrants were welcomed as they provided the cheap, unskilled labour needed for a booming economy. As economic recession hit in the 1970s the need for such labour declined rapidly.

Immigration is now tightly controlled and in 1979 only 195 000 immigrants entered the UK. Only 41 000 came from the New Commonwealth, the vast majority came from the white Commonwealth and from countries of the European Economic Community.

▶ Figure 3.15 shows the main effects of different Immigration Acts between 1948 and 1981. Write a paragraph to describe how the law has changed towards immigration during this time.

What makes immigration such an important issue in Britain today is that the most recent immigrants, unlike the Irish and the Jews, are black. As they live together their communities are more 'visible' and certain RESIDENTIAL PATTERNS can be noticed.

▶ Study Figure 3.16 which shows where England's black population is located. Describe the distribution of black people in Britain. Compare this map with a map showing population density in England. What do you notice?

1948 BRITISH NATIONALITY ACT: confirmed the right of all citizens of Commonwealth countries to enter Britain freely, work and settle.
1962 COMMONWEALTH IMMIGRANTS ACT: restricted entry to people holding work permits and to close families of residents and permit holders.
1968 COMMONWEALTH IMMIGRANTS ACT: was rushed through parliament in three days to deny entry to British subjects of Asian descent. These people, mostly resident in East Africa, had been promised British protection. When they were threatened with expulsion from Kenya, the British government decided not to protect them after all.
1971 IMMIGRATION ACT: was an attempt to say in more acceptable terms that Britain preferred white immigrants. It invented the word 'patrial' to describe anyone with at least one British grandparent, or who had been naturalised or lived for five years in Britain. Patrials and their close families, and families of other Commonwealth citizens legally resident in Britain before 1973, might enter freely. EEC citizens, including the Irish, might also enter freely. All others – with British, Commonwealth or foreign passports – needed permits.
1981 BRITISH NATIONALITY ACT: restricts British citizenship, with full right of residence, to people already legally settled in Britain, or who have one British parent and have been registered abroad at birth. All others have no right to enter Britain.

Figure 3.15   Immigration Acts in Britain

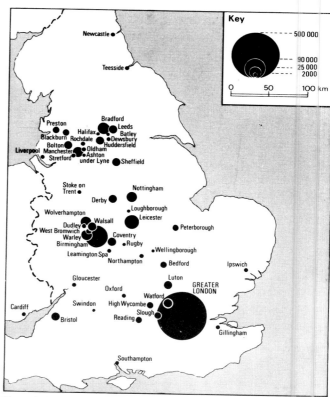

Figure 3.16   England's black population

There is a pattern to where immigrants live in Britain. Liverpool is well-known for its large Irish community. Large communities of Jews live in London, Leeds and Manchester. Black immigrants have been attracted to the large, industrial cities of Birmingham, Bradford, Nottingham and Leicester, as well as to London.

Residential patterns also exist within cities. In London a large Irish population can be found in Kilburn in the north-west of the city. Jewish people are numerous in the Golders Green area of north London, and Haringey is known for its Greeks, Cypriots and Turks.

The urban riots of 1981 reminded people in Britain that our cities are multi-racial and that some parts of our cities are deprived. Concentrations of black people exist in inner city areas where the housing is poor, unemployment is high, and poverty widespread. Local and national government will need to provide more help for these communities.

▶ 1 Write down a definition of an 'immigrant'.
2 Study Figure 3.15 again. Write a paragraph to explain how the different Immigration Acts have affected black immigrants and white immigrants. Have they been treated in the same way or a different way?
3 Make a copy of the map of London shown in Figure 3.17. The number of each London borough is marked on the map. The numbers correspond to the numbers in the table, Figure 3.18. Shade or colour each square in the key (making the shading or colours darker towards the top of the key). Then, using your key, shade or colour each London borough according to the information in column 3 of Figure 3.18. Give this map the title: 'The Residential Pattern of West Indian Immigrants in London'.
4 Now draw a second map using the information in column 4 of the table. Use the same shading or colour key. Give this map the title: 'The Residential Pattern of Asian Immigrants in London'.
5 Describe the pattern which each map shows. What are the similarities and differences between the maps? What reasons can you suggest for the similarities and differences?

Number on Map	Borough	People Born in the West Indies as a % of the Total Population	People Born in Asia as a % of the Total Population
1	Barking	0–2	6–8
2	Barnet	0–2	6–8
3	Bexley	0–2	2–4
4	Brent	8+	8+
5	Bromley	2–4	2–4
6	Camden	2–4	4–6
7	Croydon	4–6	4–6
8	Ealing	4–6	8+
9	Enfield	2–4	2–4
10	Greenwich	2–4	6–8
11	Hackney	8+	6–8
12	Hammersmith	8+	2–4
13	Haringey	8+	2–4
14	Harrow	0–2	0–2
15	Havering	0–2	0–2
16	Hillingdon	0–2	4–6
17	Hounslow	2–4	8+
18	Islington	8+	2–4
19	Kensington & Chelsea	8+	4–6
20	Kingston-upon-Thames	0–2	2–4
21	Lambeth	8+	2–4
22	Lewisham	8+	0–2
23	Merton	4–6	4–6
24	Newham	8+	8+
25	Redbridge	2–4	4–6
26	Richmond-upon-Thames	0–2	2–4
27	Southwark	8+	0–2
28	Sutton	0–2	0–2
29	Tower Hamlets	2–4	8+
30	Waltham Forest	4–6	6–8
31	Wandsworth	8+	4–6
32	Westminster	8+	6–8

Figure 3.18   Data on immigrant residential patterns in London

Figure 3.17   Outline map of London boroughs

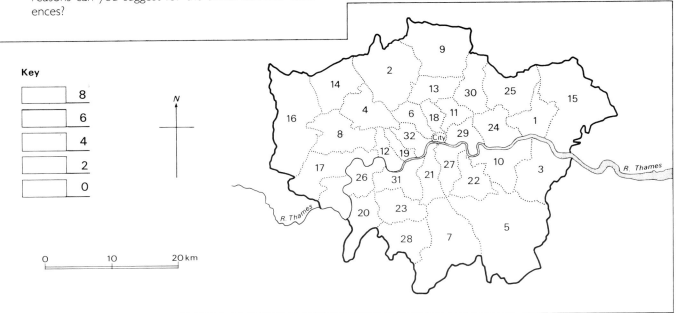

Immigrants and the city – the developing world

Population movement is a worldwide feature. Sometimes people move from one country to another but more often they move within a country. People move to improve their lives, so they move from the poorer to the richer parts of a country. In the developing world this usually means moving from the countryside to the city, and this rural to urban migration has resulted in cities becoming full with newcomers – immigrants from the countryside.

The process which involves this shift of population from rural to urban areas is known as URBANISATION. Urbanisation has been very rapid in the developing countries of South America. For example, in 1940 Brazil had only 31% of its population living in cities, by 1960 46% of Brazilians lived in cities and by 1980 the number living in cities had risen to 68%. A similar pattern can be found in most South American countries.

▶ Make a copy of the table shown in Figure 3.19. Work out the percentage change in urban population between 1960 and 1980 for each country. Put the answers in the last column of the table. Which countries have the most rapid rates of urbanisation?

Country	% Urban Population (1960)	% Urban Population (1980)	% Change in Urban Population (1960–1980)
Argentina	74	82	
Bolivia	24	33	
Brazil	46	68	
Chile	68	80	
Colombia	48	70	
Ecuador	34	45	
Paraguay	36	39	
Peru	46	67	
Uruguay	80	84	
Venezuela	67	83	

Note: Data not available for Guyana, French Guiana and Surinam

Figure 3.19   The growth of urban population in South America

The rapid increase in urban population can be explained in three ways:

● The natural growth of population in the cities.
● People moving to South American countries who choose to live in the cities.
● The migration of people from the poorer countryside to the richer cities to look for jobs in industry.

The last factor is by far the most important in most developing countries. In Brazil, cities of all sizes have grown through the influx of immigrants from the countryside. In 1970 there were 59 urban settlements in Brazil with more than 100 000 inhabitants and five of these were millionaire cities. By 1980 there were 116 settlements with more than 100 000 inhabitants and nine of these were millionaire cities. All this in just 10 years!

▶ Study Figure 3.20 which shows how Brazil's labour force and urban population have changed between 1960 and 1980. The graph shows the rapid growth of urban population. What else does the graph show which might explain Brazil's rapid urbanisation? What do you think will happen to urban population and the different parts of the labour force between 1980 and 1990?

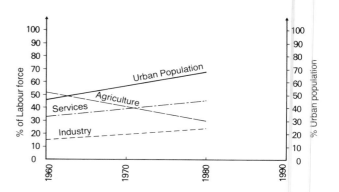

Figure 3.20   Changes in Brazil's labour force and urban population

In Brazil, urbanisation has developed hand in hand with industrialisation. As industry and services have developed in the towns and cities, people have been attracted from the surrounding countryside. The urban population has grown and employment in agriculture has declined.

It has been estimated that 75 000 people move from the countryside to towns and cities throughout the world every day. Studies have shown that the two most important reasons for migration from the countryside are better job opportunities and higher incomes in the cities. Compared with the countryside the cities seem very attractive:

● Very little investment takes place in rural areas. The poor countryside gets poorer and the rich cities get richer.
● Poor countries which receive aid from richer countries often get it in the form of food aid. This can help push down the prices that local farmers receive for their own produce.
● Cities can provide work opportunities for resourceful migrants – if not a job in a factory then maybe a job shoe-cleaning, refuse collecting or at worst, begging.
● Incomes are higher in urban areas — on average three times higher than in the countryside.
● Chances of a college education are seven times better, chances of seeing a doctor are ten times better and there is nine times more credit available.

However, problems come with this massive drift of population from rural to urban areas. Slums and SQUATTER SETTLEMENTS have sprung up around the edges of cities as people have tried to solve the housing crisis by building their own makeshift homes. The demand for such basic facilities as sanitation has been almost impossible to meet. Figure 3.21 shows the proportion of people living in the squatter settlement areas of the main South American cities.

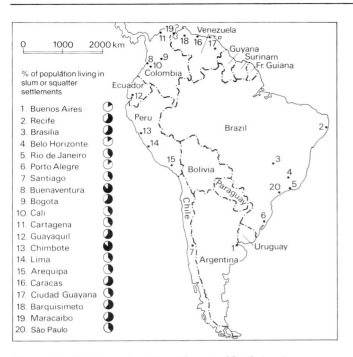

Figure 3.21   The slum and squatter settlements of South America

% of population living in slum or squatter settlements

1. Buenos Aires
2. Recife
3. Brasilia
4. Belo Horizonte
5. Rio de Janeiro
6. Porto Alegre
7. Santiago
8. Buenaventura
9. Bogota
10. Cali
11. Cartagena
12. Guayaquil
13. Chimbote
14. Lima
15. Arequipa
16. Caracas
17. Ciudad Guayana
18. Barquisimeto
19. Maracaibo
20. São Paulo

Figure 3.22   The 'suburbio' of Guayaquil, Ecuador

Guayaquil is Ecuador's largest port and industrial city. Its population has grown from a few hundred thousand to over a million in the last ten years. Much of the expansion has been taken up by the 'suburbio', a vast squatter settlement which is swamped at high tide. Figure 3.22 shows the suburbio of Guayaquil. The settlers have built their own small houses using bamboo and corrugated iron as building materials. They do their own urban planning by building the streets and housing blocks on a grid pattern. The city authorities have started to fill in parts of the tidal swamp and install basic services such as water and electricity.

Although squatter settlements are unhealthy and overcrowded they are a self-help solution to the housing problem of cities in developing countries. But, where city authorities have tried to install services and improve the environment, the quality of life has improved for the urban poor. In the long run improving life in the countryside is the only way in which the flow of people to the cities can be stemmed.

1   Explain what is meant by the terms 'urbanisation' and 'squatter settlement'.
2   Write a paragraph to explain why people are leaving the countryside and moving to the cities in developing countries.
3   Study Figure 3.23 which shows Colombo in Sri Lanka. Using an Oxfam financed brick machine the housing is being improved. Describe the improvements.
4   Write a story about someone who leaves a poor farming area in the countryside and moves to the city. Do some background research first, choosing a particular country and city, and plan the storyline before you write the final version.

Figure 3.23   (top and bottom) New brick and plaster houses with old houses in the background, Colombo, Sri Lanka

The unequal city

Just as rich and poor countries exist within the world, and rich and poor regions exist within countries, so rich and poor areas exist within cities. This is true of cities in developed and developing countries. All cities are unequal. They offer a comfortable and secure life to the well-off and a difficult and uncertain life for the poor. These different groups of people occupy different areas within the city.

Figure 3.24 shows the pattern of housing quality in Lima, the capital of Peru. The best housing is found near the city centre. Here the middle classes of the city live in great comfort. They have all the facilities of modern homes, such as electricity and clean, piped water. Immigrants to the city from the surrounding countryside began to arrive in recent years and have set up squatter settlements on the edge of the city on the only land available. This pattern of the rich living near the centre and the poor living on the edge of the city is typical of many cities in developing countries.

Cities in developed countries such as Britain are also unequal. Rich and poor areas can be distinguished in every town and city. However, the gap between rich and poor is not usually as great as that in developing countries and the residential pattern is also different.

Figure 3.25 shows the pattern of housing quality in London. Here housing quality is poorest nearest the city centre and gets better towards the edges of the city. In cities of the developed countries, a distinction can usually be drawn between the INNER CITY AREAS and the SUBURBS. The richer, more mobile middle classes live in surburban areas where facilities are better and where there are few problems of overcrowding and poor environment. Poorer, less mobile people are left to the lower quality housing and poor physical environment of inner city areas.

▶ 1 Describe the main differences between 'suburbs' and the 'inner city'.
  2 Study the photographs of an inner city area and a suburban area shown in Figure 3.26. From evidence in the photographs, write down a list of differences between the suburb and the inner city area.
  3 Draw a map of your own town. Try to mark on those areas of different housing quality. Can you identify areas which look different and which are occupied by different groups of people?

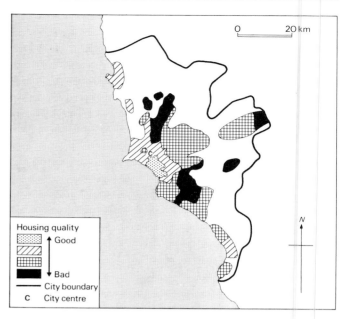

Figure 3.24   Housing quality in Lima, Peru

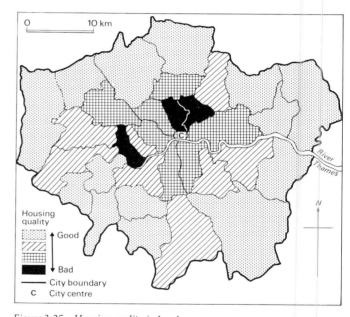

Figure 3.25   Housing quality in London

Figure 3.26   Coventry, suburb

. . . and inner city

3.3 Remaking Cities

People and planners

Towns and cities are constantly changing as older parts decay and newer parts are added. In the past 40 years, there has been a great deal of such activity in British cities. Pressure for urban change has come from a number of different directions:

● Bombing in World War II left many areas near the centre of Britain's large cities in ruins.
● Population growth in the 1950s and 1960s led to urban growth — a demand for more houses, more factories and more shops.
● More people now have cars and urban transport systems have had to be changed to cope with the volume of traffic.
● Many of the houses built in Victorian times have become old and need renewing and replacing.

At the same time, a group of people has been trained to deal with these problems. They are known as PLANNERS. It is the job of the planners to say what needs changing, when, and in what way. Planners try to renew our urban environments for the benefit of people living there and they have to manage some of the conflicts which arise.

▶ Study Figure 3.27 which shows some cartoonists' views of planners and the world of planning. What are the cartoonists saying about planners? Is it a kind view or not? Why?

Planners started getting a bad reputation in the early 1960s. This was largely because of the policy of wholesale redevelopment of areas of old housing. Under this policy, areas of old housing in inner city areas were demolished and people were either re-housed on suburban estates or in high-rise tower blocks. This led to the break-up of communities and to social problems.

The situation became even worse in the late 1960s and 1970s when planners demolished houses to build urban ring roads and urban motorways. Shopping patterns were also forced to change as small high street shops and markets were replaced by large covered shopping centres. All of these developments were encouraged by land speculators and property developers.

The face of planning started to change in the late 1970s and 1980s. Much more attention is now paid to people and the communities they live in. Wholesale demolition of housing has stopped. The emphasis is now on renovating houses rather than replacing them. This means communities can stay together. High-rise tower blocks are no longer built for residential purposes.

The most successful attempts at urban planning have been where planners have involved the people for whom they have been planning, kept communities together, and created environments that people want to live in.

Figure 3.27 The world of planning

▶ 1 Write down a definition of 'planners'.
 2 Study Figure 3.28 which shows existing and proposed land use in a small redevelopment area called Camlachie in inner Glasgow. Copy the key from Figure 3.28 and put a plus or a minus sign next to each land use to show whether it has increased or decreased after development. Who has gained?
 3 Write a paragraph to explain what the planners are trying to do in this area. Refer to evidence from the two maps.
 4 Design some cartoons which are more sympathetic to planners.

Urban renewal

Many of the cities in western Europe grew rapidly in the nineteenth century. Today this has left them with old centres which are in need of renewal. There has been widespread URBAN RENEWAL in Paris, a city that has been changing rapidly in the past twenty years.

▶ Study Figure 3.29 which shows those parts of central Paris which are being renewed and preserved. Write a paragraph to describe the pattern of urban renewal in central Paris.

Paris is the largest city by far in France. There has been a great deal of commercial and political pressure behind many of the urban renewal schemes, but the planners have decided to preserve many of the older historic areas at the centre. However, urban renewal in this historic zone has caused a great deal of controversy. The area known as Les Halles became a battleground for residents, politicians, planners and conservationists before it was redeveloped.

The Front de Seine area (Figure 3.30) is another area undergoing urban renewal in Paris. In some ways it is typical of many areas being renewed. Its 29 ha site was once a run-down inner city area which had grown up in the last century. 1560 dwellings and 731 other buildings had to be demolished to make way for the new development. Many old factories, warehouses and other semi-derelict buildings were removed.

Front de Seine had been redeveloped using some of the 'futuristic' planning and architectural ideas of the 1960s. It consists of 15 multi-story apartment towers containing 4000 apartments, 4 office towers creating 110 000 m^2 of office space, 6500 garages, a luxury hotel, shops, social and sporting facilities. An artificial ground level, which is for pedestrians only, is set above roads and garages which are on normal ground level.

The main problem with urban renewal schemes is that they help to push out poorer people and traditional jobs. New apartments can only be afforded by richer people and most of the new jobs created are service jobs, mainly white-collar office jobs. As traditional industries decline, for example the clothing industry, working class people move to other parts of the city or out of the city altogether. Between 1954 and 1975, Paris lost nearly 20% of its population, which fell from 2.8 million to 2.3 million.

Figure 3.28   Planning in Camlachie, inner Glasgow

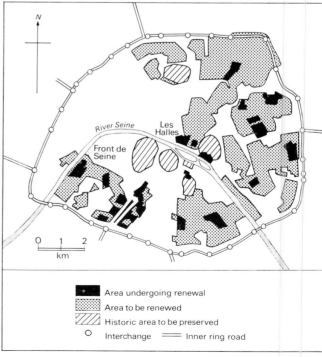

Figure 3.29   Urban renewal in central Paris

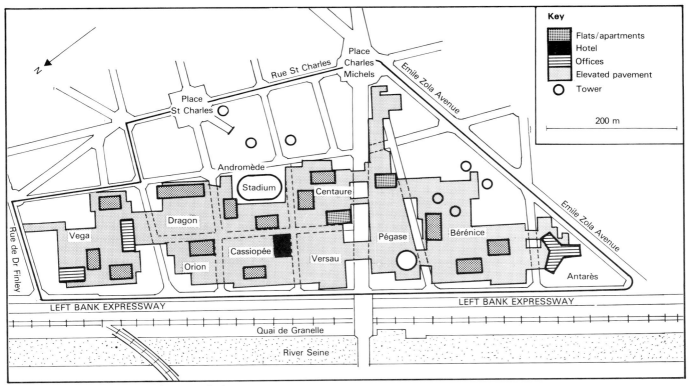

Figure 3.30   The Front de Seine urban renewal scheme

Urban renewal is, therefore, leading to a decline in the population and traditional functions of Paris. Politicians are prepared to see people and traditional jobs go because they are trying to make the city attractive to large multi-national companies who may set up offices in the city. The future function of Paris increasingly seems to be as an international business and financial centre.

▶ 1 Write down a definition of 'urban renewal'.
   2 Study Figure 3.29. On a piece of tracing paper draw a grid of squares (1 km × 1 km) using the scale on the map. Use this to estimate the total area of central Paris, the area to be preserved, the area to be renewed, and the area being renewed. What else can be said about the pattern of urban renewal in Paris?
   3 Imagine that you work for an advertising company which specialises in promoting cities as suitable locations for businesses. You have been approached by Parisian politicians to promote Paris as a location for the headquarters of large national and multi-national companies. Design a publicity sheet which could be used to help 'sell' Paris. Use an atlas and any of the information from this section.

City of the future

An alternative to renewing old towns and cities has been the creation of completely new settlements. Many NEW TOWNS have been built in Britain in the past 40 years. Some have been built to take overspill population from nearby cities. Others have been built to attract industry to problem regions. Milton Keynes is one new settlement which has attracted much attention.

Study Figure 3.31 which shows the location of Milton Keynes. Copy the following and fill in the missing words:

▶ Milton Keynes is in an excellent location, situated about half way between the cities of _____ and _____. It has good transport links and is served by the _____ road and the _____ motorway. A modern, electric railway line runs between _____ and _____. Air connections are also good with _____, _____ and _____ airports all within a reasonable distance.

Figure 3.31   The location of Milton Keynes

With such a good location it is not surprising that Milton Keynes has developed rapidly. When Milton Keynes was designated in 1967, it was decided that it should be a new city rather than a new town, and that it was to be a major national economic growth point. People and industry have flocked to the city in the 1970s and 1980s. In 1971 Milton Keynes had a population of just under 50 000, by 1981 it was just over 100 000 and by 1990 it should reach 200 000. In the past ten years 23 000 new houses have been built and 30 000 jobs have been created.

The planners of Milton Keynes were keen to give the city a modern and carefully constructed layout. They had to work around the existing railway lines and the small settlements of Bletchley, Stony Stratford and Wolverton. Figures 3.32 and 3.33 show the layout of the new city.

▶ Write a few paragraphs describing the layout of Milton Keynes. Think carefully about what the planners are trying to do and say something about the following features: grid pattern of roads, position of Central Milton Keynes, links between employment centres and transport routes.

In many ways Milton Keynes is a city of the future. The Milton Keynes Development Corporation want to encourage the city's 'high technology' image. They feel this has been successful in attracting both people and jobs.

▶ 1 Write down a definition for 'new towns'.
   2 Think about the differences between a new city such as Milton Keynes and an older city such as London. Make a list of the advantages which the new settlement offers for the following groups of people when compared with the old city: those living in the city, industrialists, those responsible for public transport.
   3 Study Figure 3.34 which shows the area known as Central Milton Keynes. The city is only part developed at present. Discuss with your neighbour or in groups what the sites for development could be used for. Think carefully about the needs of a developing city which will eventually have a population of 200 000. When you have discussed the possibilities fully, present your ideas to your class.

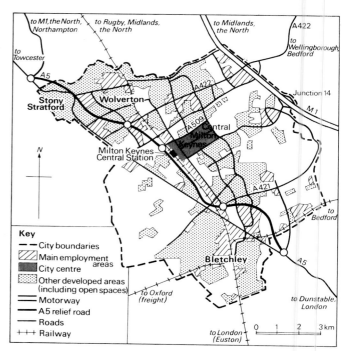

Figure 3.32   *The layout of Milton Keynes*

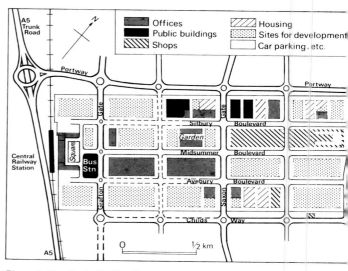

Figure 3.34   *Central Milton Keynes*

Figure 3.33   *Milton Keynes: before*

. . . *and after*

Key Points: Urban Environments

- Britain's inner city areas are declining rapidly. As people and jobs leave these areas they become centres for poverty, poor housing and social unrest.

- Many of the problems which face cities in developing countries are caused by urban growth.

- More and more of the world's population is living in towns and cities. The growth of millionaire and multi-millionaire cities is very rapid.

- Immigrants have been making homes for many years in British cities. Often, distinct residential patterns are formed.

- Rapid urbanisation in developing countries can be explained mainly by rural to urban migration. Squatter settlements result from this rapid inflow of people.

- Economic and social well-being varies in different parts of cities. In cities in developed countries the rich live in the suburbs and the poor in the inner city areas. This pattern is often reversed in cities of the developing world.

- As urban environments and urban problems have become more complex, the role of planners has become more important. Planners try to manage change in urban environments.

- Many cities in developed countries have older centres which need redeveloping. This urban renewal causes conflicts of interest between developers and conservationists.

- New towns have been built in Britain to take overspill population from large cities and to attract industry to problem regions.

Chapter 4 INDUSTRIAL ENVIRONMENTS

Changing raw materials into manufactured articles is a widespread activity. There are some areas, or regions, where this activity is so important that we call them industrial or manufacturing regions. The signs of manufacturing industry are clear, especially if it has been established for a long time. These signs include:
- Factories (often with chimneys) where goods are made.
- Roads, railways and canals used for delivering raw materials and taking away the finished products.
- Housing for the workforce close to the factory and often with individual houses close together.
- Piles of waste materials.

▶ Can you identify all of these features in Figure 4.1?

Such areas may not be particularly pleasant to live in, especially if they are old. However, over a period of many years, the picture may change.

Figure 4.1   The Seraing district of Liège in Belgium

4.1 Industrial Change

With the passage of time, factories may no longer be able to sell their goods, and new products may replace old ones. Factories may close and people working in them may lose their jobs and have to search for new ones. The first section of this chapter is about an industry in Britain which is well over 100 years old and which is now experiencing major changes. This is the steel manufacturing industry. At the present time the British steel industry has the ability to make more steel than is required. In other words, it has a surplus of CAPACITY. Some steel-making plants are old with out-of-date equipment, while others are situated where it is now difficult for them to obtain supplies of raw materials such as coal and iron. Changing circumstances threaten the future of these plants in particular.

Consett and Ravenscraig: the uncertain future of steel

▶ Look at the map of N.E. England, Figure 4.2b, and find the area on a map of England in your atlas. Think of some reasons why it was a good place to manufacture steel (think of raw materials, of transporting both the raw materials and the finished goods). Can you also think of any reasons why it would be at a disadvantage now — how far is it from the coast?

Consett

Consett is a volcanic island of industry thrown up by the nineteenth century on the rolling moors of County Durham. At the very heart of the town is the steelworks — erupting fitfully in flame and smoke. The British Steel Corporation 240 ha site is a scrapyard of chimneys, blast furnaces, gas holders and gantries tied untidily together by skeins of huge pipes. The plant actually spills across the main road, and, even as you watch, smoke pumping from one of the tall chimneys turns from white to red, depositing another layer of dust on the landscape!

The Sunday Times, 7 September 1980

On 12 September 1980 the British Steel Corporation closed Consett steel works. It was closed because there was already a huge surplus in the country of the kind of steel it was producing. British Steel produced figures to show that the works were losing £15.2 million a year, and that if they were closed the Corporation would save £40 million a year. 3700 men lost their jobs.

What did the Consett workers think of this decision?

Mr Kenneth Robson (51) who worked at Consett for 25 years:

'You are talking about an entire town. What are we supposed to do? Throw away all the facilities here?

Figure 4.2a   Consett steel works: ex steel worker looks on

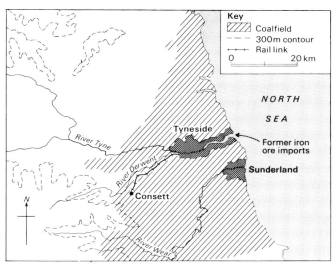

Figure 4.2b   N.E. England

What about the schools, the new sports centres, the civic centre, the community; do we carry those with us, and more to the point where do we go? I don't think they even realise that it can cost £1 to travel by bus from Consett to Newcastle. That is just one way!' Another worker:

'Consett will never be the same. People will move if they can and that may mean that a lot of old people are left there. It will probably not be a very happy place early next year when the hardship begins to bite and when people have grown weary of job searching!'

▶ Imagine that you were a steel worker at Consett who was 30 years old and had a young family to support. What would your feelings be on learning that you were to lose your job? Would you expect any help from B.S.C.? Would your feelings be very different if you were 55 years old, and unlikely to get any other type of job at all?

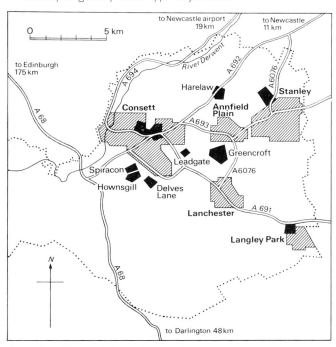

Figure 4.3   The new industrial estates of Derwentside

One year later, September 1981

Many of the Consett workers were still unemployed, and dependent upon their redundancy money. Others had been more fortunate.

John Lee fought hard to save the works: he was leader of the campaign to keep Consett open. At 50 he decided to take a degree course at Newcastle Polytechnic, and the closure has not affected him financially.

John Reay worked at the plant as a driver for 14 years. Before that he had been a cobbler by trade. When the town's cobbler died, he used his redundancy money to buy the business. He said 'I think people have not felt the pinch this year. That will come later.' He is now making a reasonable living.

Dennis Freek (who had worked as a fitter at the plant for 38 years) found employment with a new company, D.J.H. Models, who make model kits and model trains. He is delighted with his new job, for he has really turned his hobby, model making, into a full-time job.

B.S.C. Industry Limited: bringing new jobs to Consett

To help attract new businesses and industry to steel-closure areas, the British Steel Corporation set up a new company known as British Steel Corporation Industry Limited. At Consett, where 3700 people lost their jobs when the steel plant closed, B.S.C. Industry Ltd set up a special area to which they hoped to attract new employers. This area was named Derwentside and Figure 4.3 shows its extent.

In order to attract new firms, B.S.C. Industry had to offer cash grants and other incentives. The range of incentives that were offered on Derwentside are summarised diagrammatically in Figure 4.4.

Figure 4.4   Incentives for new industries on Derwentside

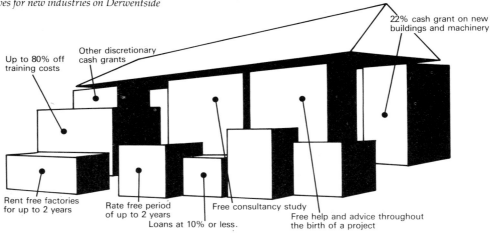

- Up to 80% off training costs
- Other discretionary cash grants
- 22% cash grant on new buildings and machinery
- Rent free factories for up to 2 years
- Rate free period of up to 2 years
- Loans at 10% or less.
- Free consultancy study
- Free help and advice throughout the birth of a project

Figure 4.5   Muggleswick Common to the west of Consett

▶ Not only does B.S.C. Industry have to attract new companies, but also key personnel from other parts of Britain, such as the south. Using the photograph (Figure 4.5), suggest what features of the countryside newcomers might find attractive. What doubts might new managers or technicians have about moving to a new part of the country? What other details of the area around Derwentside would they be anxious to know?

Ravenscraig

Ravenscraig steel works at Motherwell in Scotland was opened in 1962 in order to provide Scotland with a new and modern steel-making plant. It is fed with iron ore from the terminal at Hunterston and uses locally made coke. It is one of the five major steel plants in Britain, the others being Redcar in Cleveland, Scunthorpe in Lincolnshire, and Port Talbot and Llanwern in South Wales.

Figure 4.6   Ravenscraig steel works

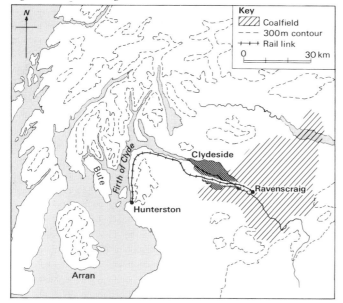

Key
- ///// Coalfield
- --- 300m contour
- +++ Rail link

0   30 km

N

Bute
Firth of Clyde
Clydeside
Ravenscraig
Hunterston
Arran

▶ Look at Figure 4.6 showing the position of Ravenscraig in central Scotland and find the area on an atlas map. What similarities are there between the position of Ravenscraig and that of Consett? Make a list of these similarities.

Recently Ravenscraig lost a major market for its steel when the car-making plant at Linwood, near Glasgow, closed. This event, and the decline in demand for steel in Britain, has put Ravenscraig under a threat of closure, even though the plant is only just over 20 years old. 'Closing Ravenscraig would tear the heart out of Scottish steel-making and pose a threat to the prospects of the nearby plate rolling mills it feeds with steel for making North Sea oil rigs and ships. Total job losses would reach 10 000,' said one worker.

Although Ravenscraig was saved from closure by a Government decision in 1982, a new plan for its future was suggested in early 1983. This new plan involved another steel-making plant 4800 km away on the other side of the Atlantic Ocean, namely the Fairless works near Philadelphia on the east coast of the USA. Figure 4.7 shows the location of the Fairless site and its sources of raw materials.

▶ In what ways does the Fairless site differ from that of Ravenscraig?

Despite the advantages of the Fairless works, it does have some disadvantages. For instance, its method of steel-making is out of date. At Ravenscraig, the new oxygen furnaces make 300 tonnes of steel in 45 minutes. The older open-hearth furnaces at Fairless take 11 hours to make the same amount. The plan involved closing part of both the Ravenscraig and the Fairless plants. As you have seen, Ravenscraig is more efficient at producing raw steel, and its steel-making capacity would be kept working. However, the mills where the steel is rolled out would be closed, and the steel shipped to Fairless for rolling. Fairless, in its turn, would lose its steel-making furnaces but would keep its rolling mill.

Figure 4.7   The Fairless works, Philadelphia

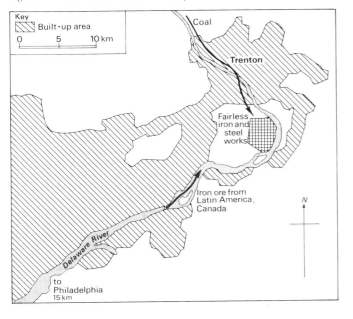

▶ The table below summarises the position at Ravenscraig in Scotland and Fairless in the USA. Some of the boxes are completed for you. On a copy of the table, fill in the missing information in the boxes.

	Ravenscraig	Fairless
Location	Located at Motherwell 30 miles from tidewater	On estuary of Delaware River
Advantages		
Disadvantages	No market in Scotland for rolled steel	
Closure plan		Steel-making plant closes. Rolling mill stays open using Ravenscraig steel
Loss of jobs	2000 in rolling mills	3000 in steel-making plant

The workers from both sides of the Atlantic had this to say about the plan:

Tommy Brennan, Ravenscraig:
'We are producing one tonne of steel in just over four man hours which is as good as, or maybe better than, anywhere else in the country.'

Jimmy Reddiex, Ravenscraig:
'Our conversion costs from steel slabs into steel strip are probably the lowest in the country. We've got an automated well-equipped plant. Now they want to close us down. It makes me very angry.'

Al Lupini, Fairless:
'We're in this fight together. This deal is no good for us and it's no goddam good for the boys in Scotland.'

Bill McLean, Fairless:
'If this deal goes through I'm not just going to lose my job, I'll probably lose my home.'

▶ Hold a class discussion around the following questions which highlight the main points of the Ravenscraig-Fairless issue:
 1 Do you think it is a good idea to ship Scottish steel across the Atlantic to be finished in the USA?
 2 Is it a good idea in general to combine the operations of steel plants which are located so far away from each other?
 3 Would it be better to close Ravenscraig anyway, since there is not a large enough market for its steel in Scotland?

4.2 Industry on the Coast

Industries which develop inland often find themselves at a disadvantage when they come to rely on seaborne raw materials. For example, Ravenscraig receives its iron ore from a terminal some 50 km away to the west. Many industries now find it much more to their advantage to locate on the coast where the materials can be received and processed in one place. Two examples of coastal industry are studied in this section of Chapter 4. They are the Esso oil refinery at Fawley on Southampton Water and the Europoort complex of the Netherlands.

Esso Fawley

The Fawley oil refinery was the first large coastal refinery to be built in Britain. It was opened in 1951 and today it has a capacity of 15.6 million tonnes. It employs approximately 2100 people.

▶ On an atlas map of England locate the port of Southampton and the Fawley oil refinery. Using the map (Figure 4.8) to help you, study the photograph (Figure 4.9) and prepare a sketch map from it showing:
- Southampton Water and the jetties at which the super-tankers berth.
- The main 'tank farms' where the crude oil is stored.
- The main plants where the crude oil is refined into other products.

The refinery has attracted other industries to it. These are the petrochemical and power industries and together with Esso Fawley they have created what is called an INDUSTRIAL AGGLOMERATION. In the case of the Fawley agglomeration the petrochemical plants are strongly dependent on the oil refinery for their supply of raw materials, while both the power stations are oil-fired.

▶ Now add the location of the petrochemical plants and pipelines to your sketch map.

Esso Fawley lies close to the New Forest, an Area of Outstanding Natural Beauty. Esso has made every attempt to reduce the impact of the refinery on the scenery, but the high chimney stacks can be seen over a very wide area. Extensive tree screens have been planted around the tank farms in order to obscure them from the road and residential areas to the west, as well as from parts of the estuary shore. However, such a vast industrial complex is not easily hidden, and people enjoying the quiet of the New Forest can still see the refinery from some miles to the west.

▶ Now complete your sketch map by adding:
- The areas of housing adjacent to the refinery.
- The main tree screens planted around the refinery.
- The area occupied by the New Forest.

Your sketch map of the Fawley industrial agglomeration is now complete. What would you say were the main impacts of Esso Fawley on the surrounding area? Are all the impacts necessarily bad ones?

1 Esso refinery	1a Refinery depot	5 Hythe Chemicals
2 Marchwood power station		6 Air products
3 Fawley power station		7 Monsanto
4 E.N.I. Chemicals		8 RE Chemicals

Key
- ═══ Road
- +++ Single track railway

Pipelines
- – – – Heavy fuel oil
- ×—× Ethylene
- ⊂⊃ Butadiene

0   1   2   3 km

Figure 4.8   Southampton Water and Esso Fawley

Figure 4.9   Aerial view of Esso Fawley

Rotterdam — Europoort

Rotterdam handles more traffic than any other port in Europe. The port's total tonnage is about 300 million tonnes per year, and the bulk of it is crude oil. The petroleum port consists of the three main areas of Botlek, Europoort and Maasvlakte as Figure 4.10 shows.

▶ Study the map and the photograph accompanying it. In what ways do the petroleum installations appear to differ in layout from those at Fawley? (Fawley is also located on an estuary.)

In what order to you think that the three sections of the petroleum port were developed?

The photograph was taken approximately from the BP refinery looking across to the Maasvlakte. List some reasons why the Maasvlakte looks an attractive area for industrial development.

Figure 4.10   Rotterdam – Europoort; the photograph shows western Europoort and the Maasvlakte

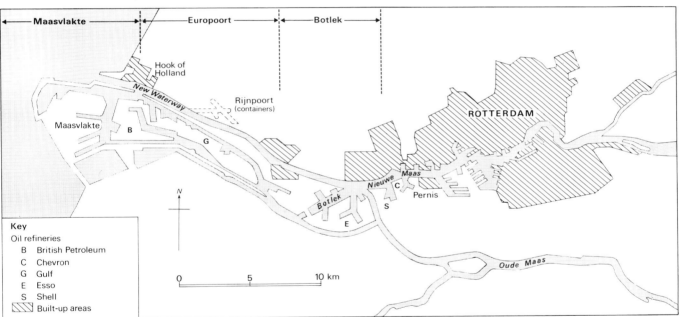

Why the Maasvlakte never got its steelworks

Much of the seaward end of the Rotterdam-Europoort area is described as environmentally sensitive. The expression 'environmentally sensitive' means that the area, made up of mudflats and sandbanks and backed by sand dunes, has a varied and attractive wildlife. It is also a popular recreation area for people who live in Rotterdam. Industrial development, with its noise, waste and air pollution, would do much damage to such a 'sensitive' area.

In the late 1960s, two proposals were made to develop a site in the Maasvlakte district for an iron and steel works. One set of proposals came from an American company and resulted in a site being reserved in 1968 and the option on the site being extended until 1969. During 1969 a Dutch company, Hoogovens, made a fresh proposal to develop a huge iron and steel

works. Rotterdam Council approved the plan in late 1969 by a decisive majority (80%). However by April 1971, a motion opposing the new steel works was carried by 35 votes to 5. Why did such a remarkable change of opinion occur?

The people of Rotterdam, and particularly those from the areas nearest the oil refineries, were becoming very aware of the increasing amount of air pollution coming from the refineries and the constant rumble from the plants in the Pernis and Botlek areas. In 1970 a protest body, 'Clean Randstad South', alerted the public to the possibility of a 'cocktail' of pollutions combining emissions from the proposed steel works with those from the existing refineries. Feelings ran very high at public meetings, especially in the Hook of Holland area which would not only be the closest residential district to the new site, but also immediately downwind of it.

▶ Study Figure 4.11 which shows the number of officially registered complaints concerning air and noise pollution made in Rotterdam between 1968 and 1975.

Draw a simple graph to represent the information given in Figure 4.11. Use the vertical axis of your graph for the number of complaints, and the horizontal axis for the years.

How did the number of complaints change between 1968 and 1975?

What reason could account for the dramatic increase in complaints in 1970?

What might explain the decline in complaints between 1974 and 1975?

Year	No. of Complaints	
	Air Pollution	Noise
1968	2107	252
1969	6633	899
1970	14777	2566
1971	22698	4810
1972	12403	2475
1973	17132	1818
1974	11231	1222
1975	6710	969

Figure 4.11   Rotterdam: air and noise complaints

Thus the reason for the surprising change of heart by the Rotterdam City Council seems to be clear. Councillors would have been well aware of public feeling and this was reflected in the way they voted in April 1971. Maasvlakte lost its steelworks; the citizens of Rotterdam could breathe cleaner air. Remember this study as an example of how environmental considerations can have a clear and decisive influence on industrial location.

4.3 Industry for Tomorrow's World

High technology industry is already with us. It includes the manufacture of a wide range of electronic equipment, especially computers and control systems using microprocessors. High technology industry is an ASSEMBLY INDUSTRY because it uses large numbers of intricate components. These are usually manufactured elsewhere and supplied in bulk to the assembly factories.

High technology demands a highly-skilled labour force, and inventive and thrustful research and managerial teams. Consequently manufacturers of high technology equipment are very concerned to attract the best brains to work in their factories. The surroundings in which researchers and workers operate must be pleasant and attractive.

Since close access to raw materials is relatively unimportant, manufacturers of electronic devices tend to choose areas which their workforce will find agreeable. For instance, Silicon Valley, one of the greatest centres of high technology in the USA, is in California, and two large plants owned by IBM in France are located in Nice and Montpellier in the south of the country.

M4: high technology corridor

In southern England, the route followed by the M4 motorway has become a high technology corridor for a number of reasons.

New industry in the M4 corridor has not stopped with the computer companies. In their wake have come the service industries, the precision engineering shops, the banks and insurance centres. Berkshire County Council has recently completed a survey of job prospects and found that 51 per cent of new firms in the county expect to hire more staff in the future. Only 3 per cent of new firms and only 12 per cent of established firms expected any job losses.

These industries along the M4 corridor are called GROWTH INDUSTRIES and they have an important influence on other industries once they have become established. They are the industries of the last decades of the twentieth century and of the first decades of the next century, and are very different from the declining and troubled steel industry at Consett and Ravenscraig.

Swindon: growth centre on the M4

Swindon grew up as a railway town. I.K. Brunel chose it as the centre for the Great Western Railway's workshops in 1848. It became very dependent on these workshops as a source of employment and, as circumstances have changed, it has now deliberately set out to attract a wider variety of firms to give it a broader INDUSTRIAL BASE. The contrasts between the old and the new are considerable.

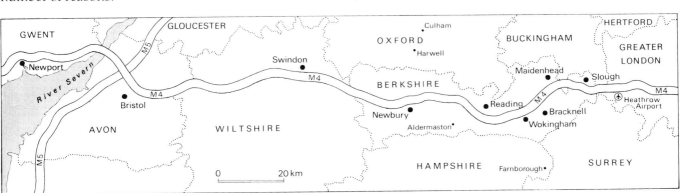

Figure 4.12   The M4 corridor in southern England

▶ Figure 4.12 shows a simple map of the M4 corridor. Find the M4 on a good atlas or road map and, on a copy of Figure 4.12, mark on the Cotswold Hills, the Chiltern Hills, the Wiltshire Downs and the Vale of Whitehorse.
What characteristics of the towns shown on the map in Figure 4.12 might make them attractive for high technology manufacturers?
Why is access to a major international airport important to makers of high technology products?
What features of the countryside might attract new firms to the M4 corridor? Use the photograph on the right in Figure 4.12 to help you answer this question.

	Distance in Kilometres					
	Swindon	London	Birmingham	Southampton	Bristol	Oxford
Oxford	47	90	103	108	119	0
Bristol	66	193	138	121	0	119
Southampton	103	125	209	0	120	108
Birmingham	120	190	0	209	138	103
London	130	0	190	125	193	90
Swindon	0	130	120	103	66	47

Figure 4.13   How central is Swindon?

For modern industrial firms like Intel, easy access to other towns is a very important factor when locating a factory. The table in Figure 4.13 is printed in Swindon's 'fact file' for industrialists and it claims to show how central Swindon is within southern England.

▶ To check this claim of centrality add up the six figures of each row. This will give you the total distance between the town on the left, e.g. Oxford on the top row, and all the other towns. The town with the lowest score in kilometres will be the most central. Which one is it?

How Swindon's industrial base differs from the rest of the country can be measured by using a location quotient. This is a simple figure obtained by dividing two percentages. A location quotient for industry can be worked out by using percentage employment figures, in this case for Great Britain as a whole and for Swindon.

For example:
In Britain as a whole, 1.9% of the workforce is employed in agriculture, whereas only 1.7% of Swindon's workforce works in agriculture. By dividing the value for Swindon by that for Britain the location quotient of 0.89 is obtained, i.e. $\frac{1.7}{1.9} = 0.89$. As you can see, this figure for agriculture is below 1.00: this means that proportionally fewer people are employed in agriculture in Swindon than in the country as a whole. If the location quotient value was above 1.00, it would mean that proportionally more people are employed in a particular job than is, the average for the rest of the country.

▶ Figure 4.14 gives percentage employment data for Swindon and the UK for ten groups of occupations.
Work out the location quotients for each of the occupational groups listed.
In which occupations are proportionally more people employed in Swindon than in the country as a whole? (N.B. quotient values above 1.00)
In which occupations are proportionally fewer people employed in Swindon than in the UK as a whole? (N.B. quotient values below 1.00)
In the UK the percentage of people employed in manufacturing industry is falling while that in services is growing. Does Swindon appear to be following the national trend? Refer to the 1968 percentage figures to answer this question.

Employment has declined in both vehicle manufacture and in mechanical and electrical engineering, but it has grown in 'other manufacturing'. This sector includes the new high technology industries which the town has been anxious to attract.

▶ Analyse the information given in Figure 4.15. How many of these American companies are concerned with   i) vehicles or mechanical and electrical engineering, and   ii) electronics? Does the evidence that you have seen suggest that Swindon is being successful in broadening its industrial base? If you were an industrial consultant to the town of Swindon, what further changes would you like to see in its industrial structure by 1990? What measures could you take to bring about your proposed changes?

Figure 4.14   Swindon's employment structure

Occupational Group	% of Swindon's Workforce in 1984	% of UK's Workforce in 1984	% of Swindon's Workforce in 1968
Agriculture	1.9	1.7	3.2
Manufacturing (all types)	37.2	33.5	47.1
Vehicles	10.6	3.3	16.6
Mechanical & electrical engineering	14.0	8.2	20.2
Other manufacturing	12.6	22.0	10.3
Construction	4.7	5.5	6.8
Distribution	15.6	12.2	11.1
Office jobs:			
Finance & business	4.7	5.3	1.0
Other services	29.7	33.3	23.8
Public administration & utilities	6.2	8.5	7.0

Swindon Based Company	Date Established	Type of business
AMI Microsystems	1972	Semiconductors
Barnes Hind	1971	Distributors of ophthalmic products
Book Club Associates	1975	Mail order book sellers
Brown Brothers	1966	Motor car accessories
Emerson Electric	1969	Electrical and electronic equipment
Harris Press & Shear Division	1982	Selling, installation & commissioning of shears & balers
Intel Corporation UK Ltd	1979	European HQ for sales, distribution and service of microprocessors
Johnson Control Systems Ltd	1979	Environmental control & energy conservation systems
Magnaflux	1970	Non-destructive testing equipment
Metallo Medical	1966	Orthopaedic implants
Monsanto	1972	Test instruments
P.H.H. Services	1980	Vehicle fleet management
Raychem	1966	Heat shrinkable plastics
Soilax	1980	Industrial cleaning chemicals
Spectrol Reliance	1966	Electronic components
Square D	1959	Electrical control equipment
Sundstrand Hydratec Ltd	1981	Hydraulics
T.F.E. Industries – Europe	1981	Engineered plastics
Tennco Exim Ltd	1980	Electronic component distributor
Torin Corporation	1963	Air moving equipment
Tran Telecommunications Ltd	1978	Computer peripherals
Union Carbide (UK) Ltd	1968	Wear resistant coatings
Vishay Resistor Products (UK) Ltd	1976	Electronic components
T.D. Williamson (UK) Ltd	1970	Engineered pipeline equipment
F.W. Woolworth	1972	Distribution depot
Zimmer Deloro Surgical Ltd	1980	Manufacture of surgical joints

Figure 4.15   American companies operating in Swindon

4.4 Governments and Industrial Location

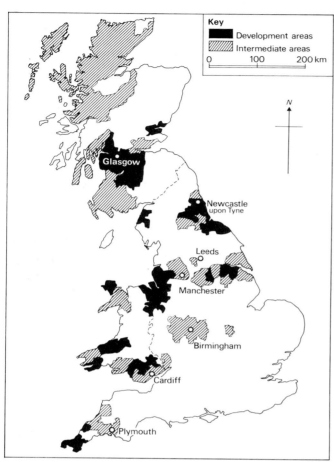

Figure 4.16   Development areas in Great Britain

Figure 4.17   Development areas in Wales

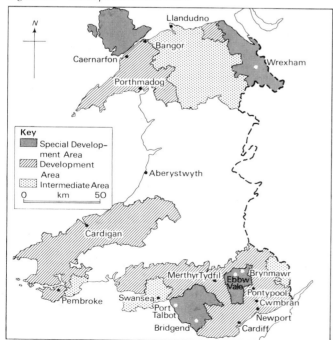

Regional policy in Britain

In the first section of this chapter you saw how industry is changing. Industries close down, people become unemployed and whole areas begin to decline because jobs are lost. Often these areas fail to attract new growth industries because firms find other parts of the country more attractive and better placed.

In order to assist areas of declining industry the Government is prepared to offer companies grants, loans and other incentives in the hope that they will locate there. The setting up of Derwentside after the closure of the Consett steel works is just one example of this form of assistance. In Britain, financial help is available on a regional basis and it is part of the country's REGIONAL ECONOMIC POLICY. Certain regions qualify for more help than others and some do not qualify at all. Areas which do qualify are known as DEVELOPMENT AREAS. The present distribution of these areas is shown on Figure 4.16.

▶ Describe the distribution of the UK's development areas and attempt to explain the pattern.
  Why do you think that different types of development area are needed?

New industries for Wales

Wales qualifies for a good deal of development assistance from the government. Figure 4.17 shows large areas of North and South Wales that have been, and continue to be, aided. In fact, a wide range of incentives is on offer to firms locating in certain areas of Wales and the Welsh Development Agency places large advertisements in most of the nation's newspapers. A part of one of these advertisements is shown in Figure 4.18.

▶ Make a list of the incentives on offer through the Welsh Development Agency under the headings of 'Financial Incentives' and 'Other Incentives'. Which parts of Wales have qualified for the greatest amount of assistance? Use Figures 4.17 and 4.18 to work out the answer to this question.

One aim of the Welsh Development Agency is to attract a variety of industries to Wales so that the country's industrial base is as broad as possible. A recent advertisement with a different theme has been placed by the Agency in newspapers and has also appeared as a television commercial. It is reproduced here as Figure 4.19. The words are set to the famous Welsh hymn tune, Cwm Rhondda, which is often sung by Welsh male-voice choirs.

▶ Make a list of all the companies mentioned in the advertisement and attempt to find out what each one makes. Does each firm make the same sort of product or is the industrial base of Wales really broadening?

Figure 4.18   A Welsh Development Agency advertisement

Figure 4.19   New industries in South Wales

Where do the new companies come from?

Development areas aim to attract firms from all over the world, not just from within the UK. In fact many of the new companies in Wales have very strong overseas connections. One of these companies is Matsushita Electric (UK) whose premises are shown in Figure 4.20.

Matsushita Electric established their colour television (National Panasonic) and stereo tuner (Technics) factories on the outskirts of Cardiff in 1976 and 1978 respectively. In 1979, National Panasonic music centres began to be produced in the same location. Matsushita is the third biggest manufacturing company in Japan and it was anxious to establish a plant in Britain which could supply both the British and the European markets.

Matsushita decided on their Cardiff site for a variety of reasons. For a start, Cardiff was in a Development area and this was a major influence on their decision. Help was given through both the Welsh Development Agency and the Welsh Office. Sony, another Japanese company, was already operating at Bridgend in South Wales and Matsushita were very impressed by the success of their operation. The right type of skilled labour was available in the Cardiff area and relations between the company and labour organisations were unlikely to be a problem. Matsushita's plant is located close to the M4 motorway, which means that both the component parts for assembly and the finished products can be easily transported to and from the plant. Matsushita find that their only problem in South Wales is finding and keeping the highly skilled work-

ers that are vital for their factory. This difficulty has arisen because of the competition provided by the many electronic companies now operating in the Cardiff area and in coastal South Wales as a whole. Remember how the M4 appeared to be an important factor in the high technology belt in southern England? It appears to be an important influence in South Wales too, and here, of course, Government help is also available. However, Matsushita could have chosen to locate in either of the nearby Special Development Areas in which case the company could have received even more financial help from the government.

▶ Can you think of any reasons why Matsushita did not locate in either of these Special Development Areas? Refer to Figure 4.20 and a good atlas map of the area to help you work out your answer.

Figure 4.20   Matsushita's premises near Cardiff

Of course, Japanese firms are not the only overseas companies to take advantage of locating in Wales. Figure 4.21 shows the distribution of all the companies in Wales which have foreign links.

▶ Compare Figure 4.21 with Figure 4.17. How do the two maps compare, and can you explain the pattern of distribution of the companies shown on Figure 4.21. Also use an atlas.

Using Figure 4.21, add up the number of overseas firms and work out the percentage in each group, e.g. American, European and so on. List the different countries of origin in rank order and place the country with most firms in Wales at the top of your list. What reasons can you think of that might explain this rank order?

Will the overseas companies stay in Wales?

Companies do not have to stay forever in the development areas. A great deal will depend upon how satisfied they are with the area and on how long it remains a suitable location for their particular manufacturing operation. The following comments were made by industrialists who have moved to Wales to take advantage of the incentives on offer:

Control Data (USA, computers) located at Brynmawr:

'A significant reason why we chose Wales was the economic factor. Training grants allowed us to train all our people, day by day, for a period of six months. Interest relief grants added up to about £1 million, which was a very good start.'

Ford Motor Company (engine plant) located at Bridgend:

'The basic problem we find with people who work in Wales for the Ford Motor Company is that it's difficult to persuade them to move elsewhere.'

▶ What is the general tone of these two comments and what theme is common to both of them? What could entice firms away from development areas such as those in Wales?

Paris or the provinces? Government and changing industrial location in France

'The Paris region has 21% of the nation's skilled industrial workers, 39% of the professional and managerial workers, 48% of the nation's qualified engineers and 72% of the total research workers. The region accounts for 56% of the output of the aircraft industry, 80% of the private vehicles, 68% of the precision engineered products and 75% of the radio and television sets. The region contributes 35% by value of the nation's exports.'

This passage appeared in a Geography book published in 1970 and it was making the point that Paris had a major share of some of the most important industries in France. The city is a very old established industrial centre and it has continued to act as a magnet for new industries, often at the expense of other areas which are attempting to industrialise. Many workers from within France and from overseas (particularly North Africa) have migrated to Paris in order to find a job. As a result, the population of Paris has grown at an alarming rate, and housing and welfare services have become overstretched. Towns and cities in the rest of France have grown much more slowly because industry has tended to avoid them.

The French Government, well aware of this growing gap between the capital city and the rest of the country, has tried to encourage industries to locate in the rest of France and to discourage industries from setting up or expanding in Paris. In the 1960s it was proposed that eight other city-regions should be encouraged to grow in order to counterbalance the attraction

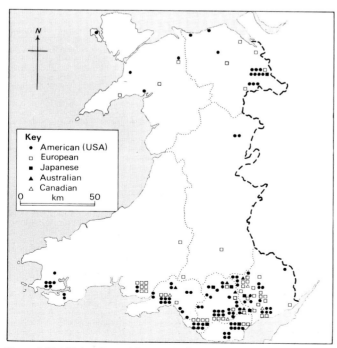

Figure 4.21   Wales: firms with overseas connections

Figure 4.22   Paris and the Metropoles d'Equilibre

of Paris. These cities have been termed METROPOLES D'EQUILIBRE which, literally translated, means 'cities of balance'. Their location is shown in Figure 4.22; they are clearly a long way from Paris.

Apart from the idea of encouraging other cities to grow, the French government has also introduced extra measures designed to encourage industry to set up and expand in other parts of the country. Governments can adopt two approaches to changing the pattern of industrial location in a country. They can, as in Britain, encourage firms to locate in areas like Wales by means of special loans and grants. Alternatively, they can actively discourage them from operating in areas which are considered to be sufficiently industrialised already. This latter approach has been adopted in the region of France known as the Ile de France. By means of a tax on floor space, the attraction of Paris has been reduced.

▶ Study Figure 4.23 which shows the nature and extent of the tax on floor space in the Ile de France. What can you say about the distribution of the lowest rate of tax? Are there any exceptions to the general pattern of the lowest tax charged? What purpose might the new towns (Cergy-Pontoise etc) serve?

Like Britain, France also offers financial advantages to firms prepared to locate in those areas of the country where industry needs to grow. Figure 4.24 shows those parts of the country which qualify for help in the form of a regional development grant. A greater proportion of the country is eligible for help than in Britain, with much of the south-west qualifying for the maximum rate of assistance.

▶ Compare Figure 4.24 with an atlas map of France. Identify the regions of the country where government help is available at the maximum and intermediate levels, and try to give some reasons why western France appears to be more in need of help than areas in the north and east.

The success of French regional policy can be assessed from Figure 4.25 which shows the new locations of jobs that were once in Paris but have now moved to the provinces.

▶ Examine Figures 4.24 and 4.25 closely and attempt to answer the following questions:
  1 Have many jobs moved far from Paris into the areas that need them most?
  2 Which parts of the country qualify for the most assistance but remain the least successful in attracting new jobs?
  3 How successful, or otherwise, do you think the French government has been in counter-balancing the attraction of Paris?
  4 Apart from financial benefits, what other advantages are there for companies that move from old industrial districts in Paris to new locations elsewhere? Compare the two pictures in Figure 4.26 to help you answer this question.

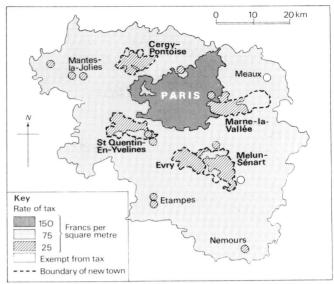
Figure 4.23   Tax on floor space in the Ile de France

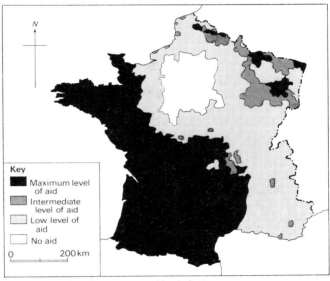
Figure 4.24   French government aid to industry

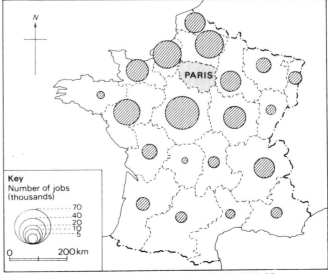
Figure 4.25   Jobs moving to the provinces from Paris, 1954–75

Figure 4.26   The old Citroen works in Paris

. . . and their new plant at Rennes in Brittany

Industry and the inner city: enterprise zones

Decaying inner city areas are usually areas of high unemployment. Once the older factories of the inner city close, new jobs are slow to arrive and the land they once occupied is likely to become derelict until a new use is found for it.

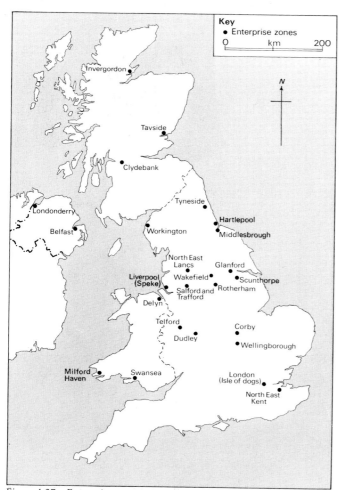

Figure 4.27   Enterprise zones in Britain, 1984

In order to help these declining urban areas, the government has created ENTERPRISE ZONES in various British towns and cities, Figure 4.27. These zones are rather like miniature development areas with existing and new industries qualifying for a range of financial incentives. These incentives include relief from local rates until 1991 and from certain other taxes as well. Enterprise zones vary in size from place to place, but the one that has been set up at Swansea in South Wales is 297 ha in area.

Swansea Enterprise Park

Swansea Enterprise Park was the first enterprise zone to be established in Britain. It is particularly interesting because much of the land on which it is located has been reclaimed from former industrial use. The Lower Swansea Valley, in which the enterprise zone is now located, was the site of one of the densest concentrations of industry in Britain in the nineteenth century. Coal could be mined easily and cheaply and the area became important for copper and zinc smelting. By 1800 there were nine copper smelters in the valley. Owing to foreign competition many of the works eventually closed down and the last zinc works closed in 1974. Steel and tin plate (steel sheets coated with tin) were also made, but again, because of cheaper and more modern methods in use elsewhere, the plants were forced to close in the years between 1940 and 1961.

When the various works closed, much of the land was left to become derelict. Waste tips remained, together with the factories which gradually fell into disrepair. Railways and canals that were no longer needed also deteriorated.

In 1961, the Lower Swansea Valley was described as an industrial desert, Figure 4.28. The situation in 1962 is shown on the lefthand map of Figure 4.29. As you can see, there are numerous tips and a good deal of neglected and derelict land. By 1978, Swansea City Council had acquired 300 ha of this land and much of it had been RECLAIMED. This means that it had either been brought back into use, or that it had been made ready for use in the near future. The righthand map of Figure 4.29 shows the changes that had occurred by

1979. One of the most noticeable changes occurred in the Hafod district where a massive copper waste tip, covering five ha, dominated the locality. During 1972 and 1973 it was removed with considerable difficulty, and in 1976 a brand new school was opened on the same site. Figure 4.30 shows the 'before' and 'after' character of the site.

Small wonder, then, that the Lower Swansea Valley became the site of Britain's first enterprise zone. The area was in urgent need of new jobs and a ready-made site was available. Factory units were built by Swansea County Council and the Welsh Development Agency in the first instance, but private companies are now developing other sections of the zone. In the first 18 months of its life, Swansea Enterprise Park attracted 22 manufacturing companies. Half the new factory floorspace is given over to warehousing and it is expected that half the new firms and new jobs will be in the service sector.

▶ Compare the two maps in Figure 4.29 and write a short account of the changes that have taken place in the area since 1962.

Enterprise zones — formula for success?

Enterprise zones are an attempt to attract both manufacturing and service industries into inner city areas in order to reduce unemployment and to halt decline. They are a relatively new idea and on the surface they appear to be a good one. But they are not without their

Figure 4.28   The White Rock copper, lead and silver works in 1961

problems, some of which stem from the simple fact that some places now have enterprise zones while others do not. Listed below are some important questions about enterprise zones and some suggested answers:

Q. Are firms being offered enough financial benefits?
A. Some people say that ten years rate free are not long enough. On the other hand, many firms have shown interest in the zones and the Swansea zone was increased in size from an original area of 263 ha to its present 297 ha because so many companies wished to locate there.

Figure 4.29   Changes in the Lower Swansea Valley between 1962 and 1979

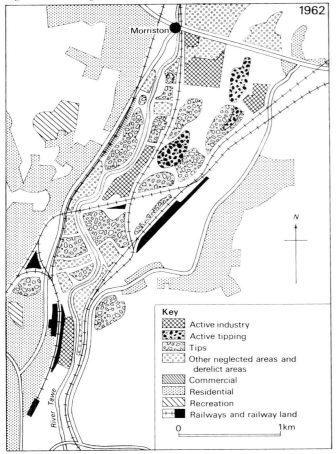

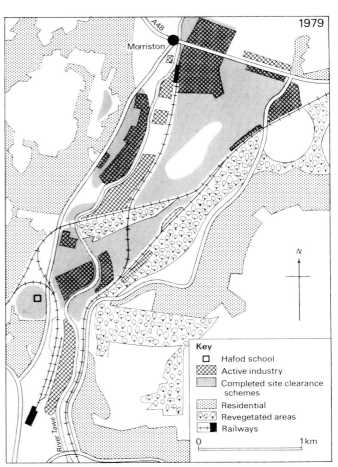

Figure 4.30   Before

. . . and after the removal of the Hafod tip

Q. Is the inner city the best place to encourage a new industry to grow?

A. Inner cities are often unattractive areas in which to work and live. Firms will not be attracted to them unless certain basic improvements are also made, e.g. improved road and rail links and schemes to raise standards of housing and recreation provision. Areas like the M4 corridor are much more attractive to new companies.

Q. Are enterprise zones unfair to existing firms who find themselves located just outside their boundaries?

A. Firms just outside the boundaries will not receive any benefits. Industrial estates just outside the zone will probably find it very difficult to attract new companies.

Q. Are enterprise zones creating new jobs?

A. Firms moving into a zone in order to enjoy the benefits do not create new jobs. They only succeed in moving old ones.

▶ Consider these questions and answers carefully. Now imagine that you are the director of an organisation, such as the Welsh Development Agency, and that you are personally responsible for making a success of an enterprise zone. What answers would you give to the four questions posed? Use your knowledge of the Swansea Enterprise Park to help you in this task.

4.5 Industry and the Natural Environment

Manufacturing industry undoubtedly benefits many people in many countries. It creates jobs and it provides most of the commodities that we take for granted as everyday possessions. For the leading manufacturing nations it also provides important earnings from the export market.

However, industry can have undesirable side-effects, and one of the most important of these is its impact on the natural environment. This impact is often harmful and must be counted as one of the REAL COSTS of industry. A real cost is one that cannot be measured accurately in monetary terms. For example, tolerating polluted air and noise may be the real cost of living in a heavily industrialised area. Poor health as a result of air pollution would be an even more severe real cost. Nowadays we are more concerned about the environmental side-effects of industry. Its disadvantages have to be weighed carefully against its advantages.

Industry produces a great range of solid, liquid and gaseous waste substances. Liquid waste often finds its way first into streams and rivers and then into the sea. In so doing, it pollutes the water and may be poisonous enough to kill fish and other forms of river and marine life. Various gases are discharged into the atmosphere and, together with dust particles, can have a harmful effect on the quality of the air we breathe.

Manufacturers are aware of these dangers and many of them do a great deal to reduce the amount of waste that is imposed on the natural environment. Increasingly tough laws on pollution are helping to improve the situation, but on their own they are not always enough. In the developed countries many industrial plants survive from the last century and they are invariably unable to cope efficiently with the disposal of all their waste products. In any case, proper waste disposal is always expensive and the level of industrial pollution in many areas is still dangerously high. Very often it takes a disaster of major proportions to bring the whole question of pollution to the notice of the public. One effect of industrial pollution that is now receiving a lot of attention is acid rain.

Figure 4.31   Trees protest in the Black Forest

head forester of a 6000 ha section of the Black Forest near the town of Baden Baden, had drawn attention to the situation in much the same way:

'Two years ago there wasn't an unhealthy tree here. Now, half my firs are sick, really sick, and a third of my spruce are going.'

What is killing the trees? The answer is believed to be acid rain. When gases are poured into the atmosphere, rather like those shown in the photograph of a factory in the Ruhr industrial region of northern Germany (Figure 4.32), sulphur dioxide and oxides of nitrogen combine with the moisture in the atmosphere to form weak acidic solutions. These solutions fall as acid rain. Acidity is measured on a scale of pH values which in theory ranges from pH 1.0 to pH 14.0. A value of pH 7.0 is neutral and the smaller the pH figure, the greater the acidity of the substance being measured. Once rain has a pH value of less than 5.6 it is sufficiently acid to be dangerous. The most acid rain that has ever been recorded fell at Pitlochry in Scotland. It had an acidity of pH 2.4 — greater than that of vinegar! In the same month a rainstorm with a pH value of 2.7 was reported from the west coast of Norway.

The rain that kills: acid rain in Europe

Look at Figure 4.31. The notice in German fixed to the trees reads, 'Dying forest, I am being killed by air pollution.' In the Black Forest of West Germany this is no joke as the minister responsible for forestry in Baden Wurttemberg pointed out in 1983:

'If pollution continues at the present rate, most of the fir and spruce trees in the Black Forest will be dead in the 1990s.'

In fact, forestry specialists have already reported that the number of healthy firs has dropped from 66% to 1% of the total stock and that in some areas 94% of the spruce trees are affected. Karl-Viktor Gutzweiler,

Figure 4.32   Air pollution from heavy industry in the Ruhr

Acid rain, once it has entered the soil, releases excess quantities of potentially toxic (poisonous) substances such as aluminium. These substances attack the roots of trees preventing them from absorbing water properly. Trees also become more vulnerable to bacteria, fungus and virus infections. In effect, they are doomed.

In West Germany, in particular, new regulations are being enforced. Although power stations are not entirely to blame, in 1983 the West German government introduced a new law requiring large power stations to install filters, or 'scrubbers', to reduce the quantity of sulphur dioxide vented into the air. The total cost of installing these filters was estimated to be £1500 million — at one West Berlin station the cost of fitting the filter was £40 million. Added to this figure is a further £7.5 million per year for running costs. Had all these costs been passed onto the consumer, the price of electricity would have risen by 20%.

Figure 4.33   People, pollution and trees

▶ 1 Find out how much your family pays for electricity in one year. Now raise this figure by 20%. How would members of your family respond to an increase of this size in their electricity bill if they knew it was for the protection of i) trees growing in this country, ii) trees growing in forests abroad?

2 Figure 4.33 is one person's view of acid rain. Draw a cartoon of your own to illustrate the causes and effects of acid rain. Power stations, remember, are not the only cause. Other factories and motor vehicles are equally to blame.

3 If your school records rainfall, start measuring the acidity of the water trapped in the rain gauge. You could relate your findings to sources of local air pollution and wind direction.

Who are the polluters?

While acid rain itself is a serious matter, it is the question of who is mainly responsible that has provoked most argument. Wind can be very effective in transferring air pollution from one country to another and the pollution may not be noted until rain brings it down to earth. Sulphur is the main chemical responsible for acid rain and it is emitted by factories all over Europe. Figure 4.34 is a list of the main flows of sulphur between the countries of Europe; there are also numerous minor flows which have not been shown in the table because reliable information is not available.

From	To	Net Amount of Sulphur☆ Transferred ('000 tonnes per year)
Spain	France	67
UK	France	172
UK	Norway	96
UK	Sweden	84
Italy	Switzerland	96
Italy	Yugoslavia	158
Italy	Austria	120
East Germany	Sweden	101
East Germany	West Germany	79
East Germany	Poland	446
East Germany	Czechoslovakia	334
Poland	Sweden	65
Poland	Czechoslovakia	98
Poland	USSR	844
Czechoslovakia	USSR	420
Hungary	USSR	373
Hungary	Rumania	132
Rumania	USSR	377
Rumania	Yugoslavia	214
West Germany	Czechoslovakia	144
Bulgaria	Greece	65

☆ This is the net amount between each pair of countries, e.g. Spain 'sends' France 67 000 tonnes more than France sends Spain in one year

Figure 4.34   Sulphur transfer by air pollution: the main flows

▶ 1 On an outline map of Europe, indicate the direction of the flows by drawing arrows between the countries listed in the table. On each arrow write the quantity of sulphur being transferred. What is the general direction of sulphur movement in Europe? What might explain this pattern of movement?

2 Study the table again. How many countries receive sulphur (i.e. are in the 'To' column) but are not listed in the 'From' column? Which of these countries i) probably emit very little sulphur into the atmosphere anyway, and ii) are heavily industrialised but whose sulphur emissions do not show on the map because they are not carried westwards?

Prepare a rank order of the countries in the 'From' column according to how much sulphur they transfer to other countries. Which countries head your list? Is this because they are more heavily industrialised than the others, or because they take less care over emission control?

The Scandinavian countries are particularly concerned about the condition of their lakes. Brown trout have disappeared from many lakes in Norway and in the four southern counties of the country, more than half the fish have disappeared over the last 40 years. In Sweden, 4000 lakes are effectively dead. The cause is again believed to be acid rain, but although the lake water itself is acidic, it is not the direct cause of fish death. Fish die gasping for oxygen through gills clogged with aluminium. The aluminium, washed from soil surrounding the lake by acid rainfall, accumulates in the lake at a rate well above the normal. As with the trees of Germany, the fish are killed though poisoning by an excess of aluminium. The Swedish Environmental Protection Board claims that 'the acid load in southern Scandinavia has to be reduced to at least one-third of today's level if all the former good fishing waters are to be saved.' The sources of the acid rain which harms Scandinavian lakes are shown in Figure 4.35.

The Scandinavian countries of Norway and Sweden hold Britain responsible for most of their acid rain. As Figure 4.35 shows, 11% of the acid rain which damages lakes in Scandinavia originates in Britain. This is less than the 17% produced by Norway and Sweden themselves, but considerably more than that contributed individually by other countries. The main points of issue in this dispute with Britain are presented in the table opposite:

Britain's view	Scandinavia's view
Only 4% of Britain's sulphur is deposited over Norway and Sweden	Only 17% of the sulphur poisoning the lakes of Scandinavia is produced in Norway and Sweden
25% of Britain's sulphur is deposited in the North Sea and never reaches Scandinavia	Britain produces 200% more sulphur per head of population than Norway and 43% more than Sweden
Long range transport of sulphur does not necessarily cause acidification of lakes	Lakes cover 10% of Sweden and are dying as a result of inaction by foreign countries, and one in particular. The forests are also threatened
Rain did not appear to become more acid in Europe between 1965 and 1975 when total emissions of sulphur rose by 35%	Any reduction in industrial emissions at all would reduce sulphur deposition. This would benefit any area where acidification was a problem

1 Study Figure 4.35 closely in conjunction with the map you drew showing the direction and quantity of sulphur transfers. Imagine that Britain alone was to reduce its sulphur emissions to zero. What difference would this make to Scandinavian lakes?

2 Consider each of the viewpoints listed in the table. Which points seem to be highly relevant to the argument and which ones appear to need more information to back them up?

Figure 4.35   Sources of the acid rain which poisons Scandinavian lakes

Malaysia: industry and environment in conflict

Problems of pollution and waste disposal are not confined to the developed industrial nations of the world. Developing countries also face difficulties especially when they are anxious to expand the industrial sector of their economies in as short a time as possible, and with the minimum of expense.

One country in this position is Malaysia in the Far East. Malaysia has supplied raw materials to the industrial nations of the Northern Hemisphere over a long period of time. Now it is beginning to develop its own manufacturing and processing industries on a larger scale than before. In Western Europe we have seen already how important it is to manage efficiently the side-effects of industry.

Developing countries, with less money at their disposal, and many urgent calls upon it, are often not able or willing to spend money on pollution control. How successful has Malaysia been?

The Mamut disaster

In the Malaysian state of Sabah on the island of Borneo, a large copper mine is operated by a group of Japanese companies at Mamut near the village of Ranau, Figure 4.36. The surface waste and spoil from the mine form ugly scars in the rain-forest nearby. In early 1977, heavy tropical storms washed large amounts of this waste into the Lohan River causing it to overflow. Vast quantities of mud were deposited over adjoining rice paddies. Between 70% and 100% of the year's vital food crop was destroyed.

Local people complained to Sabah's chief minister and the Japanese companies were forced to pay a large sum of money to compensate the villagers for the loss of their crops. A further sum was paid out the follow-

ing year when it was discovered that the paddies were still unusable. After a third year's claim for compensation, the mining companies paid for the resettlement of all the local people who wished to move away from the damaged area. A new village site was selected and 620 families were moved. Each family was given four ha of land complete with house. The whole event, from the first flood to resettlement, cost the mining companies in excess of £8 million.

Since 1977 further complaints have also been made. The mining of copper at Mamut has created pollution problems for up to 70000 people living in the villages sited on the banks of the Sugut River. For their part, the mining companies claim that neither copper ore, nor the waste from the smelting process, are being tipped into the river.

However, tests by the Environmental Agency of Sabah have revealed dangerously high levels of not only copper, but also zinc and chrome, in the water at a number of sites around the mine.

As usual with such issues, money plays an important part. The mining companies at Mamut have spent £100 million on the exploration and development of the copper ore. Eighty three million tonnes of ore remain. This quantity has a total export value of about £600 million.

▶ What action should be taken now at Mamut? Try to come to some decision about this by answering these questions:

1 Do the sums of money needed to resettle people seem insignificant beside the export value of the ore?

2 Should the people of the Sugut River area be moved for the sake of the national economy?

3 Is the country of Malaysia likely to benefit fully from the mining operation at Mamut?

4 Would it be realistic, or even right, to close the mine down?

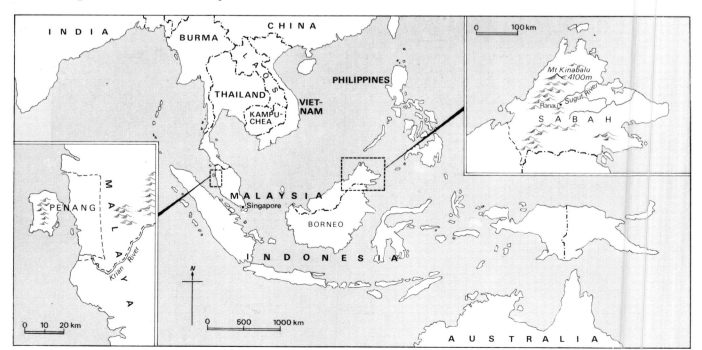

Figure 4.36   Sabah and Penang: two areas at risk in Malaysia

Pollution comes to Penang state

Kampung Teluk is a fishing village on the banks of the Krian River in the state of Penang. Catching and selling various species of fish and prawns is the livelihood of the villagers, but in this region of Malaysia, oil palms are grown widely for their valuable vegetable oils obtained by crushing the palm nut. Many of the crushing factories are located on the banks of rivers such as the Krian and waste material is freely discharged into the water. As a result, increasing numbers of fish and prawns have been found dead and dying in these rivers. Rather like the villagers living near the Mamut copper mine, the people of Kampung Teluk and other nearby settlements called a protest meeting and formed an action group.

One member of this action group said, 'The main purpose of setting up an action group is to look after the cleanliness of our rivers, because even after sending appeal letters to the various authorities, nobody came to our villages to assess the hardship faced by us. It is more effective for the villagers themselves to take care of the environment than to leave the job to the Ministry of the Environment.'

Similar situations exist elsewhere in Malaysia. At present the country has 130 oil palm mills and a further 50 under construction. Between them they discharge some half a million kilogrammes of waste material per day into various rivers and streams. Rubber factories also pour a similar quantity of waste into the country's rivers. Recent surveys show 42 rivers to be heavily polluted (some quite 'dead'), 16 moderately polluted, and the remainder all experiencing some degree of pollution.

What should be done?

Very often, controlling pollution is just as much a matter of attitude as a technological problem, and this would appear to be the case in Malaysia. Much of the machinery used in the oil palm and rubber factories has been developed in Malaysia and not bought from heavily industrialised countries elsewhere in the world. As a result, pollution control equipment is not readily available from outside sources and it has had to be designed, built and tested at home. This process has taken a long time, but new pollution control regulations were introduced in 1981. All oil palm factories are now expected to have effective systems for handling waste materials. Nevertheless, a representative of the Ministry of the Environment had this to say to the villagers of Kampung Teluk when they complained of pollution by oil palm factories: 'Malaysia is a developing country and must pursue a policy of economic growth. Our resources are in need of protection and sustained production.'

▶ 1 Compare the opinion of the member of the Kampung Teluk action group with that of the Ministry representative. How do these views vary? What sort of resources did the Ministry representative appear to be talking about and which ones does he appear to ignore?

2 Listed below are some possible options for pollution control in developing countries. Prepare a table of points for and against each option:
   ● Go for all-out economic growth and spend little on pollution control.
   ● Exercise strict control on pollution and hold back industrial development until factories are completely able to handle waste products without risk of pollution.
   ● Go for all-out industrial development in parts of the country, but create national parks, with absolutely no development, in areas having a sensitive or particularly valuable natural environment.

3 In the little sketch below, who are 'they'?

They say...

THEY SAY WE ARE THE WORLD'S LARGEST PRODUCER OF TIN... ... BUT THEY NEVER SAID WHAT IT DID TO THE LAND....

THEY SAY WE ARE THE WORLD'S LARGEST PRODUCER OF RUBBER AND PALM OIL .... BUT THEY SAID NOTHING OF THE OIL PALM WASTES IN OUR STREAMS...

Key Points: Industrial Environments

- Over time industry changes its character in response to alterations in the demand for its products.

- Industrial change can bring about social and economic change; the size and impact of these changes will vary from one part of the country to another.

- It may be necessary for governments to take special steps in order to attract new industry to areas that have declined and become centres of high unemployment.

- Modern industries, especially high technology industries, are free to locate almost anywhere. Multi-national companies have almost the entire 'western' world to choose from.

- Industry and the natural environment can easily come into conflict; destruction of the natural environment is never likely to be in everyone's interest.

Part III
Using Natural Environments and Resources

Part III considers our use and management of the natural environment and its natural resources. Of course, the natural environment is as much a natural resource as coal, oil and mineral ores, but you may not be accustomed to thinking of a landscape, coastline, or a river basin in this way. However, it only takes a little thought to realise that land for farming is an important resource for food production; an attractive landscape is a valuable recreational resource; and a river basin may well provide water resources as well as suitable land for agriculture and settlements. A natural resource is, therefore, any part of the natural environment which people find worth using in whatever way they choose. But it is how they choose to use it which really matters, as you will see in Chapters 5 and 6.

Chapter 5 considers the ways in which people use (or misuse) some of the physical systems which make up the earth's natural environment. A physical system is a working mechanism which has moving and fixed parts. Both these sets of parts may change either as a result of natural causes or because of the way in which they have been used by people. A river basin is a good example of a physical system. The valley and its slopes are the slowly changing 'fixed' parts of the system, while the main river and its tributaries are the moving and rapidly changing members. Chapter 6, on the other hand, examines how the more 'usual' natural resources are supplied for people to use. At the same time, the chapter considers the effects on the natural environment of extracting and supplying these resources in ever increasing quantities.

Land laid bare — the price of forest clearance?

Chapter 5 PHYSICAL SYSTEMS

5.1 Oceans, Seas and Coasts

What attracts your attention first when you look at a map of the world? The chances are that it is the areas of land. After all, they are usually presented in striking colours and have a lot of detail on them. In any case, geography tends to start with a study of the land, and we soon come to recognise the shapes of the continents and islands on which we live. By contrast, the oceans probably do not receive so much attention although they cover approximately 70% of the earth's surface and 'fill the gaps' between the continents. By comparison, areas of land occupy only 30% of the earth's surface — a total of 149 million km².

To help you gain a better idea of the size of our 'global ocean', consider the table of information given below:

Areas of selected oceans (km²)		Areas of selected countries (km²)	
Pacific	180 500 000	Australia	7 687 000
Atlantic	92 200 000	Canada	9 976 000
Indian	75 000 000	France	547 000
Arctic	14 000 000	UK	244 000
		USSR	22 402 000

▶ How many times can each of the countries be fitted into the oceans listed in the table?

As land dwellers, we are accustomed to putting the land first in our thinking. Most of the maps we use are drawn to help us use and understand the land. However, maps can be drawn which emphasise the size and shape of the oceans. Figure 5.1 is an example of such a map, and at first glance it is not very easy to recognise the major continents.

▶ Use an atlas map to name some of the oceans and seas shown on Figure 5.1.

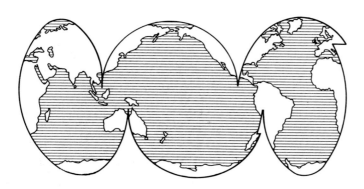

Figure 5.1   A world of oceans and coasts

Using the seas

The oceans and seas cover such a huge proportion of our planet that their condition is of global concern. In fact, their use and management are worldwide issues. Not only are we dependent upon the oceans for transport, but also for food, minerals, water, recreation and as a sink for many (perhaps too many) waste products. They also form a major component of the earth's HYDROLOGICAL CYCLE and are a major influence on patterns of weather all over the globe. The world's oceans contain 97.6% of the earth's water; the ice caps and glaciers contain the next largest store of water — a mere 1.9%!

Since 1974, the United Nations has operated the Regional Seas Programme. This programme has been particularly concerned with the health of coastal waters especially in enclosed and semi-enclosed seas. It consists of ten regions with over 120 coastal nation members. The distribution of these regions is shown in Figure 5.2. Each region has its own action plan (Figure 5.3) intended to prevent the deterioration of the marine environment. An interesting contrast is provided by Figure 5.4 which shows the global distribution of offshore activity associated with oil production and transportation.

▶ Compare the two maps (Figures 5.2 and 5.4) and name those areas of ocean which would appear to be in need of a marine action plan.
  What reasons might account for some of the busy oil handling areas not being part of the Regional Seas Programme?

It is well known that oil spillages can present serious environmental problems. In the Middle East, which produces about 30% of the world's oil, the two seas that are especially at risk are the Gulf of Suez (at the northern end of the Red Sea), and the Persian Gulf. Both come within regions covered by action plans which have special provisions for dealing with oil spillage emergencies.

The most likely causes of pollution in the Persian Gulf are tanker spills, tanker washings, pipeline breaks and offshore blowouts. The narrow entrance to the Gulf means that there is little water exchange with the Indian Ocean and thus it is all the more difficult to keep its waters clean. Figure 5.5 shows the regions of the Gulf where oil is transported and the areas where the environment is most sensitive to oil pollution.

▶ Compare the two maps in Figure 5.5 and on a simple sketch map of the Gulf, shade on those areas of the coast and open sea that are likely to experience most damage in the event of an oil spill. Use three categories of shading on your map to show: Highest risk; Intermediate risk; Lowest risk.
  Which factors combined to give the area of highest risk?

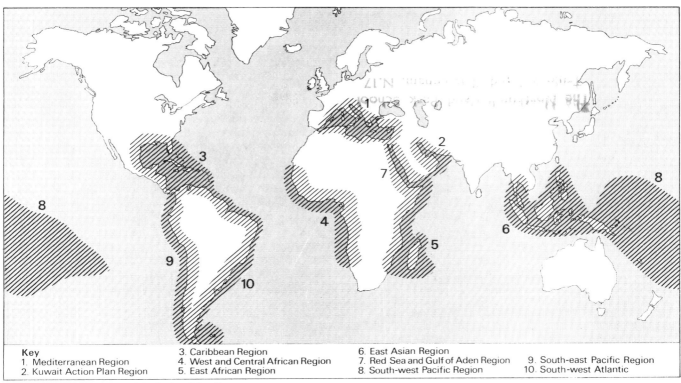

Figure 5.2   The ten regions of the Regional Seas Programme

Key
1. Mediterranean Region
2. Kuwait Action Plan Region
3. Caribbean Region
4. West and Central African Region
5. East African Region
6. East Asian Region
7. Red Sea and Gulf of Aden Region
8. South-west Pacific Region
9. South-east Pacific Region
10. South-west Atlantic

A typical action plan aims to:

- Promote agreement amongst member countries on how to control marine pollution so that all nations work together in the same way.

- Work out ways of assessing the amount of pollution so that changes can be detected and measured.

- Co-ordinate each country's efforts to reduce pollution, especially in times of emergency.

- Provide support for educating countries in the protection, development and management of marine and coastal resources.

Figure 5.3   A typical Regional Seas action plan

Figure 5.4   The main areas of offshore activity associated with the oil industry

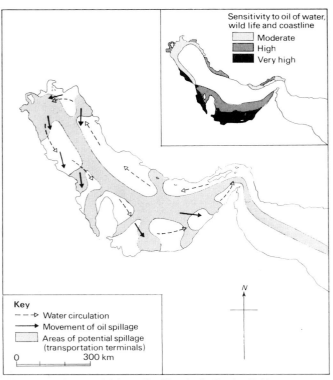

Figure 5.5 *Areas at risk from oil spillage in the Persian Gulf*

A plan for action

To combat oceanic pollution is expensive and difficult, especially as several countries are usually involved. Mounting a successful action plan means more than being able to cope with oil spills at the time when they occur. Oil spills cause more damage more quickly than most other forms of pollution, and it is important to know in advance how different types of coastline will react to oil deposition. Some will be more vulnerable than others, and some will require more urgent action. A vulnerability index for different types of coast has been drawn up as a guide for those people who have to cope with oil spillage emergencies, Figure 5.6.

One semi-enclosed coastal area in Britain which is at risk from oil is the Milford Haven estuary in the county of Dyfed, South Wales. Here the concentration of oil terminals is particularly heavy although the coastline itself is very sensitive to oil pollution in many places. Figure 5.7 is a sketch of the Milford Haven area showing the shape of the estuary and the position of some of the oil terminals.

Figure 5.6 *A vulnerability index*

Vulnerability Index	Shoreline Type	Comments
1	Exposed rocky headlands	Wave reflection keeps most of the oil offshore. Clean up frequently unnecessary
2	Eroding wave-cut platforms	Wave-swept. Most oil removed by natural processes within weeks
3	Fine-grained sand beaches	Oil does not usually penetrate far into the sediment, allowing mechanical removal if necessary. Otherwise, oil may persist for several months
4	Coarse-grained sand beaches	Oil may sink and/or be buried rapidly making clean-up difficult. With moderate to high wave action oil will be removed naturally within months from most of the beachface
5	Exposed, compacted tidal flats	Most oil will not adhere to, nor penetrate into the compacted tidal flat. Clean-up is usually unnecessary, except to prevent the oil from going elsewhere
6	Mixed sand and shingle beaches	Oil may undergo rapid penetration and burial. With moderate to low wave action, oil may persist for years
7	Shingle beaches	Same as above
8	Sheltered rocky coasts	Areas of reduced wave action. Oil may persist for many years. Clean-up is not recommended unless oil concentration is very heavy
9	Sheltered tidal flats	Areas of low wave energy and high biological productivity. Clean-up is not recommended unless oil accumulation is very heavy. These areas should receive priority protection by using barriers
10	Saltmarshes	Most productive of aquatic environments. Oil may persist for years. Cleaning of saltmarshes by burning, cutting or stripping should be undertaken only if heavily oiled. Protection by barrier recommended

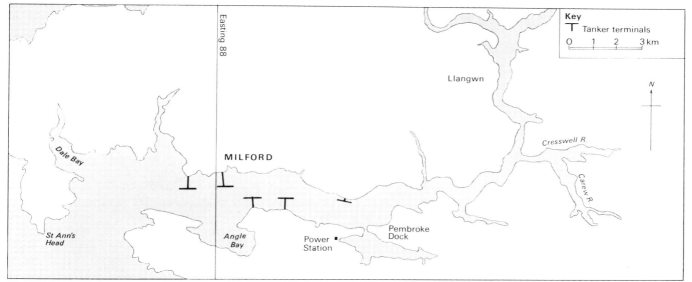

Figure 5.7   The Milford Haven estuary

You are now going to prepare an action plan for Milford Haven. To do this you will need a copy of the OS Map No. 158. Tenby, at a scale of 1:50000. You may also find the adjoining sheet (No. 157) helpful, but it is not essential. Working from the OS map, carefully examine the coast of the estuary to the east of Easting 88. Then, on a copy of Figure 5.7, put on the vulnerability index number for each type of shoreline you encounter, e.g. for rocky ledges, mudflats, shingle etc. When you have completed this mapping task, write a short report describing which areas are most at risk, and stating what measures you would take in order to reduce the effects of an oil spillage in the estuary.

There's more to manage out there than oil . . .

One European sea that is under considerable pressure is the North Sea. At the start of this century the North Sea was best known for its fish and holiday resorts. All that has now changed with the surrounding nations anxious to share in its resources, particularly oil and gas. Figure 5.8 shows the main uses of the North Sea at present and the countries which share its resources.

Which country do you believe is responsible for   i) putting most in, and   ii) taking most out of the North Sea? Are you sure of your facts?

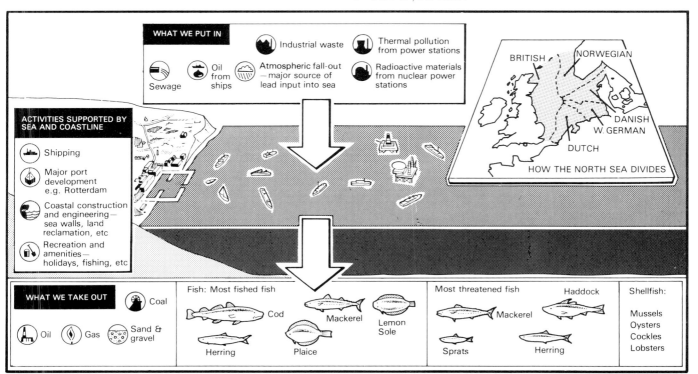

Figure 5.8   How we use the North Sea

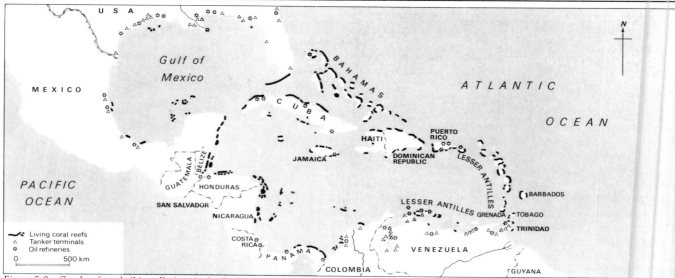

Figure 5.9   Coral reefs and oil installations in the Caribbean Sea

Another sea which is in need of care and attention is the Caribbean. Here, the coral reefs are particularly at risk from the combined effects of pollution and direct damage by collectors who sell pieces of coral to tourists. The distribution of coral reefs is shown in Figure 5.9. The locations of the main oil refineries and tanker terminals are also shown. Oil is a major cause of pollution in the Caribbean, but it is not the only one. Others include untreated sewage, chemicals used in agriculture and industrial waste materials.

Reducing pollution in the Caribbean area is made all the more difficult by the fact that 27 nations are involved. Further, all except the USA are developing countries who are highly dependent upon the resources and opportunities provided by the Caribbean Sea. In the case of the smaller island nations, tourism is an especially large source of income, but there is still very little money left over to pay for cleaning up the sea and preventing further pollution in the future.

In 1981, an action plan for the Caribbean was given a budget of $8.2 million by the United Nations Environment Programme, but an important condition was made. This condition required that the countries of the Caribbean themselves contributed $1.2 million. Some of the larger countries promised quite substantial sums, e.g. Mexico promised $250 000 and Venezuela promised $230 000. But by 1983, the larger nations had not actually paid anything and only $140 000 had been collected — not enough to allow the $8.2 million to be released by the United Nations. Of the $140 000, most came from the smallest countries such as Grenada and Barbados. The USA refused from the start to contribute to the fund because it claimed that it was already spending $160 million dollars on environmental protection in the area as a whole.

▶ Column 1 in Figure 5.10 gives information on the Gross Domestic Product per head of 20 countries in the Caribbean. (The GDP per head is a measure of economic wealth.) Column 2 is for you to complete using the map shown in Figure 5.9. Column 3 is also for you to complete from the map using a simple code letter   A = a great deal of coral reef;   B = some reef;   C = almost no reef.

Country	Gross Domestic Product per Head, US $	Number of Oil Installations	Amount of Coral Reef
Barbados	3137		
Bahamas	4693		
Belize	757		
Colombia	1237		
Costa Rica	1860		
Cuba*	900		
Dominican Republic	1041		
Guatemala	1082		
Grenada	375		
Haiti	283		
Honduras	692		
Jamaica	1420		
Mexico	1749		
Nicaragua	885		
Panama	1843		
Puerto Rico	4260		
Trinidad and Tobago	4279		
USA	11363		
Venezuela	4315		
Other countries of the Lesser Antilles**	1665		

*Estimated value   **An average figure

Figure 5.10   Who can afford to protect the reefs?

▶ When you have completed the table what conclusions can you come to about:
   i Which countries might be contributing most to oil pollution of the Caribbean Sea?
   ii Which countries can most afford to help clean up the Caribbean?
   iii Which countries have most reef to protect?
   iv Which countries have least wealth, few or no oil installations, and most reef to protect?

Seabed resources

Although it has long been known that there are valuable minerals on the seabed, it is only within the last ten years that serious attempts have been made to start mining them. The metal which has attracted most

Figure 5.11   Manganese nodules on the seabed

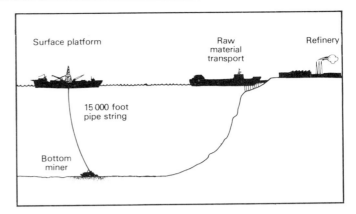

Figure 5.12   From seabed to refinery; manganese nodules

attention is manganese because large numbers of rocky lumps containing manganese have been discovered littering the bed of the Pacific Ocean. These rocky lumps have the appearance of pitted cannonballs and are known as 'nodules', Figure 5.11. They lie in about 5000 m of water and at this depth they are difficult to mine and bring to the surface for processing, Figure 5.12. On the other hand, the nodules offer a stock of minerals far greater than any that exists on land. For example, it has been calculated that they contain enough manganese for the next 400000 years at present rates of use! They also contain other minerals, but in smaller quantities. These include copper, lead, iron and cobalt.

Whose nodules are they?

Who should be allowed to mine the nodules is a difficult question. Mostly they lie in international waters and are not actually owned by anyone. However, the technology needed to collect them will be expensive and, inevitably, the developed countries will be able to afford it first. Some countries already have a number of companies involved:

USA	6	Japan	2
France	5	Netherlands	2
UK	3	W. Germany	1
Canada	2	Belgium	1

The problem is that many of the world's present mineral producers are less developed countries. When the time comes for seabed mining to begin on a large scale, the economies of these mineral producing nations could be seriously affected. The USA, in particular, is keen to be independent of other nations as far as mineral supplies are concerned. How mineral resources from international waters should be shared is a global issue of the near future.

1 Find out who produces most of the world's manganese, copper, cobalt and bauxite (aluminium ore). Which of these countries could find that seabed mining would threaten their mining industries?

2 Select one of the countries sharing the North Sea's resources (see Figure 5.8) and write an essay describing and explaining how it uses the North Sea. Use the appropriate regional geography textbooks to help you with your essay.

3 Write a concise statement explaining why it is difficult for developing countries to spend money on oceanic pollution prevention although their future prosperity might depend on their seas being clean.

4 Study Figure 5.13. Put the oceans in rank order with the most polluted one at the top of your list, i.e. North American areas with 13 crosses. Now prepare a second list of the causes of pollution; sewage will be at the top of this list. Are there any surprises in your two lists?

Figure 5.13   Types of pollution in the world's oceans

Type of pollution	Baltic Sea	North Sea	Mediterranean Sea	Persian Gulf	West African Areas	South African Areas	Indian Ocean Region	South-east Asian Areas	Japanese Coastal Waters	North American Areas	Caribbean Sea	South-west Atlantic Region	South-east Pacific Region	Australian Areas	New Zealand Coastal Waters
Sewage	X	X	X	X	X	X	X	X	X	X	X	X	X	X	X
Petroleum (maritime transport)	X	X	X	X	X	X	X	X	X	X	X	X	X		
Petroleum (exploration and exploitation)			X	X	X			X		X	X	X	X		
Petrochemical industry	X	X	X							X	X	X			
Mining				X			X			X				X	X
Radioactive wastes	X	X	X					X		X	X		X		
Food and beverage industries	X	X	X		X					X	X	X	X	X	X
Metal industries		X	X		X					X	X		X		X
Chemical industries	X	X	X							X	X				
Pulp and paper manufacture	X				X					X			X	X	X
Agriculture runoff (pesticides and fertiliser)		X		X		X	X			X					X
Siltation from agriculture and coastal development							X	X	X		X				
Sea-salt extraction									X		X				
Warm water (e.g. from power stations)								X	X		X	X	X	X	
Dumping of sewage sludge and dredge spoils	X									X	X				

5.2 The Coastline

The coastline is the meeting place of land and sea. It is a valuable resource for many countries because it gives ready access to the ports of other nations. Countries without their own coastline are said to be LANDLOCKED. In Europe, Switzerland is an example of a landlocked state.

▶ What examples of landlocked states can you find in South America, Africa and Asia?

While the coastline itself marks the boundary between land and sea, it is the much wider COASTAL ZONE which is of greater overall importance to our lives. Some divisions of the coastal zone are shown in Figure 5.14. Each division is important in its own right. For example, beaches may be used by many people for recreation, while the relatively shallow water of the offshore zone may be a valuable source of seafood.

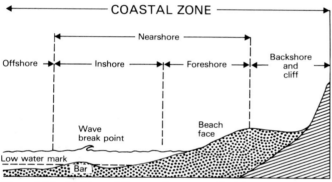

Figure 5.14   Divisions of the coastal zone: not all of them may be present everywhere

However, it is usually the combined characteristics of the coastal zone which make it attractive for so many people and activities. Figure 5.15 shows how the south coast of England is particularly popular for yachting. Marinas able to accommodate large numbers of boats have been built at regular intervals from Penzance in the west, to Ramsgate on the Kent coast in the east.

▶ Compare Figure 5.15 with an atlas map of the south coast. What parts of this coast appear to be most popular for yachting? Can you explain the distribution of the largest marinas? What sort of coastline is particularly suitable for yachting?

The importance we attach to the coastal zone shows in the way we use it and in the way we look after it. In many places steps are taken to protect the coast so that its usefulness to us may be preserved. In areas where harbour facilities have been highly developed, little of the original coastline may remain. Elsewhere, the beach and cliff may have been modified artificially in order to prevent the erosion of land lying immediately behind them. In fact, in technologically developed countries, little of the coast is likely to be free from attempts to develop it in some way, or to prevent it from changing too much too quickly. Weymouth Bay in Dorset provides a good example of how a stretch of coastline can become the location for several different activities. These activities then require that the coast itself is looked after, as Figure 5.16 shows.

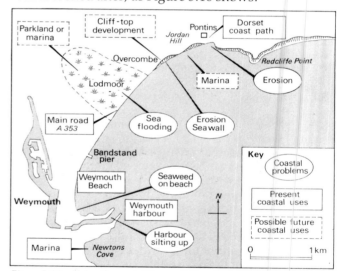

Figure 5.16   Using the coast: Weymouth Bay, Dorset

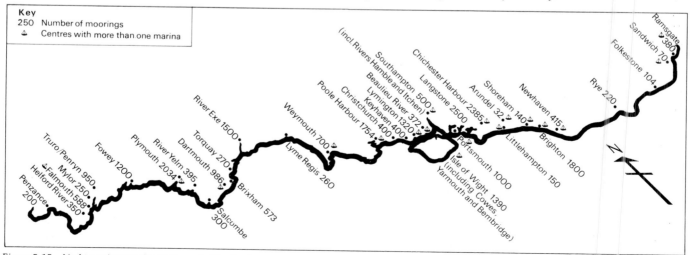

Figure 5.15   Yacht marinas on the south coast of England

Figure 5.19 Newly planted marram grass at Newborough Warren, Anglesey

Deciding how to look after, or manage, the coastal zone is not easy. It is a natural feature of the earth's surface, and it is subject to many natural forces and changes. Beaches can alter considerably between one high tide and another, while after a winter of stormy weather, cliffs may take on a very different appearance. Figure 5.17 shows an 'overnight' cliff collapse; note how the foot of the cliff has been undercut by wave action.

Popular terms such as COASTAL PROTECTION and SEA DEFENCES suggest that we tend to think of the sea as an attacking force that is directly responsible for our coastal management problems. Some people might say that this attitude can be traced back to King Canute, but it is more likely that we consider the sea to be a threat because it is a powerful force always on the move. By contrast the land stands still, and seems to need all the care we can provide. You have probably seen some stretches of coast which have been reinforced with sea walls. Others may have GROYNES built out into the sea as a means of trapping sand and shingle to make a larger and more protective beach. Two different coastal engineering schemes are shown in Figures 5.18 and 5.19. Both schemes are intended to stabilise the beach, but different methods have been used because the causes of coastal change are not the same at each location.

▶ Study Figures 5.18 and 5.19 carefully and work out the likely causes of coastal change at each location. How are the protection measures intended to work?

Figure 5.17 Cliff collapse in soft rock

Figure 5.18 Coastal engineering works on the South Hampshire coast

Coastal management

The term COASTAL MANAGEMENT is a useful one to describe how we treat and look after the coast. It suggests that certain measures are taken by official organisations, such as county councils, to maintain the coast in a condition which will allow everyday activities to continue undisturbed by the risk of cliff collapse or flooding by the sea. Coastal management is a relatively new idea. In the past, it was often assumed that the loss of land and settlements due to coastal erosion was inevitable, and that little could be done to stop it. The Holderness coast in the county of Humberside, Figure 5.20, shows how land and settlements have both been lost over many years. The map also shows new land which has been RECLAIMED from the Humber estuary, but even in this area changes have led to the loss of some small places.

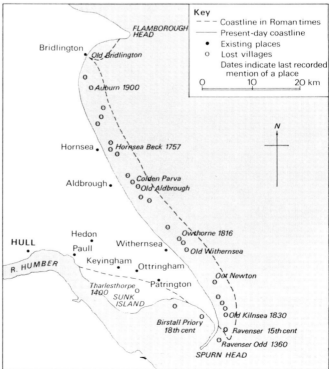

Figure 5.20 Lost villages of the Holderness coast

Change on the Holderness coast is continuing rapidly today. Much of the coastline to the south of Flamborough Head consists of a soft sedimentary deposit known as BOULDER CLAY. It is easily eroded by the action of the sea, and the material carried away to help form the SPIT of Spurn Point. The pace and scale of change are described in Figure 5.21, a short article printed in *The Sunday Times* on 6 March, 1983.

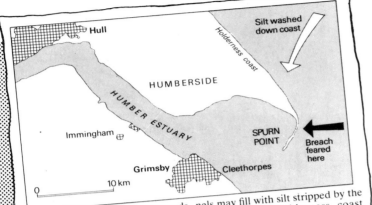

THE tiny community of coastguards and lifeboatmen on Spurn Point, a sand and shingle spit sticking out into the Humber estuary, have anxiously ringed the date of the next spring tide, on their calendars. For that is the day they fear their three-and-a-half miles of Yorkshire will be severed from the mainland and turned into an island.

Spurn is hanging on by an 'increasingly tenuous thread', according to George Boer, a Hull University geographer. 'Another storm surge could do it. It depends on a combination of spring tides, which come every fortnight, and north-westerly gales.'

Without the barrier of Spurn, he says, the Humber's navigable chan-nels may fill with silt stripped by the sea from the Holderness coast further north – which is eroding at about 2.7 m/yr, faster than any other in the world.

One channel already needs dredging so that supertankers can reach Immingham. Already 250,000-ton tankers have to come in only part-laden. Increased silting would leave Associated British Ports with a choice between more expensive dredging, or greatly reduced access to Immingham, Goole, Grimsby, and Hull. And if Spurn disappeared, the area around Cleethorpes, on the North Lincolnshire coast, could be at greater risk from flooding.

Sunday Times, 6 March 1983

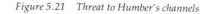

Figure 5.21   Threat to Humber's channels

'Heritage coast'

Flamborough Head itself is the subject of a coastal management project. It is part of the national heritage coast scheme designed to conserve stretches of attractive and interesting coast. In many parts of Britain recreational and tourist developments on the coast have caused severe environmental damage. The heritage coast scheme is intended to protect the natural scenery of the coast while still allowing farmers, residents and visitors to use it. Flamborough Head is a spectacular headland made of chalk, and it is a popular tourist attraction. Soil erosion is a serious problem and is partly caused by people clambering down the cliffs at the easiest places. Signs have been put up directing people to use certain footpaths only, the idea being to protect the already damaged areas from further erosion. Figure 5.22 shows the coast at Flamborough and one of the signs. The sign also includes the heritage coast symbol used at Flamborough.

Longshore drift

One important natural activity which can lead to coastal change is known as LONGSHORE DRIFT. It is a process which moves large amounts of beach material and it arises from the action of waves. Waves rarely approach beaches exactly at 90°. If they did, they would merely move shingle and sand up and down the beach over the foreshore and backshore. It is more usual for waves to approach the coastline at an angle, and then they have the double effect of moving beach material up and along the beach. The rush of water up the beach following each wave-break is called the SWASH; it moves sand and shingle up the beach in the same direction as the approaching waves. The BACKWASH occurs as the water forming the swash loses its energy and returns directly down the slope of the beach to the sea. As it does so, it drags some beach material with it. In this way, sand and shingle are moved along the coast. In Figure 5.23, although the approaching waves are from the south-east, they create a longshore drift towards the north.

Figure 5.22   (above and right) Heritage coast at Flamborough Head

For longshore drift to take place two basic conditions are necessary. Firstly, as you have seen, waves must approach the coastline at a suitable angle. Secondly, a good supply of beach material is needed because the waves must have something to move if drifting is to occur. Beaches receiving plenty of fresh material by longshore drift are likely to be well built and able to 'repair themselves' after storm damage. On the other hand, where a beach no longer receives new material, losses of sand and shingle may never be made up. On Figure 5.23 the construction of a large enough groyne from point X out into the sea could well deprive the beach to the north of its supply of material, and cause it to shrink in size. In this case, coastal change could not be blamed on natural processes, but rather on the building of the groyne which interfered with the northerly movement of beach material.

Some parts of our coastline have been changed dramatically by people failing to understand how the sea and beach behave towards each other. One example of change caused by this misunderstanding can be seen at the abandoned village of Hallsands on the south Devon coast, Figure 5.24. In 1850 Hallsands was a busy fishing village of 128 people. Built on a rock ledge, it was protected from the direct impact of the sea by a shingle beach 18 m wide. However, this beach was not to remain its protector for ever. Between 1897

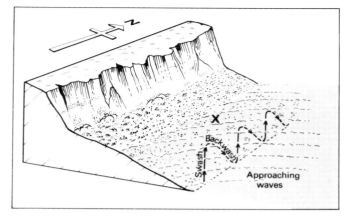

Figure 5.23   Beach material movement by longshore drift

and 1902 large quantities of shingle were removed for use in building the naval dockyard at Devonport. The beach was lowered by as much as 3.6 m as approximately 660 000 tonnes of shingle were dredged from the beach at high tide. A few years later, on the evening of 26 January, 1917, severe easterly gales and very high tides combined to bring the sea crashing into the village. By the next morning only one of the thirty houses in the village was still standing. All that remains today is shown in Figure 5.25.

Figure 5.24   Start Bay, south Devon

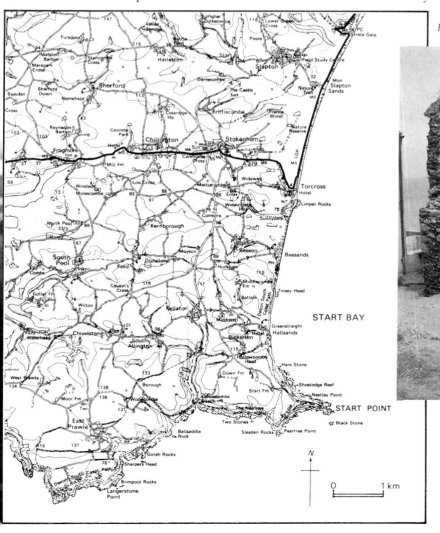

Figure 5.25   The remains of Hallsands

You might well ask why a beach which gave so much protection to a village was dredged in the first place. The answer is simple. At the time it was argued that fresh shingle would be washed ashore by the sea to replace what had been removed. It was expected that waves would bring new shingle from the Skerries Bank to the beach at Hallsands, see Figure 5.26, and that the loss would soon be made up. As you have seen, this was not to be. The Skerries Bank consists of sand and shells, not shingle. It could never have supplied shingle to the beach, even if wave action was able to transport shingle towards Hallsands. Long-shore drift has been of no help either. There is no suitable supply of material within Start Bay and, in any case, the direction of wave approach changes from south-east to north-east too often to create a regular one-way pattern of drift.

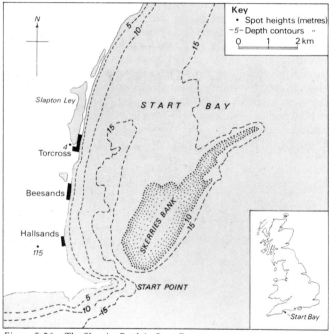

Figure 5.26   The Skerries Bank in Start Bay

Other places on the coast of Start Bay have not had their beaches dredged like Hallsands, but they have taken steps to protect themselves from storms and high tides. To the people who live in Beesands and Torcross, Hallsands provides a constant reminder of what can happen if a settlement loses the protection of its beach.

Over the Christmas and New Year period of 1979–80, heavy snowfall was followed immediately by severe storms along the coast of south-west England. Huge seas smashed against the sea front at Torcross and many houses and buildings were destroyed, Figure 5.27. All the sea front homes were evacuated as more bad weather and high tides were forecast. The local authorities arranged for round-the-clock convoys of lorries to tip massive boulders onto the seafront as a form of temporary protection. Roads blocked by snow made the whole operation very difficult, but about 13000 tonnes of rock were in place within a week. At Beesands, where a road runs between the houses and

Figure 5.27   Devastation at Torcross

the sea, lorry loads of boulders were dumped along the edge of the road to prevent waves reaching the buildings. In all, a total of 2540 tonnes of rock were taken to Beesands. In the weeks and months that followed the storms an argument raged about who was responsible for seeing that such damage did not occur again in the future. You can read some of the headlines printed in the local newspaper in Figure 5.28. To help the villagers get back to normal, a Torcross and Beesands appeal fund was started, and a total of £5000 was soon reached.

Eventually, a decision was taken to build a permanent sea wall at Torcross. Work began in October 1979 and was completed by August 1980, some 20 months after the damage had occurred, Figure 5.29. At Beesands no wall was built, but the boulder defences were strengthened. A mass of boulders now lines the seaward side of the road and obscures the view of the sea from the cottages, as Figure 5.29 shows.

1   Using Figure 5.26, draw a cross-section from the 115 metre spot height (to the west of Hallsands) to the eastern edge of the Skerries Bank. What does your section tell you about the likelihood of material from the Bank ever reaching the beach at Hallsands?
2   Study newspaper headings given in Figure 5.28. Which of these headlines suggest that:
   i   The storms occurred at a particularly difficult time?
   ii It was not an easy matter to decide what should be done to prevent a similar disaster in the future?
   iii The issue over what to do did not remain a local one?
   iv The issue was about rather more than just defending people's homes?
3   Examine the map closely (Figure 5.24). What else might the local authority wish to defend at Torcross? Try to suggest reasons why.
4   Again using the map, give some possible reasons why a sea wall was not built at Beesands.
5   Write a description of the differences between the coastline to the west of Start Point and that to the north of it. What are the main physical features to be found along each stretch?
Design a symbol (like the one in use at Flamborough Head) for a coastal management scheme for a stretch of coast that you know. For your chosen piece of coastline, write four separate statements (one sentence each) explaining the purpose of your scheme.

Figure 5.28   Local newspaper headlines

fter the snow the storm

Top level talks as high tides loom

Battle to beat the sea goes o Westminster

. . . and Beesands

EXPERTS CALLED IN AT TORCROSS

DEVASTATION AT TORCROSS

Woman claims storm tragedy could have been avoided

Defending more than seafront houses

NO QUICK SOLUTION TO TORCROSS PROBLEM

George and Mildred help Torcross fund

Torcross fund hits £5,000 target

HELP FROM DARTMOUTH

OVERNMENT TO BLAME FOR START BAY DISASTER?

Cafe collapses, other buildings wrecked

Figure 5.29   Protection by boulders at Beesands

. . . and by a wall at Torcross

Coastal development and tourism

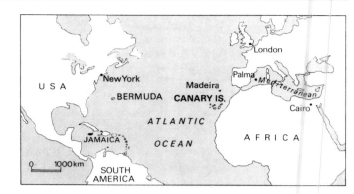

Earlier in this chapter, the coastline was described as a valuable resource. You may think that it is rather strange to call the coast a 'resource', but that is only because the word is most commonly used to refer to raw materials such as coal and oil. In fact, an attractive mountain landscape, or a fertile valley, or a sandy beach are also resources — resources which need looking after just as much as any raw materials.

Today, coastlines suitable for recreation and leisure, coupled with a warm climate, have become an important resource for many countries. Patterns of modern international tourism are heavily influenced by a combination of consistent warm weather and a coastline which provides an attractive location for a holiday with accessible beaches and good swimming. Tropical islands in particular have become major centres for coast-based tourist developments. The better known examples are the Seychelles in the Indian Ocean and Jamaica in the Caribbean. The holiday brochures stress the beauty of the coast, and tourist facilities are often built as close to the beach as possible.

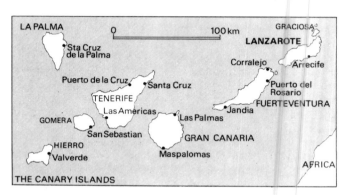

Within Europe, the Mediterranean coast of Spain probably provides the best example of a highly developed tourist industry dependent upon climate and coast. Also a part of Spain are the Canary Islands (Figure 5.30), lying about 60 km off the west coast of Africa at a latitude of 28° north. The Canaries are made up of five main islands; the best-known tourist resorts are in Tenerife. The most north-easterly island of the group is Lanzarote which, while it may still be least commercialised, is experiencing a considerable growth in coastal tourist development.

Figure 5.30   Lanzarote, Canary Islands

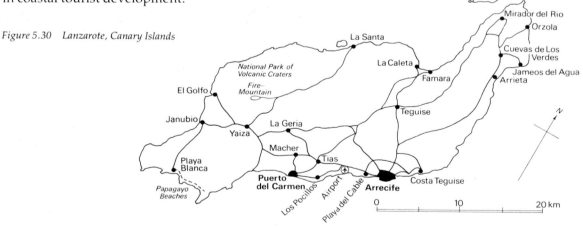

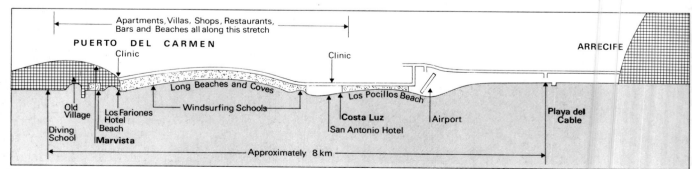

Figure 5.31   Arrecife to Puerto del Carmen

Lanzarote – coastal development on an island in the sun

Lanzarote is a volcanic island with beautiful volcanic scenery, notably the National Park of Volcanic Craters. Sunshine hours are high and the annual rainfall is very low at approximately 150 mm per year and the cost of providing drinking water for tourists and inhabitants is extremely expensive. Virtually all the residential tourist developments are to be found on the coast, but not all of them are near the main sandy beaches.

Traditional tourist development has taken place along the coast to the west of the capital, Arrecife. From Arrecife to Puerto del Carmen, hotels, apartments, villas and shops continue to be built as the tourist industry is expanded. This stretch of coast is near the international airport and has some of the largest sandy beaches on the island. Figure 5.31 is taken from a typical holiday brochure published by one British company. The photographs (Figure 5.32) show the beach at Puerto del Carmen, with the Hotel Los Fariones on the left (top), and the continuing construction of holiday apartments (bottom).

Elsewhere on the Lanzarote coast, another type of tourist development is taking place. At several locations tourist villages have been built with villas and bungalows available for limited ownership under a time-share scheme. Time-share means that you own a particular property for only an agreed period during the year, say the last two weeks in July. For the remaining weeks of the year it is owned by other people.

A major time-share development has been built recently by Wimpey (the international construction firm) at Playa Blanca in the south of the island. Known as Las Casitas (Figure 5.33), it consists of 48 villas grouped around a heated swimming pool. To own a two-bedroom villa for one week varies in price from £2200 to £2900 (1983 prices) according to the time of year. In addition, there are purchase and maintenance fees to be paid. Las Casitas is largely self-contained although the settlement of Playa Blanca provides extra shops and other facilities such as car rental.

Figure 5.32   Tourist developments at Puerto del Carmen

Figure 5.33   (above and right) Las Casitas at Playa Blanca

Similar holiday villages are to be found at La Caleta, Famara and Costa Teguise, while near La Santa a time-share sporting complex has been built. The Santa Sport complex, Figure 5.34, where the 1984 British Olympic squad trained, is a large almost castle-like, self-contained development offering a full range of sports facilities. Its position, however, is rather curious. It is located in a rather remote part of the island on a particularly inhospitable stretch of coastline. Figure 5.35 shows that the coast near the old village of La Santa is rocky and not very suitable for beach leisure activities. At La Santa Sport walled circular beaches have been artificially constructed as an alternative to the 'natural' coast of the district.

Figure 5.34   The time-share sports complex at La Santa

Figure 5.35   The coast near La Santa

. . . and the artificial beaches at La Santa Sport

The world's beaches – are they vanishing?

A recent article in New Scientist magazine started by saying, 'If you know of any beaches that are being built up today as a result of the deposition of sand, make the most of them.'

It seems that evidence has been collected which suggests that more than 70% of the sandy beaches around the world are declining in width at the rate of about 10 cm per year. Less than 10% of the world's sandy coastline is growing.

Particularly disturbing is the case of Ninety Mile Beach on the coast of Victoria to the east of Melbourne in Australia, Figure 5.36. Here much of the beach retreated 150 m between about 1870 and 1970, except near artificial breakwaters where it has extended seawards a total distance of 300 m. But Ninety Mile Beach is far from being alone. Many locations around the world's coasts are reporting similar changes. It appears that the loss of sandy beaches is often greatest where nearby rivers have been dammed, thus cutting off an important supply of sediment to the coast. Following the completion of the Aswan Dam on the River Nile for example, the delta coastline has been eroding in some places at the rate of 40 m per year. Elsewhere, the construction of breakwaters has caused the build up of sand in one place but has prevented it reaching others.

Human activity is not totally to blame, however. Natural coastal processes are still important, and even remote coastlines unaffected by human activity are displaying a loss of sandy beach. What is important now is to identify the main cause of the loss of sandy beaches, and then to see what can be done about it.

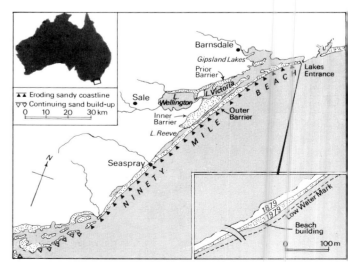

Figure 5.36   Australia's Ninety Mile Beach

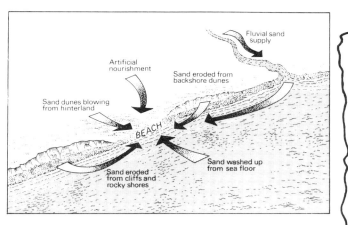

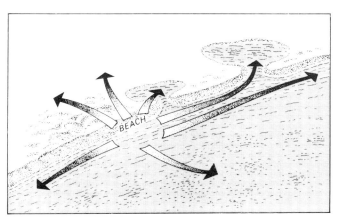

Figure 5.37 Receiving and losing sand

Figure 5.38 Suffering Sylt

Holiday isle under threat from sea

Sylt, with its promenade lamp-posts and their ornamental globes safely removed and its windows boarded over, is like a ship battened down, tense, for whatever else winter may inflict.

As the west coast along from Wenningstedt so graphically shows, this sliver of land — 42 km long but only 93 km^2 overall and less than 1.5 km across in places — is literally a diminishing asset.

The low cliffs of soft red sandstone, moraine and clay, topped by dunes of more recent formation, are being constantly eroded by storms and high spring tides, in conjunction with rain and melting snow pouring down from the higher ground. The ragged asphalt edge of the Wenningstedt promenade beyond the safety walls hangs poised to crumble away and follow the black fragments strewn all down the cliff.

Awareness of the North Sea's constant menace is everywhere. In 1976, the white fury of the sea almost cut Sylt in two, snapping 10-in wooden beams like matchsticks on Wenningstedt's lower promenade.

At Westerland basalt slabs from the promenade ramp were hurled into the air and the concrete cupola of the bandstand ended up far down the beach.

Coastal erosion is the nagging worry for the 20000 islanders. The current technique for breaking the full force of the North Sea is emplanting submerged artificial sandbanks, out from the Westerland/Wenningstedt area.

But what may eventually be left of Sylt for future generations is of less concern than sustaining the community's defences against the flood of holidaymakers from Easter into September when the car-train services transport thousands of vehicles daily.

'A road along the causeway would be the death of Sylt,' says Her Volker Hoppe, Mayor of Westerland and a key figure in the Coastal Protection Union. 'Nobody wants it — none of the visitors wants it either'.

'A letter from Sylt' by Alan McGregor. *The Times*, 3 February 1982

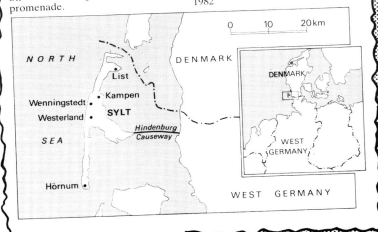

1 On a copy of the top map in Figure 5.30 draw a circle centred on the Canaries so that its circumference passes through London. The radius of this circle represents about four hours flying time. Use an atlas to find out which heavily populated parts of Europe are within this four-hour circle; mark the main towns and cities on your map. What other coastal tourist areas also lie within this circle?

2 How do time-share developments and traditional hotels and apartments differ in the ways they affect the natural environment of the coast? Which type do you consider to be the most desirable form of development?

3 To what extent are holiday developments built by foreign companies (such as Wimpey's Las Casitas) likely to contribute to the economic well-being of the district in which they are located?

4 If you were a permanent resident of one of the central towns of Lanzarote, e.g. Teguise, La Geria, Yaiza, how would you feel about most of your island's tourist developments taking place on the coast? Write a statement explaining the advantages and disadvantages to you of such developments.

5 Think carefully about the position of La Santa Sport complex. What good economic reason might explain its location on the opposite side of the island from the main tourist area?

6 Study Figure 5.36 again. What might account for the beach building that is taking place near the entrance to the Gipsland Lakes?

7 Study Figure 5.37 which shows how beaches can receive and lose sand. The labels for the bottom diagram have been removed and are listed here: Sand washed into lagoon; Sand removed along shore; Sand blown inland; Sand swept into inlet; Sand withdrawn to seafloor; Beach quarrying; Sand removed along shore.

Make a simplified copy of the bottom diagram and then fit each label to its appropriate arrow. What is meant, do you think, by artificial nourishment and beach quarrying?

8 The holiday island of Sylt in the North Sea (Figure 5.38) is a tourist island under threat. What is the main cause of the problem — the fact that erosion is occurring, or that people choose to use such a doomed piece of coastline?

Mangrove swamps — a coastline with a difference

Mangrove swamps are tidal forests that are found on all the continents in the tropical regions of the world. They also extend into the sub-tropical regions of Asia, North America, Africa and Australia as Figure 5.39 shows. In effect they form the borderline between the oceans and the tropical rainforests inland, and they serve as a nursery for many commercially valuable species of fish. They also provide raw materials for a variety of purposes and help to protect and stabilise the coastline itself, Figure 5.40.

Traditionally, mangrove swamps have been regarded as wasteland because they are difficult to explore and are full of mosquitoes. But the wisdom of this view has now been called into question. Recent studies have shown that mangroves play a vital role in land formation and that they protect low lying areas immediately behind them. To destroy them threatens the existence of millions of people, largely in developing countries, who are directly or indirectly dependent upon mangroves for their livelihood. Nevertheless, the threat of destruction is a real one. Population expansion in many developing countries is putting severe pressure on coastal areas. For example, the population of urban Calcutta in India is reckoned to be increasing by one thousand people per day due to immigration from surrounding rural areas alone. In the case of Bangladesh, where about one-eighth of the country is covered by mangroves, it is estimated that approximately one-third of the population, some 30 million people, depend on them for their income.

Mangroves are of considerable value to people in many countries. Today the main direct uses of mangrove wood are for fuel, charcoal and construction materials such as posts, chipboard and resins used in making plywood. Indirectly, mangrove swamps provide food and shelter for many species of tropical fish and shellfish, especially shrimp. They also protect coastal land against erosion and flooding, and have been deliberately planted in a number of countries to prevent the marine erosion of railway embankments and causeways located near the sea. This practice is common in Florida, Hawaii, Sri Lanka and in other countries of South-east Asia.

Figure 5.40   A mangrove forest in Bermuda

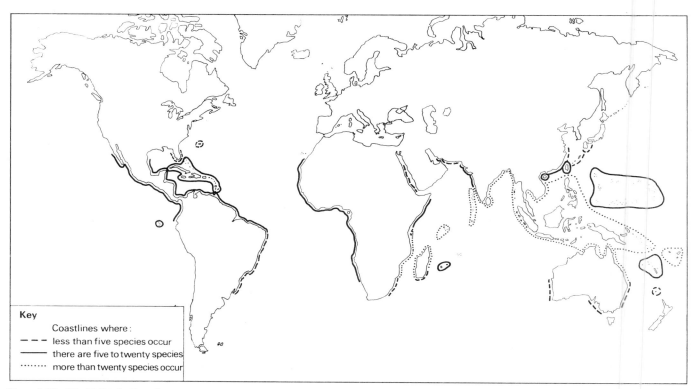

Key

Coastlines where :
- – – less than five species occur
- ——— there are five to twenty species
- ········ more than twenty species occur

Figure 5.39   World distribution of mangrove swamps

Figure 5.41   Mangrove areas now used for building in Bombay, India

The main difficulty in managing mangrove coast-lines arises from the slow growth of the mangrove plant itself. It is easy to cut down mangrove trees for their timber, but because they take a long time to grow again, the land is often cleared and used for some other form of development. For example, the mangrove area around the city of Bombay (Figure 5.41) has been reclaimed for new building.

Indonesia is one country that has attempted to develop a positive management scheme for its mangrove vegetation. Mangrove swamps line the coasts of its islands (Figure 5.42) and cover an area of approximately 3·8 million ha, but they are not distributed evenly between the nation's islands and provinces. In 1978, $4·1 million were earned through the export of mangrove products and the incentive to exploit them remains an attractive one in economic terms.

Until 1972, the Directorate General of Forestry in Indonesia attempted to conserve the mangroves with the following controls:
- By not allowing any logging within 50 m of the coastal limit of a mangrove swamp or within 10 m of any river.
- By allowing logging only in 50 m wide strips at right angles to the coastline with each strip being separated by a 20 m wide belt of untouched trees.
- By permitting only the felling of trees with a diameter of 7 cm or more.
- By insisting on replanting in areas where natural regeneration did not seem adequate.
- By insisting on a logging cycle of 20 years, i.e. leaving an area alone for 20 years after tree felling.
- By removing logs by water using boats and artificial canals where necessary.

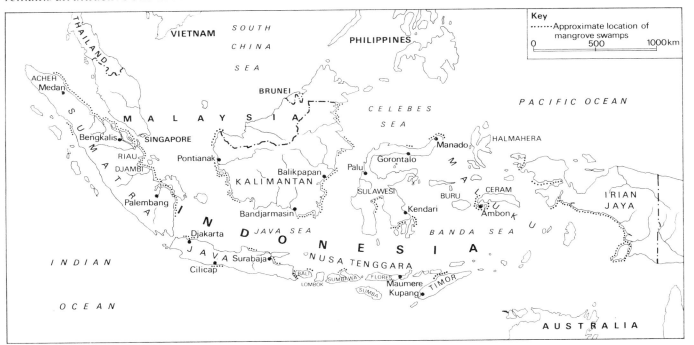

Figure 5.42   The distribution of coastal mangroves in Indonesia

More recently, the central Indonesian government has become increasingly responsible for mangrove management with the aim of attracting foreign companies into the mangrove exploitation business. The government has decided that certain mangrove areas should be available for leasing to interested organisations and 12% of the country's mangrove area has been made available for commercial exploitation. The distribution of this percentage is shown in the right hand column of Figure 5.43.

Region	Total Mangrove Area (ha)	Area Available for Cutting (ha)
Sumatra	400 000	151 000
Sulawesi	53 000	none
Irian Jaya	2 934 000	54 000
Kalimantan	275 000	250 000
Java	40 440	none
Maluku	100 000	none
Nusa Tenggera	3 678	none
Total	3 806 118	455 000

Figure 5.43   Mangrove forest areas in Indonesia

Under the new scheme, different conservation controls have been drawn up. They are:

- That the exploiting company must first carry out a survey of the area leased to it in order to establish zones of protection where the mangrove trees must be left untouched. These zones are to be 50 m in width along the coast and 10 m in width alongside rivers.
- That cutting can only proceed if at least 40 seed trees of a minimum diameter of 20 cm will be left per hectare.
- That the exploiting company carries out studies to determine how long it will take for the mangroves in the area to regenerate (grow again).
- That companies do not exceed cutting limits laid down by the Directorate General of Forestry.

The issue surrounding this new scheme is that its success will largely depend on the honesty and goodwill of the companies cutting the mangroves for commercial purposes. In effect, control of mangrove conservation has passed from the Indonesian forestry authorities into the hands of private, and possibly, overseas, organisations.

1 Which Indonesian islands appear to depend most on mangrove swamps for coastal protection?
2 Refer to Figure 5.43. In which region of Indonesia are the mangroves under most pressure, and where will supplies last longest?
3 Consider the two sets of measures intended to conserve the mangrove areas. Describe the differences and similarities between them, and explain which set you believe to be most effective for mangrove conservation.
4 It has been suggested that the destruction of the once huge mangrove forests in the coastal regions of Bangladesh may be the main reason for the catastrophic flooding of the area in the last 12 years. Given the plans for exploiting the mangrove forests in Indonesia, which island is perhaps going to find itself at increased risk from this hazard in the future?

5.3 Small Streams and Large Rivers

Rivers and coastlines have one thing in common. They are both important parts of the natural environment that people attempt to use and change in one way or another. Just like coastal areas, rivers and their valleys offer a natural resource of enormous value, and people everywhere have come to depend upon them very heavily. Using rivers and their valleys is not always straightforward, and even the smallest of streams can be difficult to manage under certain circumstances. Of course, increasing use of the land occupied by streams and rivers means that more people are affected by their behaviour. In this part of Chapter 5, you will be examining, at different scales, some of the attempts people have made to use, change and manage rivers and the DRAINAGE BASINS they occupy.

Using rivers on a world scale

A RIVER SYSTEM is an organised, and ordered, collection of rivers. The pattern may be a simple one with a single main stream receiving many smaller tributaries, or it may be much more complex. The area drained by one system is known as its drainage basin. The size of these basins varies from the very large, e.g. the Amazon Basin, to the very, very small.

Water flow within any drainage basin results from the combined effect of a number of factors and these need not concern you here. Nevertheless, by examining on a continental scale the general level of water flow within drainage basins, and by knowing how this flow is regulated, it is possible to build up a picture of the importance of river systems to people worldwide.

▶ Study Figure 5.44 and note that the units are very large.
  i What does the table tell you about the global distribution of river water?
  ii Plot a graph of general river flow (x axis) and the flow regulated by reservoirs (y axis). What is the general relationship between these two sets of figures, and which continent does not fit the overall pattern? Why are the figures for Australasia so low?
  iii Which continent regulates the greatest percentage of its overall flow?

Traditionally, dam construction has been the most common method used to regulate river flow and to create reservoirs. The extent of dam construction is another indicator of how river systems and drainage basins have become increasingly important to people. Figure 5.45 shows the pattern of world dam construction from 1840 to 1970. There are some marked differences between the eight major regions, as you can see. There are also some striking similarities.

Continent	The General Level of River Flow	Flow Regulated by Reservoirs
Europe	1325	200
Asia	4005	560
Africa	1905	400
North America	2380	490
South America	3900	160
Australasia	495	30

All units cubic kilometres (km^3) of water

Figure 5.44   The regulation of river flow

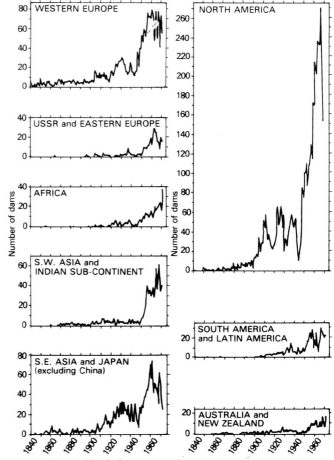

Figure 5.45   Worldwide dam construction

▶ Referring to Figure 5.45, try to explain i) why dam construction increased so much from about 1930 onwards, and   ii) why North America has built so many more dams than other regions.
  When did the world's rivers really begin to feel the impact of human efforts to manage them?

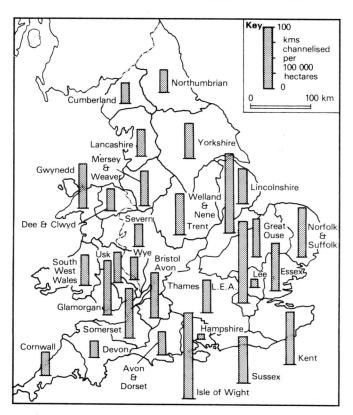

Figure 5.46   River channelisation in England and Wales

Using rivers on a local scale

Left to themselves, rivers are not always very convenient features of the landscape. They may become choked with sediment and vegetation growth and be unable to discharge all the water that runs into them. Under conditions of heavy or prolonged rainfall, the risk of flooding rises, and eventually it may become a reality.

In the past, land liable to flood was left unused and if floods did occur little damage or inconvenience was caused. But, the need to use more land for building or farming has meant that more attempts have been made recently to keep rivers in their place, rather than to avoid using the land at risk.

In Britain, long stretches of river have been CHANNELISED in order to reduce the likelihood of them leaving their channels and flooding the surrounding land. Channelisation involves modifying a river's channel so that water flow is improved. Typical approaches to channelisation include changing the cross-sectional shape of the channel and then lining it with concrete to prevent it changing back to its natural shape. Straightening a meandering river is another common technique used. Figure 5.46 shows the extent of channelisation in the local drainage districts of England and Wales. Can you suggest why some districts have a greater length than others of channelised river per 100 000 ha of land?

▶ Examine Figure 5.47 which shows how a stretch of river might be managed without encasing the channel in concrete and without straightening the whole stretch.
Prepare three lists to show the measures used in the diagram to   i) reduce the chance of flooding,   ii) reduce the amount of damage if a flood did occur, and   iii) maintain a natural appearance of the river and the flood plain land close to it.

Figure 5.47   A new approach to river management

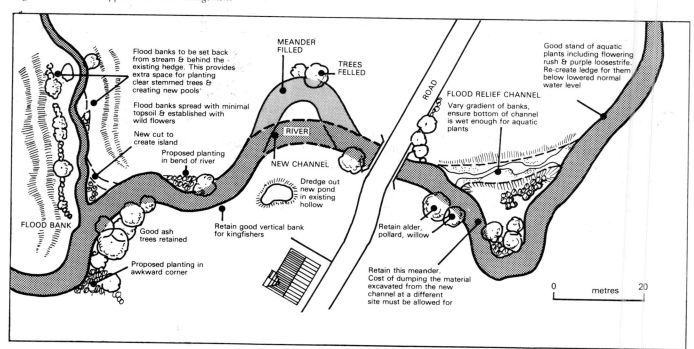

Diverting large rivers

A feature of the geography of the USSR is that many of the country's major rivers flow northwards to the Arctic Ocean. But, as a general rule, the demand for water is greatest in the south of the country and plans have existed for many years to divert the north flowing rivers in order to supply water to the south. To the east of the Ural Mountains a scheme has been drawn up to transfer the waters of the Rivers Ob and Yenesei southwards into the Aral Sea. This scheme will require a canal 2500 km long, 200 or 300 m wide and about 12 m deep.

The main issue surrounding this planned diversion is not so much connected with the transfer of water from north to south, but with the effect on the Arctic Ocean of losing one-third of the water that is normally emptied into it by these two rivers. The fear is that there will be a warming of the Arctic leading to climatic changes over a wide area. The nature of these changes cannot be forecast with any great accuracy at this time, but the possibility of some climatic change is giving cause for concern amongst environmentalists.

River diversions in European USSR

Plans have also been made for diverting rivers in European Russia. European Russia lying to the west of the Urals occupies only 23% of the whole of the USSR, but its role in the national economy is far more important than its size suggests. It accounts for 71% of the nation's population, 70% of industrial production and 62% of the country's power generation. In 1976, it produced 60% of the grain harvest, 79% of the vegetable crop and 75% of milk and meat production. However, although this level of production may seem impressive, three-quarters of the output comes from land with an inadequate supply of rainfall. Most of this land lies in the southern portion of the European USSR.

In addition to the shortage of moisture for agriculture in this part of Russia, the falling level of water in the Caspian Sea puts even greater demands on the total water supply in the region. The Caspian Sea level is falling because so much water is withdrawn from the River Volga and its other tributary streams. Shipping and fishing, especially the famous production of caviar from the roe of the sturgeon, are both threatened if the sea level in the Caspian falls further as it seems likely to do if present trends continue. Water brought from the north seems to be the only solution if there is to be enough for reliable agricultural production and for maintaining the water level of the Caspian Sea.

The proposed diversions and water transfers are shown in Figure 5.48. The plan involves the building of dams and the creation of reservoirs. Once each reservoir has filled, the water will be transferred southwards via a network of existing and new canals, and with the assistance of some very powerful pumps. As the map shows, water from the northern river basins is to be transferred into the basin of the Volga River, and hence into the Caspian Sea where it is much needed. One additional scheme to increase the amount of water available from the north involves the

portion of the White Sea known as Onega Bay. Here it is proposed to construct a dyke in order to convert the Bay into a freshwater lake and to create an extra supply of water that could be transferred south when required. The size of the water transfers in cubic kilometres is also shown on Figure 5.48. Dams and reservoirs create environmental difficulties wherever they are built, but the long-term impacts of such large water transfers as are planned in the Soviet Union are not yet known. However, in the words of one Soviet geographer, M. I. L'vovich, 'no interbasin transfer of water is possible without some sort of negative impact.'

▶ When you have decided what is meant by the term 'negative impact', write a short essay with the title: 'The Soviet Union can do whatever it likes with its rivers although the impacts may be felt far beyond its shores'. You do not have to agree with this statement, but you should attempt to find more information in support of the points you make in your essay.

Figure 5.48   Proposed water transfers in European USSR

Urban streams

Streams in urban areas are usually highly modified. In many towns and cities they are treated simply as channels, able to dispose of rainwater and often waste-water effluent as well. Where they stand in the way of new building, they are frequently piped underground and built over. The line of the original channel is often lost forever.

Brisbane's urban streams

The city of Brisbane in Queensland, Australia occupies an area of approximately 1000 km² and it contains some three-quarters of a million people. The city area is crossed by twelve streams (locally known as creeks) which either flow to the central Brisbane River or directly to the sea, as shown in Figure 5.49.

Figure 5.49   Brisbane's urban streams

Streams North of the Brisbane River	
Stream	Catchment Area (km²)
South Pine River	200
Enoggera Creek	80
Kedron Brook	70
Moggill Creek	67
Cabbage Tree Creek	44
Nundah Creek	34
Pullen Pullen Creek	31
Streams South of the Brisbane River	
Stream	Catchment Area (km²)
Oxley Creek	260
Tingalpa Creek	145
Bulimba Creek	110
Wolston Creek	47
Norman Creek	31

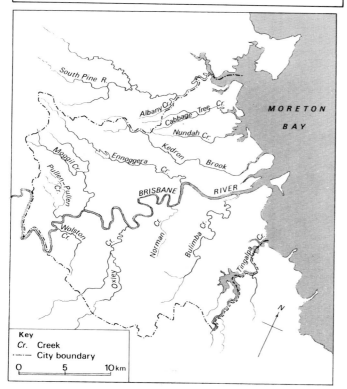

Streams in urban areas may not always seem important. But at times of heavy rainfall they provide natural flood relief channels. If they have been blocked or carelessly built over, flooding is likely to be much more severe than would normally be the case.

▶ Study Figure 5.49 carefully. Which streams have nearly the whole of their length within the city boundary, and what is the combined area of their catchments? (CATCHMENT = the area over which a river is supplied with water)

One of the effects of urbanisation is to change the nature of the ground surface. Surfaces which were once porous and allowed water to soak through e.g. grassland, become covered with buildings and roads. These prevent water from soaking into the ground and, in fact, cause it to run off very quickly. The usual result is that the urban area is flooded. In Brisbane, rapid suburban development has significantly increased the impervious area and put a substantial strain on the ability of the creeks to carry away surplus water. A major flood in 1974 was caused by a hurricane, but the effects were made worse because city building had changed the ways in which surplus water had previously flowed to the Brisbane River and to the sea.

▶ Compare Figure 5.49 with Figure 5.50.
Which parts of Brisbane, and which land uses, are found in the areas where there are most urban streams? Which parts of the city appear to be most vulnerable to flooding?

Figure 5.50   The city of Brisbane

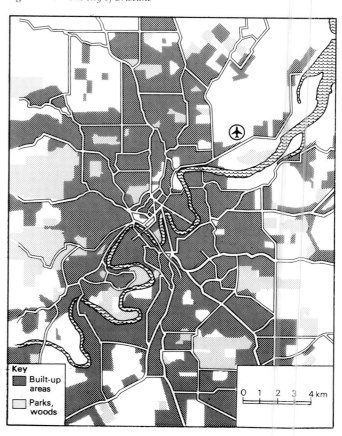

The Monks Brook — can it take it?

The Monks Brook is a small tributary of the River Itchen in south Hampshire. It rises a short distance to the west of the town of Chandler's Ford and flows close to the western edge of the existing built-up area. Its flood plain is now wanted mainly for new housing which is to be built in Chandler's Ford as part of the South Hampshire Structure Plan for the years up to 1991. Figure 5.51 shows the present extent of Chandler's Ford, the area proposed for new building and the location of the Monks Brook within this area.

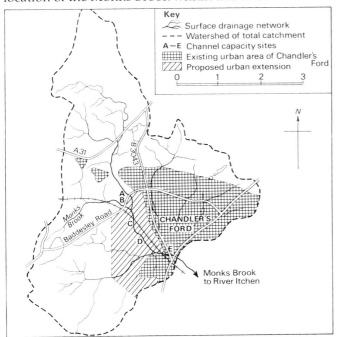

Figure 5.51 Chandler's Ford and the Monks Brook

While the flood plain (Figure 5.52) is in some ways suitable for building, it is low-lying and poorly drained. The Monks Brook occupies a small channel a little larger than 1 m in width and would not seem to pose a risk of flooding. However, the local water authority has objected to the building plans. It claims that the brook will be unable to cope with the extra water that will flow to it from a built-up surface, and that it will cause flooding of the new homes.

One way of working out the likelihood of floods is to compare the capacity of the channel, i.e. how much water it can carry, with the quantity of water it is likely to need to carry away during a severe storm. Figure 5.53 is a HYDROGRAPH for Site E on the Monks Brook, see Figure 5.51, and it shows what is likely to happen during a storm producing 72 mm of rainfall in twelve hours. River flow is measured in CUMECS (m³/s) and the hydrograph shows that for Site E at the present time, a floodpeak of 19 cumecs would occur after 12½ hours. After building, which involves covering some of the flood plain with houses and roads, not only would more water reach the Monks Brook, it would also reach it more quickly – 21.3 cumecs after 9 hours.

The problem is that at Site E, the capacity of the brook's channel is only 11·36 cumecs. Flooding will occur now, without building, and it will be even worse if building is allowed.

Figure 5.52 The flood plain of the Monks Brook

▶ Study Figure 5.54 which gives information on the channel capacity of five locations along the Monks Brook and on the capacity required to cope with a storm of the size shown at the top of the hydrograph. Can any part of the channel in the proposed building area cope with such a volume of storm water?

Finally, what measures could be taken to make the area safe from flooding? Look back to Figure 5.47. What would you need to know about the flood plain of the Monks Brook in order to plan such a management scheme?

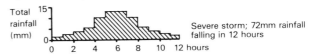

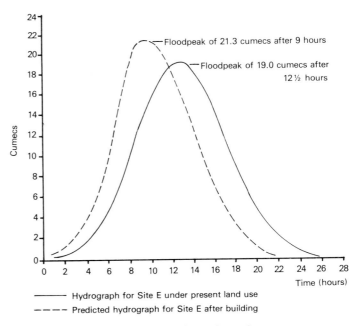

— Hydrograph for Site E under present land use
--- Predicted hydrograph for Site E after building

Figure 5.53 Hydrograph for Site E on the Monks Brook

Site	Actual Channel Capacity	Channel Capacity Required to Cope with a Severe Storm
A	0.90	7.57
B	0.50	3.59
C	6.00	10.68
D	2.40	12.01
E	11.36	24.92

Figure 5.54 Channel capacity at five sites on the Monks Brook (cumecs)

5.4 Dry Lands

Deserts cover nearly one-third of the earth's land surface and are found in over 60 countries. Their main feature is a lack of water. Figure 5.55 shows the extent of the world's deserts using the 300 mm ISOHYET to define their boundaries. Not all deserts are hot, although in some cases daytime temperatures may reach 50°C, and the ground may become so hot that it is possible to fry an egg on it.

Few people attempt to live in the deserts with the most extreme conditions, but on the edges of the main hot deserts the SEMI-ARID AREAS have attracted growing populations. The semi-arid zones have higher rainfall (above 300 mm by definition) and it is possible to grow some crops and raise animals. However, life in these zones is precarious. Conditions are only just capable of supporting people, and any good land is easily destroyed either by careless farming or by natural hazards. Therefore, it is important that the semi-arid lands are carefully treated, especially as the number of people living on them is increasing and there are more mouths to feed.

Desert mismanagement

People have been inhabiting both the true deserts and the semi-arid zones for thousands of years, although it has been difficult to live in such hostile places. Today there are too many people in the arid and semi-arid parts of the world, and because the land is of poor quality, problems of OVERPOPULATION have arisen. The only way in which people may continue to live in these areas is by better management of the water and land resources found there.

▶ Figure 5.56 shows the mean monthly rainfall and temperature figures for Death Valley, USA and for London, England.

1 Draw bar charts of the rainfall figures with the months of the year along the x axis and rainfall along the y axis.
2 What is the total annual rainfall for each place?
3 Which season has the highest rainfall in   i) Death Valley, and   ii) London?
4 What is the relationship between temperature and rainfall in Death Valley? How does this increase the problem of management of arid areas?

The population density for England is 363 persons/km² and for Mali in Africa, it is 4.5 persons/km². Population density is the average number of people living on one square kilometre of land. Find Mali in the atlas.

5 In which desert is Mali located?
6 Why is the population density in Mali so low and that in England so high?
7 Which country, England or Mali, is likely to experience problems of overpopulation?

Figure 5.55   The extent of the world's arid areas

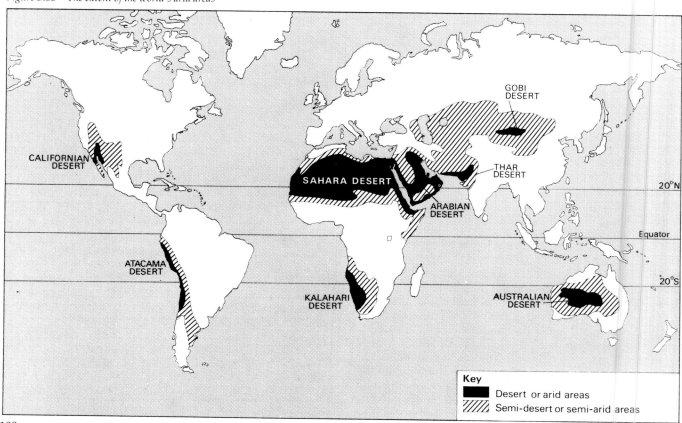

Death Valley, California, USA												
	J	F	M	A	M	J	J	A	S	O	N	D
Temperature (°C)	11	13	19	24	29	34	38	37	32	24	16	11
Rainfall (mm)	2.5	*	2.5	2.5	5.1	2.5	7.6	7.6	5.1	*	2.5	*
* too little to measure												
London, UK												
	J	F	M	A	M	J	J	A	S	O	N	D
Temperature (°C)	3.9	4.4	6.7	8.9	12.2	15.6	17.8	17.2	15	10.6	6.7	4.4
Rainfall (mm)	50.8	38.1	35.6	45.7	45.7	40.6	50.8	55.9	45.7	58.4	63.5	50.8

Figure 5.56   Mean monthly rainfall and temperature, Death Valley, California and London, England

Water management

The need for water management and control is found in all desert areas. It is probably more important in the semi-arid regions where there is water available and where there are more people using it. Two aspects of water management are important. These are WATER QUANTITY (the amount of water available), and WATER QUALITY (its purity). It is of little use if the water provided is so poor in quality that it cannot be used.

Water can be obtained in deserts from three sources. GROUNDWATER is the water which is stored in rocks beneath the earth's surface. A rock which is able to store water in this way is called an AQUIFER. The water can be pumped out of the aquifer through a WELL or it may flow out of the ground naturally as an ARTESIAN WELL.

Water can also be obtained from RIVERS which flow in desert areas. These rivers usually start in wet, mountainous regions and then flow across desert areas on their way to the sea. The River Nile is an example of this type of river, and it flows all the year round. In other cases the river may only flow after very heavy rainfall. These seasonal streams are not as useful as a supply of water.

The third source of water, which is of limited importance at the present time, is the production of fresh water from salt water by DESALINATION. About 97% of the water in the world is sea water, which can be purified by removing the salt. Unfortunately it is expensive to build desalination plants and to provide the fuel to run the machinery. So far, it is only the oil-rich states such as Kuwait or the more wealthy countries such as Israel that can afford to purify salt water on a large scale.

The problems

The main problem facing desert communities is the pattern of the rainfall. Rainfall tends to be very low and much of the water falls at the hottest time of the year and evaporates very quickly. Desert rainfall is also very unpredictable. An area may not have any rain for several years and then it may rain heavily for several days. It is this unevenness of the rainfall which makes management so important, yet so difficult.

A second problem which is becoming more acute as the population increases is the removal of too much water from the ground. Electric pumps are very efficient and in many areas groundwater supplies are being used up faster than they are being recharged by the rain. Wells are becoming dry and near coasts, salt water is contaminating fresh water supplies. This has occurred on the island of Bahrain in the Persian Gulf.

Where reservoirs have been built to store water during the wetter times of the year, other problems have been found. Lakes lose a great deal of water by evaporation and by seepage through the bottom of the reservoir. Up to 60% of the stored water may be lost in this way.

Finally, there is the problem of SALINISATION. This affects areas which have been irrigated but where there has been no attempt to drain the water away. Desert soils contain a large number of salts and these may be dissolved by water which is used to irrigate crops. If the water cannot drain away easily, it will be evaporated at the surface, depositing salts in the topsoil. Too much salt is poisonous to plants and they die, leaving the land barren and useless. In extreme cases, the salt may form a hard white crust which is almost impossible to break up. This problem has affected thousands of hectares of agricultural land in the Sind in Pakistan and is the result of bad drainage of the water provided by the Indus River Project.

The solutions

Finding solutions to the complex problems of water management is difficult and often expensive. The problem is so serious that it is a top priority in many developing countries, as water is basic to human survival.

Attempts at providing water throughout the year vary from place to place. Some schemes are very expensive multipurpose projects where dams and reservoirs are built to store water and produce hydroelectric power. Canals are built to transfer the water to the fields. The Aswan High Dam in Egypt is an example of this type of scheme.

In other areas, much simpler schemes are used in which pumps lift water from the ground and ditches to distribute it over the fields. Increasingly, such irrigation schemes are being developed at village scale with the help of government, or development agency, experts. Many of these projects combine irrigation and water drainage projects, so that the problem of salinisation of the soil is avoided.

Water is also being applied more efficiently by sprays and sprinklers which can direct the water exactly to the point at which it is needed. For rows of crops, trickle irrigation is used, which waters the roots of the plants and does not waste water by irrigating the soil between them.

Significant steps are now being taken to overcome the problems of water loss from reservoirs. In Namibia, sand-filled reservoirs are used. Water is stored in the sand and the water level is kept below the surface of the ground. A well allows the water to be tapped and evaporation losses can be reduced by up to 90% in this way. Other methods of water storage include using chemicals, wax or covers for the reservoirs, but these tend to be rather expensive. Seepage has also been reduced by the use of clay to line the reservoirs.

It seems that future water management in arid areas is likely to concentrate on finding new ways of providing fresh water easily and cheaply, and on improving the efficiency of water use. The aim is to increase the length of time that the reserves will last.

▶ Figure 5.57 shows two lists, one which summarises the main problems of water management in deserts, and one which suggests some of the solutions. The lists do not match. Draw up a table and match each problem to the appropriate solution.

Problems	Solutions
1 Variability of rainfall	A Clay lined reservoirs
2 Evaporation from reservoirs	B Building reservoirs
3 Seepage from reservoirs	C Reduce pumping from groundwater
4 Salinisation of the soil	D Building sand filled reservoirs
5 Drying up of wells	E Building drainage ditches

Figure 5.57   Problems and solutions of water management

Turning the desert green

The area examined in this case study lies within the countries of Egypt and Sudan. Here much of the land is rock and sand desert. Good farming land is scarce and the best is to be found in a narrow strip which follows the River Nile. In Egypt, 42 million people use only 4% of the land. In the desert lands, a few water holes or oases have allowed small villages to grow up, but many of these are threatened by moving sand dunes that can completely bury them.

Figure 5.58 is a map of North-east Africa showing the main sources of water. Many schemes are in operation to use this water and to improve the desert lands. It is hoped that much of the land can be brought into use for growing food, and that the water may also be used to produce electricity for industry, lakes for fishing and sites for tourism. The major schemes are:

● A plan to dig a 75 km canal from El Alamein to the Qattara depression. Water from the Mediterranean Sea would then flow into the depression. A hydroelectric power station would be built to produce electricity from the water as it flows over the edge of the depression. The water would evaporate and the depression would slowly fill with salt. In addition to hydroelectric power, the scheme would help to develop fishing, industry and tourism in the area.
● The Faiyum Oasis is an area of farmland reclaimed from the desert by the ancient Egyptians. Originally it was watered by the river being allowed to flood each year. Today water is provided all year round by a series of canals and ditches.
● The Aswan High Dam was completed in 1964 and it provides water for irrigation and hydroelectric power. It was a very expensive scheme because of its size. The dam is important for flood control along the river. Many problems exist such as loss of water by increased evaporation from the surface of Lake Nasser, the loss of good agricultural land taken up by the lake, and the erosion of land by water released through the dam.
● The Sadat Canal is being built to prevent Lake Nasser overflowing. Excess water can then be drained into a depression. This will allow more land to be improved for agriculture.
● The Jebel Aulia Dam, 40 km south of Khartoum, was built in 1937. It raised the level of the river and helped control the floods. Irrigation ditches and canals were provided with regular supplies of water.

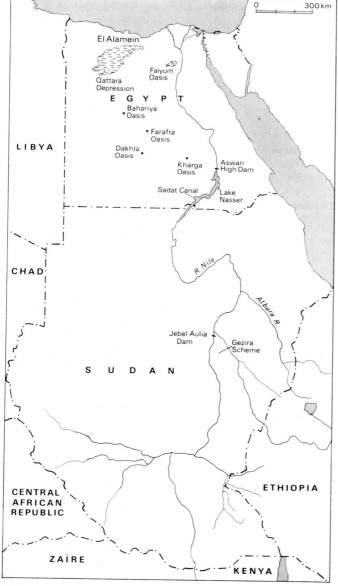

- The Gezira Scheme is a large-scale irrigation scheme in the Sudan between the White Nile and the Blue Nile rivers. The land is watered by a system of canals and ditches, providing an improved food supply and allowing large-scale production of cotton.
- Some people believe that a large reservoir of water exists underground in the Libyan Desert. If so, pumps could bring the water to the surface and it could be used for farming. However the water may be ancient water. This means that it is not being replaced by today's rainfall and may be used up quickly.
- The Kharga Oasis, the Farafra Oasis and the Bahariya Oasis are the major sources of water being used today in the Libyan Desert. Small villages and primitive farming exists here, but the livelihood of the people is being threatened by moving sand dunes and DESERTIFICATION.

1 On a large copy of the map in Figure 5.58, and using an atlas, add the following items to your map:
  i The Red Sea and the Mediterranean Sea.
  ii Egypt and Sudan.
  iii The White Nile and the Blue Nile.
  iv Cairo and Khartoum.
  v The Libyan Desert.
2 What are going to be the main problems facing the people who manage water resources in Egypt and Sudan?
3 List some of the ways that these problems can be overcome.

Land management

As well as a scarcity of water in the deserts and semi-arid regions, there is also a severe shortage of good farmland. The problem is two-fold. Firstly, as the population grows, more people need land to farm. Secondly, because the land is easily damaged, increased use can destroy it. In order to manage the land, three challenges need to be met: i Soil conservation, ii Land use, and iii Desertification.

The fragile soil

Soils in deserts tend to be thin. They lack plant material or humus, which binds the soil particles together and helps the soil retain water. This means that the soils can be removed very easily by water or wind. This process is called SOIL EROSION.

Soil in deserts is particularly prone to erosion when it is left bare. This may occur when it has just been ploughed and planted with seeds, or when it has been used so much that it is exhausted and crops can no longer grow. Fine soil particles can then be removed by the wind, which in deserts can reach very high speeds. The amount of material which can be removed by winds is enormous. In extreme cases large depressions may form such as the Qattara depression in Egypt, which has developed through the removal of 3200 km^3 of material!

The effect is to strip not only the soil from the area but also any crops which may be growing. Deflation may leave only the larger pebbles and boulders behind, forming a stone pavement. In areas where the soil is eventually deposited, blocked roads, buried crops, and filled-in irrigation ditches are common.

Water erosion is just as serious, even though rivers may only flow for a few days a year. When it does rain in deserts, it is often in the form of very intense storms. Rain water flows over the surface as a SHEET FLOOD or in channels called gullies. Large amounts of soil can be eroded, particularly in areas where people or animals have removed the vegetation cover. In Tanzania, for example, soil erosion by water was virtually absent in areas supporting the natural vegetation of thicket or grass. But the picture became very different on agricultural land. Where millet was being grown, 78 tonnes of soil/ha were lost and on bare land, 146 tonnes/ha were removed. Water erosion also caused problems of soil and seed loss, and the clogging of ditches and rivers.

Solutions to these problems come under the broad heading of SOIL CONSERVATION. It is important that the natural vegetation should be protected and that the soil should not be over-used so that it loses its fertility. It should not be left bare at any time. Cover crops of grass can be used to bind the soil together when other crops are not being grown and mulches of straw can be laid on top of the soil to protect it from the water or wind. This is particularly effective when it is combined with irrigation which keeps the soil damp and sticky. Much can also be achieved by providing demonstrations for farmers of the problems caused by poor methods. The international aid agencies, for example the United Nations' Food and Agricultural Organisation, have an important role to play here.

The land users

The population of desert areas is small. The lack of water limits the places where people can settle, but for many thousands of years they have been able to live in hostile areas by developing very specialised forms of farming.

One type is the SEDENTARY form of agriculture where farmers stay in one place, growing crops and keeping a few animals. They usually live close to rivers or to oases. The most successful crop is the date palm because it is able to tolerate salt in the water, but it still requires a great quantity of water to grow successfully.

Many people in the deserts survive by herding animals and moving them from one area of pasture to another. This is the NOMADIC way of life and these people are called NOMADS. Tribes such as the Bedouin of the Sahara keep large herds of sheep, goats and camels. Very little water is needed and in fact the date palm farmers use one thousand times more water than the Bedouin people. The drier lands are used for pasture in the wet season, while in the dry season they depend upon permanent water holes and oases. If there is a series of bad years, then the good pasture may be overgrazed by the animals and destroyed. This occurred in the Sahel in North Africa during the drought of 1967–73.

A widely used technique for growing crops is RUN-OFF farming. Long ago it was realised that crops could be grown if water from the infrequent rain storms was collected. Small terraces and dams are used to catch the rain water that runs over the surface after a storm. A more up-to-date approach is used on the Canary Island of Lanzarote. Large concrete CATCHMENTS have been built on the sides of hills. When it rains the water runs off the concrete and is channelled into storage tanks for later use. Figure 5.59 shows one of these catchments on the side of an extinct volcano.

Figure 5.59   A concrete water catchment, Lanzarote

The encroaching desert

The map in Figure 5.60 shows the worldwide pattern of a major problem. Along the edges of the great deserts valuable farmland is being changed into useless waste. In some places, land that once supported large numbers of people and animals has been stripped bare of grass and soil. The deserts are growing outwards.

In 1980, 10% of the earth's land was desert, but today the figure is closer to 25%. DESERTIFICATION is taking place. Desertification occurs where good land is being turned into desert. It is caused by many factors, both natural and Man-made. Some deserts now receive less rainfall than in the past, and are being affected by severe periods of drought more often. Good grazing land is thus put under even more pressure.

The problem is so serious that in August 1977 experts from many countries met at a conference in Nairobi, Kenya, to discuss some important questions. In particular, they wanted to know: i) what had caused desertification, ii) what its effects on local people had been, and iii) what could be done to solve the problem. Shortly, we shall look at these questions with regard to one particular country — Tanzania.

Figure 5.60   The world pattern of desertification

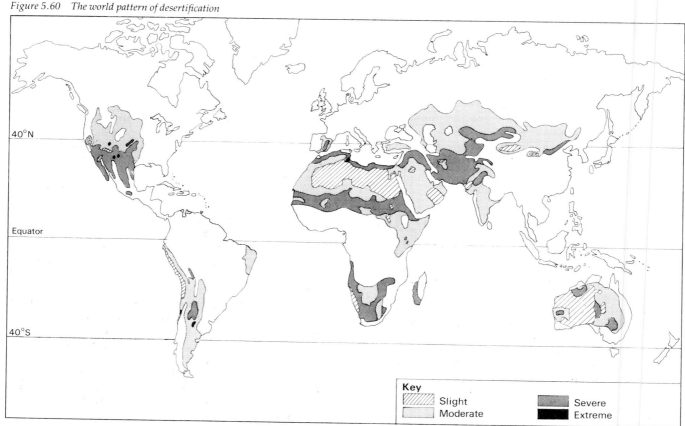

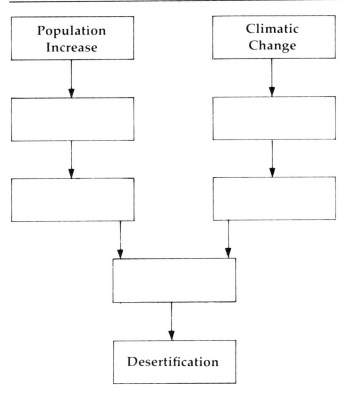

Figure 5.61   Causes of desertification

► Figure 5.61 is a flow diagram showing some of the factors which may lead to desertification. Below there is a list which contains the missing words from the diagram. Fill in the boxes, choosing the appropriate words from the list.

Overgrazing   Vegetation dies   Bare soil
Animals increase   Less rain

Desertification in Tanzania

► On an outline map of Africa mark:
  i   The main arid and semi-arid areas (from Figure 5.55).
  ii   Tanzania and Kenya.
  iii Lake Victoria.
  iv   Dar-es-Salaam.

Tanzania is one of the largest countries in East Africa, and faces many of the problems of being in the semi-arid area of the continent. It is also a developing country that is trying to raise the standard of living of its 17.5 million people by improving farming and setting up industries. One of the biggest difficulties it faces is that much of the country is suffering from desertification.

The two maps in Figure 5.62 show the areas of Tanzania that are affected by the problem, together with the main features of rainfall and relief. The regions with the most serious problems are in the north and centre of the country, the zone from Dodoma to Lake Victoria. These are the regions with the lowest rainfall in the country (between 500 mm and 800 mm per year). In the west and east, where rainfall is generally higher, desertification is not a problem.

The main symptom of desertification is the erosion of the soil and the development of gullies on slopes. This in turn means that most of the vegetation is lost and cannot be replaced. The gullying is very severe in the 'badlands' area around the town of Kondoa, to the north of Dodoma. Here much of the farmland has become useless and measurements in the early 1970s of the build-up of material in the bottom of reservoirs near Dodoma showed the amount of soil being eroded

Figure 5.62a   Desertification in Tanzania

Figure 5.62b   Rainfall in Tanzania

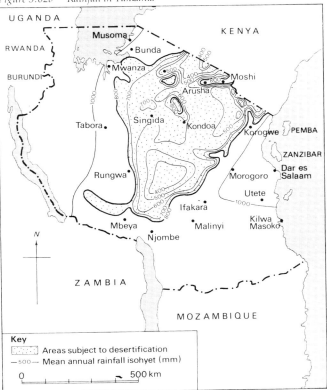

from the land surface was up to 730 m³/km². This quantity of soil is enough to fill five semi-detached houses.

The problem is clearly serious and since 1923 there have been six major famines. But what are its causes? A common suggestion is that slight variations in rainfall from year to year, and the resulting droughts, are the cause of vegetation loss and famine. In this part of Tanzania, however, this is not the cause. Records suggest that the climate today is similar to what it was long before desertification started.

A better suggestion is that it is related to rapid population growth. Figure 5.63 shows the growth of population in the semi-arid areas of Tanzania and indicates a rapid increase. This is the result of population growth in Tanzania as a whole and the pressure on people to move into areas not used before.

Year	Population (million)
1948	2.25
1957	2.61
1967	3.49
1978	5.98
1997 (est.)	7.98

Figure 5.63   Population growth in the semi-arid areas of Tanzania

The original inhabitants of the Dodoma region (the Gogo people) were cattle-grazers, who, in moving from place to place, did not overuse the vegetation. Districts were grazed for a while but then abandoned and allowed to recover. Population growth has led to farmers becoming settled, producing the following problems:

- The area can support cattle safely at a density of one animal/2.5 ha but the number of cows means that the average density is actually one animal/1.9 ha of land. Improvements in veterinary care have allowed more cattle to survive, even though the land cannot support them.
- The farming that has developed is cotton and vegetable growing. Few measures have been taken to prevent soil erosion and poor farming techniques are one of its major causes. It is a particular problem in the areas around the larger villages and the new settlements.
- Attempts to stop sleeping sickness (trypanosomiasis) in the area have involved clearing the vegetation in which the tse-tse fly, the disease's carrier, lives. This clearance has exposed the soil to increased wind and rain erosion.

Another part of the problem has been the clearance of woodland from mountain slopes because the timber has been needed for charcoal. Between 1959 and 1970, the use of firewood increased by 35% and it is estimated that the need for charcoal will increase eleven times by the end of the century. The removal of trees from slopes causes very rapid erosion of the soil, making the land unusable.

As yet very little has been done to overcome the problem. One solution which has been attempted is the reafforestation, or the planting of trees, to prevent soil erosion and to provide a future source of firewood. The government has set up tree nurseries and by 1981,

106

7700 ha had been replanted. Other measures include schemes to help prevent soil erosion through terracing of the land, plans to reduce wood consumption by using other sources of energy (e.g. wind power) and attempts to train local people in improved farming methods. The problem is still a serious one, however, and predictions of the population growth suggest that action must be taken now if the land is to be useful for farming in the future.

▶ Write an essay on desertification in Tanzania. In your essay, attempt to answer the following questions:
  i What is the evidence for desertification in Northern Tanzania?
  ii What seem to be the main causes?
  iii What remedies have been tried?
  iv In what ways does economic growth seem to have caused the problem of desertification in Tanzania?
  v What are the future prospects for managing desertification in Tanzania?

Dry Europe: the case of Iberia

Arid and semi-arid lands are commonly believed to exist only in Africa, the Middle East and Central Australia. One area of Europe, however, suffers from the same problem. Figure 5.64 shows the climatic features of the Iberian Peninsula which consists of Spain and Portugal. Over 80% of this area receives less than 1000 mm of rainfall each year, while 35% has a total of less than 500 mm. The driest regions are in the valley of the River Ebro around Zaragoza (less than 300 mm) and to the south of Madrid in New Castile. The main source of the management problem stems from the pattern of rainfall throughout the year. Most rain falls in the winter months, while there is a long period of drought in the summer. This presents a problem because the main growing season is the summer and so irrigation schemes are necessary to provide water for crops. Furthermore, the summer rainfall tends to come in heavy showers, which can cause soil erosion.

As early as the 1920s, both Spain and Portugal recognised the need to manage their water resources. Figure 5.65 shows the vast number of reservoirs constructed in Iberia. Spain has built one dam per month since 1939. At present 12% of Spain is irrigated, and that area produces 40% of the crops.

The benefits of irrigation are clear to see, especially along the Mediterranean coast. This dry area now produces huge quantities of crops to support and feed the large number of summer tourists. Near to Barcelona, the huertas (irrigated lands) grow maize, rice and vegetables to supply the Costa Brava. Around Valencia the use of wells and reservoirs has allowed the large-scale production of rice, olives, vines and citrus fruits. Further south in the drier and hotter areas around Alicante and Murcia, a canal system brings water from the mountains of the Betic Cordillera to allow crops to be grown all year round, including bananas and sugar cane.

The benefits, however, have to be balanced against the problems. Only by careful management of irrigation and terracing can problems of soil erosion and desertification be stopped in this type of climate. Overall, 10% of Spain is now affected by severe desertification, and in the arid areas this figure rises as high as 80%. The most seriously affected areas are inland from the Mediterranean coast on the slopes of the Iberian Mountains. Here the agriculture is poorer, and a lack of suitable farming techniques has allowed soil erosion to take place. Removal of the oak and scrub forests has caused gullying on the slopes. In some areas, especially around Ugijar near Almeria, the soft rocks are easily eroded.

As they are more developed than Tanzania for example, Spain and Portugal are fortunate to have some money available to help overcome these problems. Much progress has been made in water resource management, and this has greatly helped the economic development of the two countries.

▶ By referring to the studies of Tanzania and the Iberian peninsular, draw up a list of key points which describe the causes of, and the responses to, desertification in both these areas of the world.

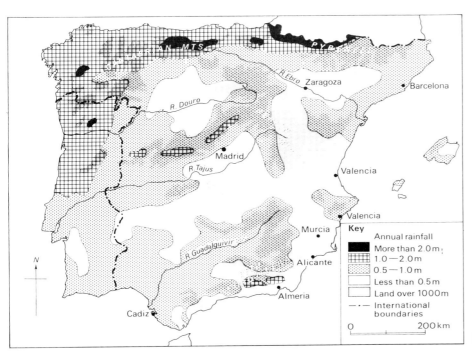

Figure 5.64   The Iberian peninsula

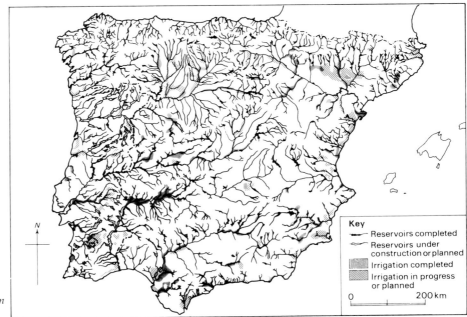

Figure 5.65   Water resource management in Spain and Portugal

5.5 The Disappearing Forests

The world's forests are slowly disappearing. Today, 33% of the land is clothed with forest. Three hundred years ago the figure was 60% and as recently as fifty years ago it was 45%. By the end of the century it will be 25%, and still declining. The reason for this great disappearance is two-fold. There has been a huge increase in demand for timber and farming has spread into forested areas to feed the world's growing population.

Where are the world's forests?

The map in Figure 5.66 shows the location of the world's forests. Three main types can be found:
Broadleaved Evergreen Forest. These are the rainforests of the Equatorial lands. A great number of species are found (up to 200/ha) and trees such as mahogany, teak, ironwood and greenheart are common. They are found where the climate is hot (25°C) and wet (1500mm+) throughout the year. They make up half of the world's forest, e.g. the Amazon rainforest and the jungles of South-east Asia.
Deciduous Forest. Outside the Tropics, many areas have forests dominated by trees that lose their leaves during part of the year. The oak and beech forests of England are typical and they contain 20 to 40 species/ha. They occur where the temperatures are warm in summer (10–25°C), but sufficiently cool in winter (0–10°C) to prevent tree growth.
Coniferous Forest. These consist of evergreen trees with needle leaves, and usually only contain 1 to 5 species/ha. In the mountains of mid-latitude areas, species such as Douglas fir and redwood may be important, while in the large forests that cover much of the high latitude areas spruce and pine are more common. These latter areas are called Boreal Forest or Taiga. They are found where the climate is cool (5–10°C) throughout the summer and cold in winter (below 0°C).

▶ 1 Study the figures in the table in Figure 5.67.
  i Which continent is most covered with forest?
  ii Which continent has the greatest resources of forest per person?
  iii Draw a pie chart to show the distribution of the world's forest areas by continent.
 2 Compare the map of forests in Figure 5.66 with a map of natural vegetation in an atlas. 'Natural vegetation' is the vegetation that would be found in an area if human activity had never influenced it.
  i Estimate how much of each of the three types of forest still remains.
  ii Which of the three types of forest has been most affected by human activity?
  iii Try to explain your answer to ii.

Continent	Forest Area (m ha)	% of Land	Hectares/Person
Europe	140	29	0.3
USSR	910	34	3.3
North & Central America	815	36	3.0
South America	908	47	5.3
Asia	534	19	0.3
Africa	639	23	2.4
Oceania	81	11	5.4

Figure 5.67   The distribution of the world's forests

Figure 5.66   The world's forests

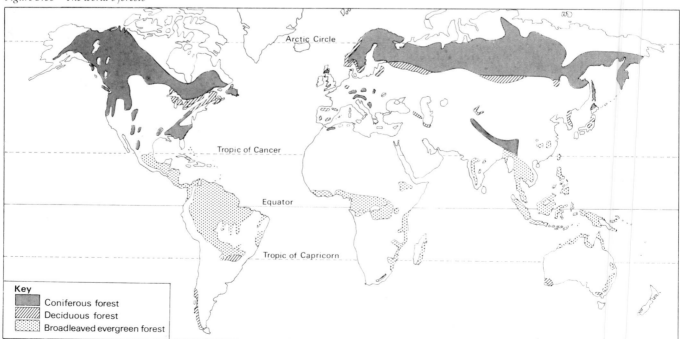

Key
▓ Coniferous forest
▨ Deciduous forest
▒ Broadleaved evergreen forest

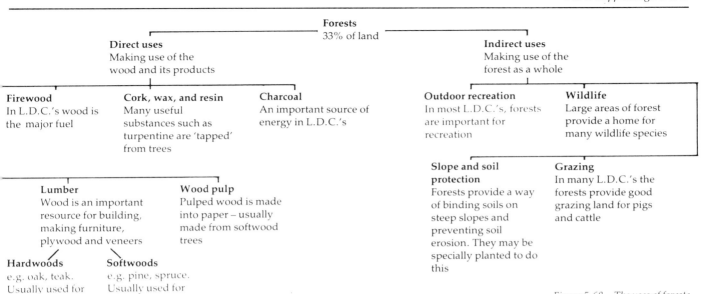

Figure 5.68 *The uses of forests*

The use of forest

Forests are useful to people in many ways, and the main uses are shown in Figure 5.68. In most countries of the world, forests are used for all these purposes, although their relative importance varies, both direct and indirect uses bring management problems.

► 1 Place the five direct uses of forests in your estimated order of wood use in, i) developed countries, and ii) developing countries.
2 Which of the indirect uses of forests would be of most importance in, i) Great Britain, and ii) India?

Direct uses

Most direct uses of forests result in trees being cleared from the land and the timber being used in some way. In the world as a whole, 42% of the wood cut each year is used for firewood, while 37% is used for industrial purposes and building. The other main uses are for wood pulp and paper (11%) and making pit props (4%). The amount of timber used is increasing very rapidly, as Figure 5.69 shows.

	1960	1975
Logs	629	815
Wood pulp	226	493
Fuel	1088	1199

Figure 5.69   The main uses of wood, 1960 and 1975 (million cubic metres)

In many parts of the world, careful management makes sure that new planting replaces cut down trees. However, there is still an annual loss of 40 million hectares of forest – an area about 1½ times the size of Britain. Many problems result from this loss:

Soil erosion. By removing the cover of forest, the soil beneath is exposed to the force of the rain which had previously been intercepted by the trees. This has the effect of washing away the soil. In the Atlas mountains of Tunisia the natural oak woodland was gradually cleared from Roman times onwards. Much of the land is now covered with deep gullies, with little soil left on the surface. It is therefore of little value for farming, which might have taken over the cleared land.

Loss of fertility. Trees contain many minerals and nutrients taken from the soil. These are normally returned when the tree or leaves die and decay. If trees are removed, as much as one-third of an area's nutrients are taken with them, and the soil is left impoverished. The nutrients that are left are also more liable to be removed by water passing through the soil, for the absence of decaying matter (humus) means they are no longer held in the soil. In Indonesia wasteland formed in this way is known as BELANG.

Damage to the atmosphere. One great fear that many environmentalists have is that the clearing of the forests may cause damage to the world's atmosphere. Trees are important in absorbing carbon dioxide (CO_2) from the atmosphere and giving out oxygen (O_2) — a giant air purifying system! Without the trees there may be a slow build-up of carbon dioxide which will have the effect of raising the temperature of the atmosphere by a small amount. In the long term such a rise of temperature could cause worldwide problems, e.g. the melting of part of the Polar ice, or the movement of the world's climatic belts, perhaps changing the weather and rainfall over the main food producing regions.

Wildlife loss. The world's forests, particularly in the Tropics, contain many hundreds of species of plant and animal. The clearance of the forest causes them to lose their habitat and there is a serious chance of many becoming extinct. This is a problem because the loss of species is seen by many as a great loss to the quality of the natural environment, and because many species may prove to be useful to people in the future. Recent research has shown that a vaccine to prevent or cure leprosy (a previously incurable disease) can be obtained from a tropical forest animal, the armadillo. Had the species become extinct, this cure would not have been found. Many drugs useful for the treatment of diseases, including cancer, have recently been obtained from tropical trees.

Figure 5.70   The message behind today's reafforestation in the Tennessee Valley, USA

Indirect uses

Indirect uses are those which do not involve the removal of the trees but use the forest as a whole for some other purpose. The importance of each of the main types varies in different parts of the world.

Grazing. This is most common in the deciduous and coniferous forests away from the Tropics. Farmers in Eastern Europe use the woodlands for grazing pigs on the tree nuts, and in the coniferous Taiga, reindeer are herded. These tend to do little damage as they feed on tree products or small plants. Little woodland grazing takes place in developed countries of the world.

Wildlife protection. In order that some species of forest plants and animals should be preserved, areas of forest are increasingly being set aside for wildlife protection. In Britain, woodlands in Cannock Chase in Staffordshire are preserved as the breeding ground of the nightjar, while in Plitvice in Yugoslavia, bears and wolves occupy protected zones in the forests. In some areas the need for protection means that access is only allowed with a permit.

Outdoor recreation. Forests are a popular place for recreation, particularly in the developed countries of the world where greater wealth allows people more free time and the opportunity to visit areas far from their home. The peace of the woodlands, the attractive scenery, and the variety of wildlife that can be seen are the main attractions. Management is very important at a number of levels. Roads to woodlands may become overcrowded and car parks and picnic sites require careful siting. Erosion of footpaths in the woodlands can be a problem, and there is the threat of damage to wildlife and of fire being started accidentally. Careful management of recreation is therefore necessary.

Slope and soil protection. When trees are removed from slopes there is a serious threat of soil erosion. In many regions, attempts have been made to protect vulnerable slopes by planting forests. In the Tennessee Valley, in the USA, tree felling in the century before 1933 caused serious soil erosion, which in turn caused the River Tennessee to flood more often than before. One of the solutions used by the Tennessee Valley Authority (T.V.A.) to halt the problem was to encourage REAFFORESTATION on the upper valley slopes. This still continues today, but also for a different purpose, see Figure 5.70. Similar schemes have worked in the Atlas Mountains of Tunisia, and along the River Hwang-Ho in Central China.

Managing the woodlands

In order that the best use should be made of the forests, careful management is necessary. Each specific use has to be managed itself, but an overall plan is necessary, too. Figure 5.71 shows the main problem facing forest managers which is that the forests often cannot be used in several ways at once.

▶ Study the table in Figure 5.71. Explain why each use is compatible with some other uses, but not with all of them.

It would seem that the only solution to the problem is to divide the forests into areas where different uses can occur. This process is called LAND USE ZONING. In the USA the National Forests (those owned by the

Uses	Direct Uses			Indirect Uses		
	Areas of Felling	Areas of Growing	Grazing	Wildlife Conservation	Recreation	Slope Protection
Areas of felling	– – –	X	X	X	X	X
Areas of growing	X	– – –	X	√	√	√
Grazing	X	X	– – –	X	X	√
Wildlife conservation	X	√	X	– – –	X	√
Recreation	X	√	X	X	– – –	√
Slope protection	X	√	√	√	√	– – –

Figure 5.71   The range of different forest uses   √ = Uses are compatible   X = Uses are incompatible

government) are managed in this way, with each area of a forest being used for the purpose best suited to it. A similar scheme is operated in the Netherlands, where the best areas of woodland are used for timber and the poorest for recreation. Here, because of the large population (390 people/km²) and the ease of importing timber, over 75% of the woodlands are used for recreation and wildlife conservation.

In contrast to the Netherlands however, Finland has a small population (15 people/km²) and so concentrates on using its land for timber production. Forest products account for 50% of the country's income and 70% of the country is forested. There is, therefore, little danger to the woodlands from recreation.

Keeping the forests growing

Even when large amounts of timber are removed from an area, it is possible to manage the forest to maintain a supply of timber. By removing a small proportion each year and replanting the same amount elsewhere in the forest, little damage is done. The forest's yield can also be increased by replanting with fast-growing species. In New Zealand, for example, many areas were cleared of woodland in the years from 1850 to 1950, and the native trees were replaced with fast-growing 'exotic' species (exotic means 'not native'). By now, 360 000 ha of these new species, particularly pine, are available for management, with 10 000 ha cleared and replanted each year.

The only problem that arises from this approach is that forestry is made easier if only one type of tree is planted over large areas. Many environmentalists complain that this spoils the landscape, and there is also the danger that disease could wipe out the forest completely. Budworm, a disease of spruce trees, has threatened to do just this in a number of places in the USA.

In general, however, a constant supply of forest products can be maintained by following two rules:
- Always replant as many trees as are felled each year.
- Never cut more timber than the forest produces by new growth each year.

Managing Northern Ireland's forests

Many parts of Western Europe have seen a great change in their forests over the last 3000 years and Northern Ireland is a typical example. Before 500 BC most of Northern Ireland was clothed with a forest of oak, ash, elm and alder but then an increase in rainfall made the conditions less suitable for deciduous trees. More importantly, however, the forests began to be cleared by people. First the Iron Age Celts slowly cleared small areas, then in the 11th century AD the Normans arrived and began to remove the trees at a greater rate. Deer and rabbit were introduced from France and over the next 700 years the forests were removed to make way for farming. By AD 1800, only small areas were left.

The need to provide timber for building, firewood and scenic value caused some wealthy landowners to start replanting in the 19th century, but little progress was made. Only since 1921, when the Northern Ireland Ministry of Agriculture took over responsibility for the province's forests, did reafforestation, begin in earnest. By 1976, nearly 50 000 ha had been replanted, and the aim is to have reclaimed 120 000 ha by AD 2000.

Most of the new forests (Figure 5.72) are on land at high altitudes (more than 250 m). Here low temperatures and high rainfall prevent much farming. 96% of the trees planted are conifers, mostly sitka spruce (62%), Norway spruce (8%) and lodgepole pine (8%). These species were chosen because they grow quickly in poor conditions and provide useful timber. The trees are planted in straight lines, with occasional gaps to provide a firebreak. Harvesting is made easy in this way but objections are raised from environmentalists who claim that large areas with straight lines of a single species are unattractive and more importantly, only a fraction of the number and varieties of plants and animals common to mixed deciduous woodlands may be found in pine forests.

The forests are not only used for timber, however, they are also seen as important for recreation, conservation of certain types of wildlife and improving the scenery. More than 400 000 people a year visit the forests and so facilities such as car parks, cafeterias, information offices and toilets have been provided. Some rare bird species such as peregrine falcons, hen harriers and buzzards use the woods for breeding, and a number of rare butterflies can be found at Drum Manor Country Park.

Figure 5.72   Northern Ireland's forests

Key

🌲 Forest parks and forests which have a wide range of recreational facilities

♧ Forests with only basic facilities

▒ Land over 250 metres

0   50 km

Ballypatrick Forest Park, near Ballycastle in County Antrim, is typical of most of the province's forests (Figure 5.73). In 1946, 1460 ha of moorland were first bought and planting started in 1948. Today there are 1300 ha of mature coniferous forest, mainly of sitka spruce, lodgepole pine and Japanese larch. In 1966 a small car park was built, and later additions included a caravan site, a number of forest trails for walkers, an 8 km forest drive and an information centre with displays. An area of moorland has been left to provide a refuge for moorland birds, including raven and grouse, and to allow local people to dig peat for fuel. Conservation is also important in the woodland where predators such as kestrels have moved in and insect and mice populations have grown. An ancient Iron Age burial mound is also preserved for tourists to visit.

▶ 1 The forests of Northern Ireland are managed for 'multiple use'. What does this mean? Give examples to illustrate your answer.

2 Use the map in Figure 5.73 to describe what you would see on a drive round the forest at Ballypatrick Forest Park.

3 What do you think the attitude of the following groups of people would be to the growing of new forests in Northern Ireland?
  i The Government.
  ii A company importing timber from Finland into the United Kingdom.
  iii A conservationist.
  iv A local resident near a 'new forest'.

4 Explain the reasons for the following management ideas:
  i Growing mainly coniferous trees.
  ii Using high land.
  iii Planting in straight lines with occasional wider gaps.
  iv Encouraging recreation in the forests.

Figure 5.73   Ballypatrick Forest Park

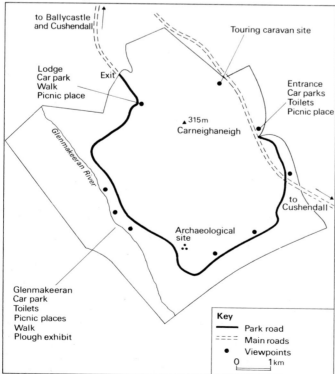

Forest clearance in South-east Asia

Half the world's remaining forest (1000 million ha) is found in the Tropics, with one-third of that total growing in the area shown in Figure 5.74 — South-east Asia. It is an enormous resource for it contains many hundreds of species of trees, and thousands of varieties of other plants and animals. It is therefore a resource under pressure. Each year across the globe 2.25 million ha are cleared, which is equivalent to an area the size of Wales being cleared each month. The World Bank predicts that by AD 2000 only 900 million ha will remain. By AD 2050 only 500 million ha will still be left and virtually all will have gone by AD 2100.

Figures 5.75 and 5.76 show a series of tables which illustrate the problem.

There are two main causes of the loss of forest. First, there has been an increase in the demand for tropical wood from the rest of the world, as Figure 5.75a shows. Most of the countries with tropical forest are poor and need to earn as much foreign money as possible from the sale of their forest products. They are therefore keen to increase production. Second, there is great pressure from population growth. Half the world's population lives in the countries with tropical forest, and the need for farmland is pressing.

East Kalimantan is a major part of the island of Borneo, in Indonesia. Of its 21 million ha, 17 million are forested, and the government is seeking to use this resource fully. The six-fold rise in log production between 1960 and 1980 is being further increased by granting permits to 100 foreign logging companies. They will clear 13 million ha over the next two decades. The timber will earn foreign income, while the cleared land will be used for resettling people from the overcrowded parts of Indonesia. Thousands of people from Java, Bali and Sulawesi are being moved to the area in order to develop agriculture.

A number of problems arise from the forest clearance, however. Little attempt is being made to replace cleared forest by replanting, and so the resource will soon be lost for ever. Secondly, the soil left behind is of low value because most of the nutrients are removed with the trees or leached by heavy rain. Thirdly, of the several hundred species of plant in each hectare of forest, only 20 trees, on average, are removed for sale. The rest are burned and destroyed and their value is wasted. Finally, many forest animals are losing their habitats, including rare species such as the orang-utan.

A second example comes from Malaysia. Very rapid population growth has forced the national government to make considerable use of forests. Two-thirds of the lowland areas of the Malaysian Peninsula are now used for logging, and a number of important agricultural development schemes have been started. In the Jengka Triangle (Figure 5.77), a scheme started in the 1950s has established farming villages in the forests to grow oil palms or rubber trees. Over a quarter of the country's palm oil comes from this area. Another scheme is the Pahang Tenggara Project, which covers 1 million ha. 150000 ha have been cleared, and 150000 people have moved in to farm the area, based in 18 townships.

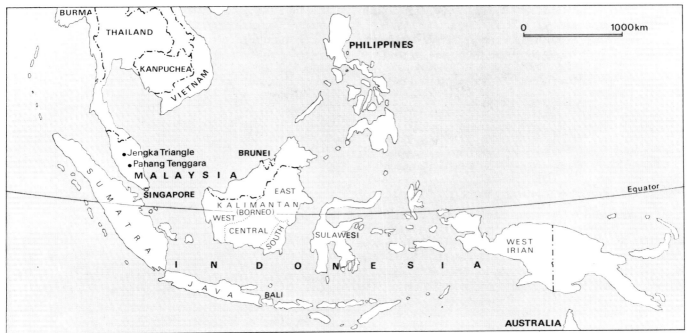

Figure 5.74   South-east Asia

a Tropical Wood	
Year	Demand (million m^3)
1973	109
1980	145
1990 (est.)	215
2000 (est.)	303

b Tropical Wood Products		
Product	Main Producer in South-east Asia	Main Market
Logs	Malaysia	Japan
Sawn wood	Malaysia	Singapore
Veneer	Philippines	USA
Plywood	Singapore	USA

Figure 5.75   Increasing demand for tropical wood and tropical wood products

Country	Forest Loss (million ha/yr)
Thailand	0.3
Laos	0.3
Indonesia	0.3
Philippines	0.26
Malaysia	0.15
South Vietnam	0.03
North Vietnam	0.01
Papua New Guinea	0.01

Figure 5.76   The annual loss of forest in South-east Asian countries

The management of forests in South-east Asia seems to consist only of clearing them and replacing them with farming. The natural forest is only being preserved in a number of nature reserves, e.g. the Bukit Timah Nature Reserve in Singapore. There are a number of arguments for and against the clearance of forest and these are considered opposite:

Against the clearance
(Common views of conservationists in developed countries.)
● The forests preserve many rare species of plant and animal.
● The wildlife may provide as yet unknown drugs for future use.
● Clearing the forest may damage the world's climate by cutting down oxygen production.
● Most forest clearance leads to soil erosion.
● Replanting must take place if future hardwood supplies are to be maintained and it takes several hundred years for a tropical forest to reach maturity.

For the clearance
(Common views of governments in developing countries.)
● The sale of the timber provides much needed money, and there are few other resources that can be used to obtain such money.

Figure 5.77   Forest and farmland in the Jengka Triangle

- Farmland is needed to produce food for rapidly growing populations.
- The clearance wouldn't be so rapid if developed countries weren't increasing their use of tropical wood.
- There is no hard evidence of the supposed damage to the climate.
- Rare wildlife is being preserved in nature reserves.

▶ In what ways does the management of forests in the tropics differ from that in Northern Ireland? What accounts for the differences of management and what are the main issues?

Firewood in Nepal — a burning issue

Most of you will have heard of the 'Energy Crisis' — the problems that developed countries have in obtaining enough oil, gas and coal at low prices. In many developing countries the energy crisis exists too — but in their case the difficulty is in obtaining enough firewood. Forty two percent of the world's timber cut each year is used for firewood and in some developing countries this figure is as high as 80%. Ninety per cent of people depend on wood for fuel. With growing populations more and more is needed and this is leading to a rapid loss of forest land.

Nepal in the Himalaya Mountains is one of the world's poorest countries and covers an area the size of England (Figure 5.78). Many of the lower slopes of the mountains are naturally covered by mixed forest, but since 1953 half the forests have been cut down and at present rates, all will have gone by the year AD 2000. The reasons are simple. In the last ten years, the population has doubled to 13 million people as a result of improved health care for children. This could increase to 20 million by the end of the century. To feed these people, woodland has been cleared so that the farm terraces on the hillsides can be extended, and more cattle are now kept to provide dairy goods. These are fed on forest 'litter'. Most important, however, has been the pressure for firewood. Eighty seven per cent of the country's energy comes from wood. Each person uses 600 kg per year, but the country's forests only grow by 80 kg per person per year. The forests are dwindling. In Katmandu, the capital, firewood prices trebled in two years in the late 1970s. In some places, four day's supply of firewood now takes a whole day

to collect because of the disappearance of woodlands nearby. Ten years ago it took only one hour to collect.

The main difficulty is soil erosion for the soil on the cleared slopes is easily washed away. The rains remove 30 tonnes of soil from each hectare of Nepal every year, and up to 80 tonnes in some places. Soil is a vital resource, and its loss causes direct problems. The beds of many rivers are being built up by 30cm each year, causing an increased risk of flooding. The rivers flow out of Nepal into India and Bangladesh and the areas alongside them now suffer four times as much flooding as they did 25 years ago.

How can the problem be tackled? In the early 1970s the Nepal government started to take action, with the help of money from abroad. Many schemes were set up, e.g. in the Phewa Tal Valley, south of Pokhara, an integrated scheme was begun. Small check dams were built across mountain streams to trap the sediment and eroded soil. Many areas were reafforested, while others were planted with grass and then fenced off. The forests are managed so that no more timber is cut than grows, and all animals are stall fed on grass only. Experiments have shown that this has already reduced the soil loss by 90%.

Reafforestation is vital. One million ha need to be replaced in the next ten years to provide enough timber. One approach is through schemes run by local communities. The village of Chotra, for example, has set up its own tree nursery and sells trees for replanting to surrounding villages,

The ultimate solution, however, lies in finding an alternative fuel. Solar panels have been used in some towns, but these are expensive. Cost is also a problem with large hydroelectric power schemes, such as that at the Kulakani Dam. More successful are small local water power schemes, and most promising of all is the introduction of methane bio-digesters. These convert cow dung into methane gas, which can be used as a fuel. Their advantages are low cost, ease of use, and the fact that they use a plentiful raw material!

▶ 1 Why is firewood collecting a problem in Nepal?
2 What problems does the firewood shortage create for:
  i Local people.
  ii The Nepal government.
  iii The people of Northern India and Bangladesh?

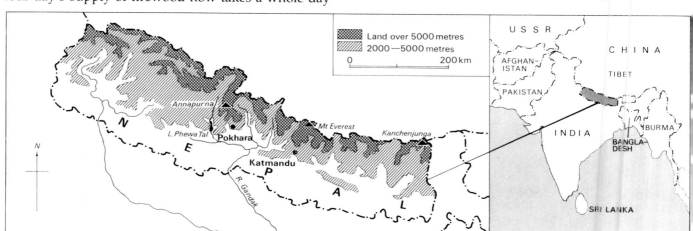

Figure 5.78   Nepal

5.6 Grass, Grain and Game

Grass has been called 'the forgiveness of nature'. All the world's grain crops are simply varieties of grass, used by people for food.

In many parts of the world grasslands are entirely Man-made. They were formed by clearing woodland to allow farming to take place. This process occurred in Britain in the Middle Ages as the population grew and the need for food increased. In other regions, though, grass is the natural vegetation and would be there even without human interference. Figure 5.79 shows where grasslands are to be found today.

Study Figure 5.79 and answer the following questions.
1 Which continent has most grassland?
2 Which continent has least grassland?
3 Which continent has most Man-made grassland? Explain why this is so.
4 Using an atlas to help you, describe in as much detail as you can the distribution of grassland in Africa. Make a list of the countries which have extensive grassland and note the areas in which they occur. If the atlas also has maps of rainfall and temperature describe the climate of the areas with grassland. Identify the *types* of climate in which grassland occurs.

The natural grasslands can be divided into two types:

Temperate grasslands
These are found in areas about half-way between the Poles and the Equator, at latitudes between 40° and 60°. In the USSR these areas are called the steppes, while those in Canada are known as the prairies. They consist of a thick cover of grasses of many types (see Figure 5.80). Trees are not common, except along the sides of rivers where more water is available, and the grasses are usually fairly short. These grasslands occur

Figure 5.80   Temperate grassland

in areas where there is not enough rainfall to support tree growth, and where the temperatures in winter are low. Figure 5.81a shows the climate of an area with temperate grassland.

Tropical grasslands
These are found between the world's hot deserts and the dense tropical rain-forests along the Equator, between latitudes 5° and 20° north and south. In Africa they are usually called savannas, while in South America they are called llanos in Venezuela and campos in Brazil. There are many different species of grass in these grasslands and they often grow to heights of two or three metres, see Figure 5.82. Near the Equator the savannas merge into the rain-forests as rainfall increases. There is also a much greater variety of animal and bird life than in the temperate grassland regions.

Figure 5.79   The world's grasslands

Key
Natural grasslands
Man-made grasslands

a Temperate grassland, Cheyenne, USA												
	J	F	M	A	M	J	J	A	S	O	N	D	Total
Temperature (°C)	−4	−3	1	5	10	16	19	18	14	7	1	−2	
Rainfall (mm)	10	15	25	48	61	41	53	41	30	25	13	13	375

b Tropical grassland, Hall's Creek, Western Australia												
	J	F	M	A	M	J	J	A	S	O	N	D	Total
Temperature (°C)	30	29	28	26	21	19	18	21	24	28	31	31	
Rainfall (mm)	137	107	71	13	5	5	5	2	2	13	35	79	474

Figure 5.81   The climate of the grasslands

Figure 5.81b shows the climate of a tropical grassland area in Australia, and two features are clear from the two figures. Firstly, the temperatures are very high, exceeding 30°C at the hottest times of the year; secondly, the rainfall comes only at certain 'wet seasons', some areas having one, some having two. During the dry season the grass dies back and the rivers are dry, but in the wet season the vegetation grows rapidly and the rivers are full — some may even flood. This variation of weather into distinct seasons is called SEASONALITY.

▶ 1 Draw graphs of the statistics in Figure 5.81 to show the climates of grassland areas.
2 Describe carefully the climates of the tropical and temperate grassland areas.
3 Explain the following words:
  Grassland Savanna Steppe Llanos Seasonality

Grassland uses

Until the last 150 years the world's natural grasslands had not been used on a large scale, for they were areas with few people. Also, their temperature and rainfall pattern made farming a problem. In the temperate grasslands the lack of water and the low winter temperatures made the growing of crops difficult. The tropical grasslands had the same lack of water problem, but this was combined with high temperatures. Here the only users were local native peoples who hunted the large numbers of wild animals or herded livestock. The Masai people of East Africa, for example, used the grasslands for herding cattle.

More recently greater use has been made of the grasslands. In the late 19th and early 20th centuries, the temperate grasslands were developed for the grazing of beef cattle (ranching), as in Argentina or Uruguay, or, more commonly, for large-scale growing of cereal crops, as in the USA and USSR. By keeping cattle or sheep at low densities, i.e. few animals per hectare, as in Australia, the grass was able to support some farming. Sheep could be kept at densities of 1 sheep/ha on very large farms, but the rainfall proved to be too low to provide enough grass to keep any more.

It was possible to grow grain because wheat and barley need less than 750 mm of rain per year and so could be produced in these marginal areas. As with ranching, however, the chief factor that caused the development of grain production was the great demand for food from the cities combined with the growth of rail and ship transport. This allowed production at great distances from centres of population.

Figure 5.82   Tropical grasslands

The tropical grasslands have only come into more widespread use in the last 30 to 40 years. Population growth in developing countries has caused farming to spread out on to the dry savannas. Local people have developed farms for arable crops, and in some areas cattle ranching has grown up to supply meat for export. Even more recently, interest in the wildlife of the savannas (lions, antelopes, elephants and many others) has led to the growth of a tourist industry.

Managing temperate grasslands

Water supply
The dry climate of the temperate grasslands makes water supply a great problem. Successful farming must have adequate water which can be supplied only by storing it and perhaps directing it to the places that need it. An example of such a scheme can be found along the River Murray and River Murrumbidgee in New South Wales, Australia. Here, the rivers are used to supply water to large areas of grazing land.

A further problem is the great variation in rainfall from year to year. Since the rainfall is low anyway, a small change in amount makes a big difference to the farmers and to the yield of their crops. Droughts may occur in three or four years out of ten. Droughts in the Steppes of the USSR in the 1970s led to the Russians buying large amounts of grain from the USA.

Soil management
The soils of temperate grasslands are usually very fertile, for the continual decay of the grass builds up large amounts of humus within them. Humus contains many important nutrients and these areas have been very successful for growing wheat and barley, as, for example the Canadian Prairies. The use of the soil for agriculture, however, causes a number of management difficulties. Under arable farming there is a tendency for soil erosion to occur. Fallow periods expose the soil to the strong winds, and rain, when it does occur, comes in heavy downpours which can quickly erode bare soil. Keeping crops on the soil all the time is the best remedy. Grass is a good COVER CROP. In addition, the crops themselves take away many of the minerals from the soil and weaken its structure. Fertilisers can help, but planting crops such as alfalfa grass, which add nutrients and nitrogen to the soil, is a popular method. The use of heavy machinery also weakens the soil and means it is more easily eroded.

Under ranching, soil erosion can also develop. Overstocking (keeping more cattle or sheep than the land can support), leads to severe trampling or consumption of the grass cover which then leaves the soil exposed and easily removed by wind and rain. The most serious problems of soil erosion occurred in the 1930s on the Great Plains of the USA. A series of dry years caused arable crops to be very poor, and severe soil erosion developed over a large area. Wind erosion was the main cause, and the area became known as the 'American Dust Bowl'.

Destruction of the natural environment
The growth of farming on the grasslands creates change or loss of the natural vegetation. The varied animal life may lose its habitat, and may disappear from some areas. Also, the great variety of plant life may change. Temperate grasslands have up to 10 000 species of grass but the search for the best grass for grazing animals has meant that many species have been removed or replaced. In New Zealand, for example, fescue is now the main grass type on the grazing lands, and this has resulted in many of the traditional insects and animals disappearing. Only rodents such as mice thrive on this grass, and they are increasing in numbers and becoming pests.

This problem is a serious one, for it is difficult to know how valuable these species might be in the future either for agriculture or medicine. There are also many people who feel that the natural grasslands should be preserved for the enjoyment of future generations, rather than replacing them now with farming. In fact, there is probably very little truly natural grassland remaining in the temperate lands. Most of it has already been changed by human activity.

Managing tropical grasslands

Many of the problems of the tropical grasslands are similar to those of the temperate areas. Water supply and soil management again present difficulties, but control of pests, diseases and big game add to the management problems.

Pest and disease control
The hot climate of the tropical grasslands is responsible for many human and animal diseases that prevent the areas from being fully used. In much of Africa the worst problem is sleeping sickness (trypanosomiasis) which affects both people and cattle. It is carried by the tse-tse fly which lives in wooded areas within the savanna. Only when chemicals such as D.D.T. and Dieldrin have been sprayed in such areas does it become possible to graze cattle. However, because the flies have developed resistance to these chemicals and have started to increase in number again, new methods of control are needed. There is also the problem of these chemicals being passed on to other animals through food chains. In the end, it is not always just the flies that die. Other diseases are also present and they include rinderpest, cattle lung sickness and foot-and-mouth disease. In many areas these diseases are endemic (always present).

Game control
The tropical grasslands support huge herds of animals such as elephant and antelope which move between different areas thoughout the year. This movement is a hazard for developing agriculture because crops are trampled and eaten by the animals. It has become necessary to restrict wildlife by keeping animals in limited areas — usually game reserves or national parks, like Luangwa National Park in Zambia. When kept in these parks, however, any increase in animal

numbers leads to overgrazing. Control by culling (shooting selected animals) is one method used to protect both the environment and the health of the remaining animals.

Tourism

Tourism is now very important to many developing countries because it provides them with foreign currency. Especially popular with tourists are visits to the game parks and national parks in the savannas. The building of hotels in these areas provides jobs, and the creation of the reserves also helps in the management of tourism. By keeping visitors in limited areas the rest of the environment is protected.

Botswana — growth on the grasslands

Botswana is one of the world's poorest nations. In 1978, the country earned only $498 per person, in comparison with the USA which earned $9590 per person. A look at an atlas map of southern Africa will show its position and its huge area – 2¼ times larger than Great Britain. However, only 900 000 people live in Botswana.

Most of its income is earned by mining and selling diamonds, copper and nickel, but most of its people, are poor farmers of the Tswana tribes. To raise the standard of living of its people, the Botswana government is trying to improve mining and, more importantly, farming. This involves the increased use of the savanna which covers 90% of the country — the other 10% is the Kalahari Desert (see Figure 5.83).

The government believes that the best use of the savannas is for keeping beef cattle, whose meat can be exported to South Africa, Europe and North America. This type of farming started as long ago as the 1890s and by 1979, meat made up 17% of Botswana's exports. However, there are many management problems to be overcome.

The first of these is rainfall. Most of Botswana receives less than 400 mm of rainfall per annum, and this varies greatly from year to year. Only four reservoirs have been built, and these are near the main towns in the south-east. Irrigation is only available near the River Limpopo. Cows can therefore only be kept at low densities in most places. Secondly, there are a lack of services. Meat can only be produced if there are enough abbatoirs, packing stations and roads and railways to transport it. These exist only around the capital of Gaborone, elsewhere this lack of INFRA-STRUCTURE hinders development.

Environmental damage is another difficulty. If rainfall is low, then large numbers of cattle damage the grassland by overgrazing. Since 1966, herds have tre-

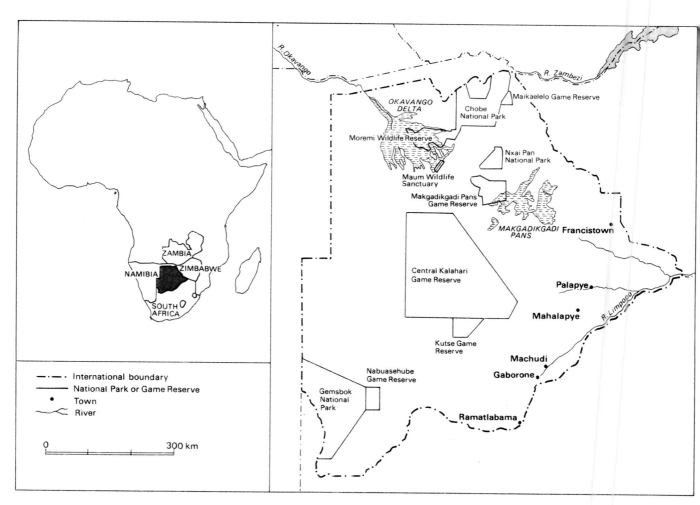

Figure 5.83 Botswana

bled in size and many rangelands have been destroyed in bad years. Herds have grown because of improved veterinary care, and the encouragement of modern methods by the government.

Cattle diseases are also a problem. Foot-and-mouth disease and rinderpest produce regular epidemics, killing many cattle, but the sleeping sickness carried by the tse-tse fly is the main problem. Much of northern Botswana and the Okavango Delta are still infested by the tse-tse fly and remain unsuitable for beef cattle.

Finally, many people are concerned that much of the savanna wildlife will be lost if ranching spreads too far. Since 1950, 17% of the country has therefore been set aside to form eight game reserves, the largest being the Central Kalahari Game Reserve (see Figure 5.83). It is estimated that by 1990 there will be few large herds of wild animals outside these reserves.

Despite all these problems, however, progress is being made. The government has set up the Botswana Meat Company to process and export the meat and in 1979 a Ranch Management School was set up at Ramatlabama, to the south of Gaborone.

> 1 Why is developing ranching on the savannas so important for Botswana?
> 2 What problems and conflicts has the scheme faced?

Tourism in Kenya

Glossy holiday brochures advertise many trips 'on safari' in East Africa. Holidays spent visiting the huge game reserves of Zambia, Tanzania and Kenya are becoming more common as their cost comes within the reach of more people. The tourist industry represents an important use of the savannas for these developing countries.

Kenya is one of the most important countries for safari holidays. In 1952, 6000 tourists arrived in the country, while by the late 1970s the figure was 291 000, most of whom were visiting the game reserves and national parks. Figure 5.84 shows where these national parks are located. Their attraction lies in the chance to watch and photograph animals in their natural surroundings, with large herds of antelope, wildebeest or zebra and many carnivores such as lions, cheetahs and hyenas. The reasons for encouraging this type of tourism are numerous:

Money
Most of the tourists are foreigners who spend large amounts of money in Kenya. Nearly half the tourists come from Europe, with 15% from North America and in total these visitors spend over £25 million and are Kenya's third most important source of income.

Employment
Many local people obtain jobs either in hotels or on the safaris, while others may help construct buildings, roads and other facilities needed by the tourists.

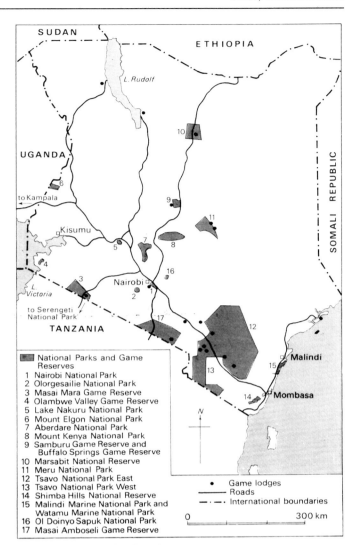

National Parks and Game Reserves
1 Nairobi National Park
2 Olorgesailie National Park
3 Masai Mara Game Reserve
4 Olambwe Valley Game Reserve
5 Lake Nakuru National Park
6 Mount Elgon National Park
7 Aberdare National Park
8 Mount Kenya National Park
9 Samburu Game Reserve and Buffalo Springs Game Reserve
10 Marsabit National Reserve
11 Meru National Park
12 Tsavo National Park East
13 Tsavo National Park West
14 Shimba Hills National Reserve
15 Malindi Marine National Park and Watamu Marine National Park
16 Ol Doinyo Sapuk National Park
17 Masai Amboseli Game Reserve

• Game lodges
— Roads
-·-·- International boundaries

0   300 km

Figure 5.84   National Parks and game reserves in Kenya

Construction
Tourism's need for hotels, airports and roads to the safari areas has encouraged the national government to build good services that would not otherwise have developed. These services have helped local people very much and have also encouraged industry and agriculture to develop.

In order to make the most of the safari tourists, the government has set up the Kenya Tourist Development Corporation. This organisation aims to help the expansion of the tourist industry by advertising, building hotels, and providing general support. It is planning to increase the country's earnings from tourism by 12% each year over the next decade.

> Collect some holiday brochures from a local travel agent and study the holidays on sale in Kenya.
> 1 What attractions do they claim for Kenya?
> 2 On an outline map of Kenya, and using Figure 5.84 to help you, mark the main areas visited by the tourists.
> 3 Do you notice anything particular about the pattern you have mapped in 2?
> 4 Which other countries seem to encourage safari holidays?

5.7 Polar Regions

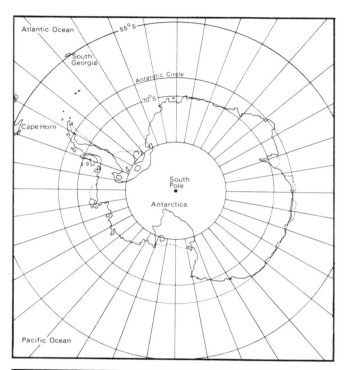

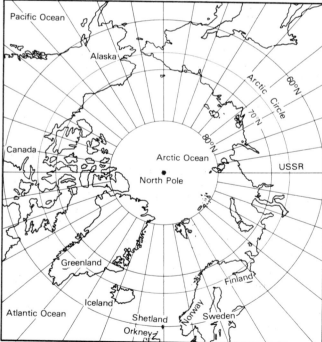

Figure 5.85   *The polar regions*

The areas around the North and South Poles are called the Arctic and Antarctic polar regions respectively. The Arctic polar region extends from 60°N to 90°N while the Antarctic polar region reaches from 55°S to 90°S. Figure 5.85 shows the location of these regions.

In the polar areas there are less than six months with temperatures above 6°C, the critical temperature for plant growth. Figure 5.86 gives details of the climate for two places in the polar region. Everywhere the temperature is low and even in the warmest month it rarely rises above 10°C. Temperatures are not high enough to cause serious melting of the ice or snow found in these regions, and so the air remains dry because it is unable to pick up moisture through evaporation. As the air is dry, precipitation is kept low, and what there is usually falls as snow.

In the coldest areas (80–90°N and 70–90°S) there is frost all year round and few plants or animals survive. Some lichens, algae and insects are found, with seals, penguins and marine life living in or by the sea. In the TUNDRA areas (60–80°N and 55–70°S) it is a little warmer and some plants and small trees are to be found.

Apart from low temperatures, the polar regions also experience a different pattern of dark and daylight hours in comparison with much of the rest of the world. Most places in the polar areas have at least one day of complete daylight and one of complete darkness each year and as summer approaches the days gradually become longer until in full summer there are several months of complete daylight. After this period, the days become shorter again until darkness returns. Even in Britain we have rather more daylight in summer and more darkness in winter.

Until about 1960 very little was known in detail about the polar regions. They were known to be cold and they were not considered to be particularly important. In fact, in 1867, the Czar of Russia sold Alaska to the USA for about two pence per hectare. Recently the picture has changed. It has become certain that these areas are rich in minerals and the exploration of some regions is well advanced. Fish resources are also abundant, and the polar regions may even develop into a tourist attraction in the future.

Place	Latitude	Altitude (m)		J	F	M	A	M	J	J	A	S	O	N	D
Nome, Alaska	64°30′N	7	Temp. °C	−17	−15	−13	−8	1	7	10	10	5	−2	−10	−14
			Precipitation mm	25	28	23	15	23	30	74	76	58	38	25	28
North Cape, Norway	71°6′N	6	Temp. °C	−4	−4	−3	0	3	7	10	10	7	2	−1	−3
			Precipitation mm	58	61	58	46	48	46	66	58	84	76	74	66

Figure 5.86   *The climate of two places in the polar area*

▶ How can these areas be made productive without spoiling the environment?

1 Look at the maps, Figure 5.85 and answer the following questions:
   i Which polar region has more land in the colder zone (80° – 90°N; 70° – 90°S)?
   ii Which polar region has more land in the Tundra zone (60° – 80°N; 55° – 70°S)?
   iii Assuming that the Tundra area will be easier to settle and develop, is more settlement likely in the Arctic or the Antarctic? Why?

2 Using the climate information from Figure 5.86, complete the following table:

	Nome	North Cape
Highest temperature		
Lowest temperature		
Number of months above 0°C		
Number of months above 6°C		
Total precipitation		

A home for wildlife?

The polar regions provide a unique habitat for certain plants and animals. If the regions become developed, the natural habitat will be disturbed and some of the wildlife may be unable to survive. In a cold region plants grow slowly. If they die they may never be replaced.

Svalbard — reserves or resources?

In Norway people have been particularly concerned about the development of Svalbard, a group of islands at 78°N 15°E, Figure 5.87. Svalbard is a typical polar region and is the easiest in the world to visit. It contains both land and sea areas and is close to Europe where most of the visitors come from. The Norwegian Ministry of the Environment is responsible for managing the polar region of Norway. It controls all activites there and is required to manage natural resources, limit pollution and protect wildlife and the local lifestyle. It also organises mapping and the collection of geographical, biological and geological data.

What is there to protect?

Svalbard is a very important area for plants, birds and animals. To the west the islands are warmer while to the east they are very cold. About 170 different types of mosses, lichens and other plants are found here. Many birds visit the area but in the eastern district only 16 types breed. One of these is the Ivory Gull which is a rare bird in the Arctic. Others are the Kittiwake, Fulmar, Black Guillemot and Little Auk. There are no birds of prey because there are no lemming or other small animals (like mice) to feed upon. Only a few animals can survive in this cold climate and the Svalbard reindeer is specially adapted being small with short legs and thick, long-haired fur. However, the conditions are so difficult in the eastern area that only about 200 reindeer can find enough food to live. The Arctic fox lives close to the cliffs where it can feed on

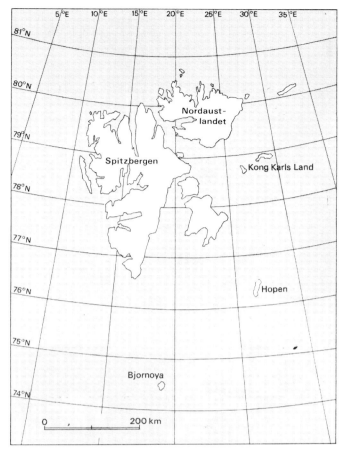

Figure 5.87   Svalbard, Norway

eggs, chicks and adult birds — in the winter it often follows polar bears over the ice to scavenge on their prey. Some seals are also found, living on the land and feeding in the water. In 1960, walrus were almost extinct (about three or four animals left) as a result of hunting but, by 1973 there were more than 300.

The most important animals are the polar bears. In winter almost all the females make dens for their newborn cubs on the shores of Kong Karls Land and Nordaustlandet. In the summer they all drift on the ice and the males and one year-old bears go south and west with the ice in the winter.

Figure 5.88 (on page 122) is a chart showing the food eaten by the Arctic animals and birds. Without enough food, some of them will die. For example, if there is a shortage of fish, seals will die.

▶ 1 If the birds die what animals will be short of food?
2 If the seals die what animals will be short of food?
3 If the plants die what animals will be short of food?
4 Why do you think it is important that the Norwegian Ministry of the Environment protects all the wildlife in Svalbard?

Protection from what?

Originally no one lived in Svalbard. The animals and plants were undisturbed. Recently people have found many reasons to visit and to live there. Figure 5.89 shows some of these newcomers to the area and the types of damage that can be done.

Their food	Polar Bears eat	Foxes eat	Reindeer eat	Fish eat	Seals eat	Birds eat
	The feeders					
Polar Bears	—					
Foxes		—				
Reindeer			—			
Fish				Smaller fish in sea	Mostly	
Seals	Main part of diet	Dead seals			—	
Birds	Eggs, dead birds	Eggs, chicks				—
Plants			Mosses	Sea plants		Yes
Seaweed	Yes					Yes

Figure 5.88   Links between plants and animals in Svalbard

Figure 5.89   The newcomers to the area of Svalbard

What is being done?

- Svalbard has 2 nature reserves, 3 national parks and 15 bird sanctuaries. There are laws to protect over half the total area of Svalbard and people are being educated about the problems they can cause.
- Where certain animals and birds have become almost extinct, special protection is given to them, e.g. polar bears, walrus and reindeer cannot be hunted. Seals can only be hunted during certain months of the year.

- Natural resources (coal, oil etc.) are being carefully managed so that damage to the land and to wildlife caused through pollution is reduced.
- Industrial activity is to be increased slowly so that the necessary shops, schools, roads etc. can be provided without disturbing the local people too much.
- Litter is collected and information leaflets on the problems of litter are handed out.
- A special team is being organised to cope with any possible oil spills. Special equipment is needed because overland transport of equipment is difficult.
- Svalbard museum has been developed and information about ancient monuments and protected buildings is available for tourists. Damage to monuments needs to be reduced.
- More money is available for mapping the area and a special research station has been built at Ny-Alesund. Visiting scientists may use the base and courses are run there.
- Arrangements are being made to improve air transport in the area. Many people cannot afford to carry out research in Svalbard because transport is difficult and the costs are high.

1 Make a list of the newcomers to the area. Alongside each name write down the types of damage they could do. Some suggestions are:
Trampling on plants
Digging up plants
Pollution — oil, air, noise, litter
Frightening animals

2 You have been asked by the Norwegian Ministry of the Environment to suggest ways in which the area should be protected. You may decide that there is no need to worry and that nothing needs to be done. You may choose to control only certain types of damage or to protect just some areas of Svalbard. Explain what *you* think the Norwegian Ministry of the Environment should be doing.

A home for people?

Although the Arctic area is very cold, it is the home of several groups of nomadic peoples: the Innuit, the Lapp and the Samoyed. They have managed to obtain food and shelter from the bare landscape because traditionally they have moved around to find it. Now they are being persuaded to make a permanent home and to settle in new villages. Can the Arctic polar region provide a living for these people, and is it right that they should be persuaded to change their established way of life?

Point Hope — what hope?

Point Hope in Alaska is a community of 400 people. The houses are scattered and untidy, there is no road and on the edge of the main town is a very large rubbish dump. The dogs that wander through the town make it very dirty. The community has become very rich because of Alaskan oil and the government is spending money on developing the area. At the moment most of the money is being spent on a community, education and social centre. New schools are planned for each age group; a sports centre, sauna and many other facilities will be provided. It will cost $6 million to build or $15 000 per person. Other improvements to Point Hope include a proper water supply. But, in order for the supply to work, the pipes must be kept heated by expensive oil and the local community is expected to pay for its share.

As an alternative, wind power is being considered for producing electricity to heat the pipes. Television is now available and many people spend the long winters and their free time in the summer watching it. Few continue to entertain themselves by carving, sewing, painting or playing music, and as a result, many traditional skills are being forgotten. The local games contest was cancelled in one village because it coincided with a television film. Modern machines are also being introduced. They are costly to run and most of them were not needed in traditional eskimo society. For example, the locals used to keep their seal meat in the almost frozen seawater, but now deep freezers have been introduced. Machines have been introduced into factories, but it is so expensive to bring in parts and fuel that fish products now cost three times as much as when local manual labour was used. The factories are managed by Americans and at school, children are taught about American life and, if they do well, they go to mainland USA to study. When they return, they often take office jobs, but many of them never return.

1. Make a list of the 'improvements' and changes that the American government is providing at Point Hope.
2. As mayor of Point Hope, what would you ask for to make your town a better place to live? Why?
3. Some locals living near Point Hope are making a study of the town. They must then report on the changes that they want for their village. You are the secretary of the group and must write this report explaining your choices.
4. What do you think will happen when the oil and building jobs end? What will the indigenous people do?

A tourist attraction?

There was a time when Greenland was one of the least accessible corners of the world. A handful of ships arrived from Denmark each summer — and that was the only contact Greenland had with the rest of the world.

Now tourists want to see this absorbing part of the world themselves. Greenland is different!

Greenland, Figure 5.90 (page 124), was a Danish colony and then a part of Denmark. In 1979, it gained self-government in certain departments such as education and it now receives about 700 million kroner (£53 million) in development aid from Denmark. In 1980 it exported goods worth 1163 million Kr, but imported goods were worth 1845 million Kr. The Greenlanders need to increase their national income as much as possible. They earn money from fishing, hunting and a little sheep farming, but the size of fish catches is variable and sealskins are less in demand. Now, trades, crafts and services are developing and there may be oil and other minerals that can be extracted. Many foreign oil companies have been allowed to explore off the west coast. Already lead and zinc are mined in northern Greenland, but much remains unexplored. One other way to increase income would be to develop tourism.

The following extracts are taken from travel brochures advertising holidays in Greenland.

● One of the last nearly untouched areas on earth.

● A country for those who dream of a life of freedom, subject only to the laws of nature, storm, sun, rain, snow, cold, night and day. It is a beautiful country with gigantic mountains, with never-ending summer days, green slopes, eternal ice, restless white and blue icebergs and with a sea that abounds with big fish.

● Qorqut with about 15 inhabitants is a true paradise. It is surrounded by lovely scenery with mountains, meadows, streams and fjords. There are many opportunities for hiking, and there will be a feast of fresh fish at the Hotel Qorqut, Greenland's first mountain hotel opened in 1974.

● Greenland's climate is Arctic and has considerable influence on travel. The weather may change suddenly. A sunny landscape can quickly be transformed by snow, storm or fog. Travellers are advised to carry with them good, warm, windproof and waterproof sportswear as well as Wellingtons.

● These regions are often filled with relics of ancient cultures, ruins from the old Norse era, eskimo encampments etc. Here are excellent opportunities for studying zoology, botany, ornithology, geology and much more.

● Your cruise calls at some of the most scenic ports of Western Greenland.

● Locally-made Greenland handicrafts — carvings in bone and soapstone, skins, souvenirs etc. are well known.

Figure 5.90   Map of Greenland

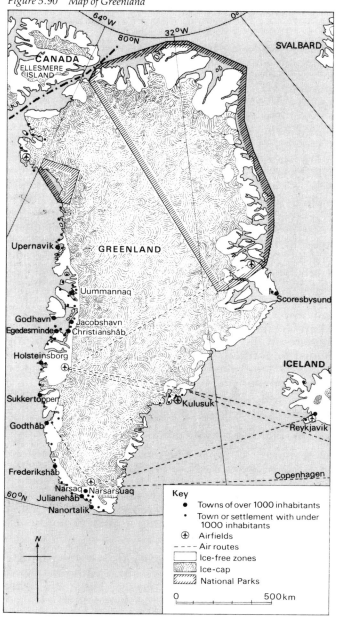

Figure 5.91   (below and right) Aspects of Greenland which attract tourists

Figure 5.91 shows a series of photographs illustrating the aspects of Greenland.

1 Look at an atlas and calculate how far Greenland is from:
   i Copenhagen, Denmark.
   ii New York, USA.
   iii San Francisco, USA.
   iv Montreal, Canada.
   v Reykjavik, Iceland.
   vi London, UK.
   vii Bonn, W. Germany.
   viii The North Pole.

2 A holiday in Greenland is expensive. From which countries do you think tourists might come? Use the extracts from the travel brochures and the photographs to help you answer this question.

3 Make a list of:
   i The attractions of a holiday in Greenland.
   ii The disadvantages of a holiday in Greenland.

4 A travel organisation in New York has money to spend on improving the tourist facilities in Greenland. Write a report describing:
   i The different types of holidays that might be provided in Greenland.
   ii The facilities that would need to be provided, the difficulties to be overcome and the possible towns to be developed.
   iii The best way in your view, to spend the money on tourism.

5 Write a letter to the New York firm explaining the benefits and the disadvantages to the native population of the proposed tourist development as suggested in 4. (Consider new buildings, jobs, way of life, quietness, foreigners etc.)

6 Is tourism a realistic possibility for the development of Greenland?

A supply of resources?

Despite the difficult environment, much of the Arctic area probably contains valuable minerals. Many of these minerals are now running out in the more accessible areas of the world and the Arctic resources are a possible supply for the future.

If there is oil – we'll get it

In March 1969, BP announced that they had found oil in Prudhoe Bay, Alaska (Figure 5.92), but it was not until August 1977, that they eventually shipped the first barrels from Valdez to the markets in the rest of the USA. Extracting and exporting the oil in such a harsh environment presented a major challenge both to the environment and to BP.

Conditions in north Alaska

Apart from people living in the towns, the remaining population of 60 000 is scattered over the rest of the state of Alaska. The North Slope area has very few people living there. It is remote and isolated with about 5200 residents living in eight villages. The land is

Tundra (marshy plain) and only low herbaceous dwarf shrubs or lichens grow in the thin soil. There is a variety of wildlife — wolves, bears, Arctic foxes, lemmings, walrus', seals, whales, sea-lions and the caribou migrate there to calve. Many birds nest in the area and fish spawn freely in the rivers.

Figure 5.93 shows the site of the drilling pads at Prudhoe Bay and the many buildings and facilities required at the surface. Each of these buildings is specially designed to resist damage by the high Arctic winds and drifting snow. Six hundred men live there all year and in winter the heat from the buildings threatens to thaw the permafrost (the permanently frozen ground). The buildings are therefore on stilts. The roads are ten metres wide with a two metres thick gravel layer below so that they can be used all year without risk of eroding the Tundra. the oil wells are drilled from special drilling pads and six to eight wells are placed on each pad so that damage to the land is limited. Underground, these wells spread out to cover a much larger area. The oil is at 82°C underground and so the bore must be insulated to prevent the permafrost from melting. The oil is then taken by pipes to the gathering centres where it is collected.

Figure 5.92   Alaska

125

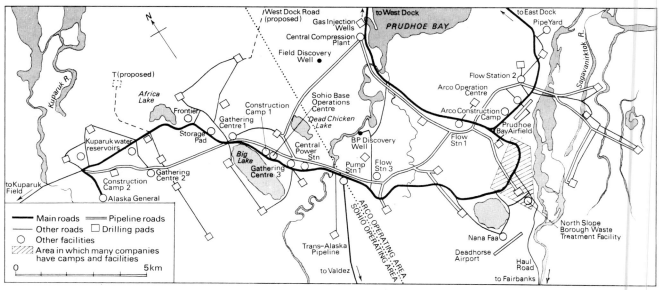

Figure 5.93   *Prudhoe Bay, Alaska*

People and food are transported by air which is expensive, but for six weeks of the year, supplies of machinery and building equipment can be brought in by sea when it is not frozen. Maintaining a warm working environment, especially in winter, is vital. The Operations Centres, where the workers live, are like small cities: they include saunas, games rooms, a running track, an exercise area, volley ball and basket ball courts, a swimming pool and a theatre. There is also a small medical unit, a library, snack bar and shop. Special parks of trees and flowers are grown indoors to help the workers forget the dark hours and bare landscapes outside. Taped television programmes, cinema films and special radio programmes are arranged and newspapers are flown in daily from the USA. The employees work from 7am. to 7pm. for eight days out of every fourteen. They usually spend their time off in Anchorage or Fairbanks. As more oil is extracted, the workforce is expected to increase from 2100 to between 4000 and 5000.

From Prudhoe Bay to the cities

Deciding how to transport the oil to cities such as Los Angeles and San Francisco was a major problem. Eventually a pipeline was planned from Prudhoe Bay to Valdez with the oil then being taken by tanker to Long Beach (California), Seattle (Washington State) and to Kitimat in British Columbia, Canada. It was then intended that it would be sent by other pipelines to towns such as Chicago, Edmonton, Houston and Tulsa. It was also expected that some oil might even be sent through the Panama Canal to the east coast to the USA.

There were many problems and it took five years for the company to obtain permission to build the pipeline. At the public inquiry, five organisations argued against its construction. They were the Wilderness Society, Friends of the Earth, Environmental Defense Fund Incorporated, the Cordova District Fisheries Unions and Five Alaskan Villages.

Difficult areas along the route		
Geomorphological	Ecological	Social
3 mountain ranges	Wildlife areas	Villages
Earthquake areas	Fish spawning	Historic sites
600 streams and rivers	grounds	Unspoilt beauty
Landslides	Permafrost	areas
Earth slumping	Areas where soil	
	would become	
	liquid and wash	
	away	

Figure 5.94   *Difficulties along the route*

The pipeline has now been built and Figures 5.93 and 5.94 show the areas that it passes through. It has been especially designed to cause as little damage to the environment as possible, and it carries enough oil to fill twenty tankers each week at Valdez. The pipeline is:

● Insulated to prevent the warm oil melting the permafrost.
● Buried underground where possible.
● Built on high bridges across rivers for fear of pollution and damage in a flood.
● Monitored to predict an earthquake and built so that oil can be emptied from threatened sections.
● Built near to existing roads.
● Built through as few villages and historic sites as possible.
● Routed to avoid the areas where landslides are a risk.

Has it been worth it?

Before the pipeline was even built $100 million had been spent. It has been estimated that the pipeline cost $8000 million to construct (e.g. $25 million for a bridge over Yukon River; $120 million worth of pipe).

By 1990, over $20 000 million will have been spent in the Prudhoe Bay area. Already one-third of the United

States oil reserves is found here. The USA is now able to reduce its imports of oil by $15 000 million each year because of its own Alaskan oil. The gas produced with the oil is reinjected into the ground and will be removed later.

▶ 1 The pipeline has a 'life' of 30 years. It will probably carry 26 400 million barrels of oil away from the area. Do you think it is worth the cost of building? Give reasons for your answers.

2 What do you think Prudhoe Bay will look like in the year 2030 AD? Why?

Starting again in Antarctica

Between 55°S and 70°S Antarctica is mostly sea, but between 70° and 90°S it is an ice-covered land mass about the size of Australia. The map, Figure 5.85 shows this land area. No one lived in this region until research stations were set up from 1944 onwards. Now, people want to exploit Antarctica for its minerals and sea-food.

Fight for Antarctica

The newspaper article, Figure 5.95, appeared in *The Sunday Times* in February 1983.

▶ Read the article and answer the following questions.
1 Who is trying to save Antarctica?
2 Why are they trying to save Antarctica?
3 What are they saving it from?
4 What do they plan to do?
5 Who wants to use Antarctica for exploration?
6 What do they expect to find in Antarctica?
7 What are the 'club of 14' explorationists doing to save the wildlife?
8 What do the conservationists want?
9 What is special about Antarctica's wildlife?
10 Using the diagram and the report explain why krill is so important.
11 What damage would a vehicle cause? Why?
12 Dr Heywood wants a 'firm international agreement' with very careful management schemes. How does his view differ from that of the conservationists (Question 8)?

Figure 5.95   Fight for Antarctic life

Fight for Antarctic life

CONSERVATIONISTS have launched an international campaign to save Antarctica, the last unspoilt wilderness on earth, from the potentially disastrous effects of drilling for oil and minerals.

An international alliance of more than 30 groups in Britian, the United States, Australia and New Zealand, including Friends of the Earth and Greenpeace, plan a campaign of publicity, political lobbying and demonstrations to try to stop any exploitation of the continent. "We intend to fight for Antarctica with the same tenacity of our campaign to save the whale," says Charles Secrett of Friends of the Earth in London.

Fourteen signatories of the 1959 Antarctic Treaty, including Britain, Argentina, the US and the Soviet Union, are currently trying to divide up exploration rights at a series of secret meetings. They hope to complete agreement by next year.

There are believed to be very rich oil deposits in the Weddell and Ross seas. Although conditions there are the most hostile on earth, there are no insuperable technical barriers to extracting the oil. On land, there are thought to be large reserves of natural gas, as well as deposits of uranium, iron, copper, coal, chromium and titanium.

The "club of 14" are drawing up conventions to protect wildlife, but there is no chance that these will satisfy the conservationists, who want Antarctica declared a permanent wilderness area. This, they say, is the only certain way to prevent catastrophic damage to its delicate environment from an oil spill.

Despite its intense cold and dark nine-month winter, Antarctica supports an abundant wildlife. Although there are relatively few species, they occur in huge numbers. Its waters support the largest mammal on earth, the blue whale, as well as the threatened fin and humpback whales. Among its seals are the Weddell seal, unique to the area, and the leopard seal, which eats penguins. The water's edge teems with birds, including the world's furthest-travelling migrant, the arctic tern, which flies halfway round the world from the Arctic to spend its summers at the South Pole.

The conservationists say Antarctica's bird and mammal life is especially vulnerable to oil damage because it is so dependent on one species – krill, a minute

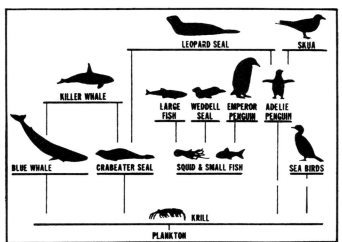

shrimp-like creature. Because of its position at the bottom of the food chain, any serious damage to krill or the plankton it feeds on would threaten birds and larger animals (see diagram).

As an unspoilt area, Antarctica is also an invaluable base for judging the effects of pollution elsewhere in the world. Dr R. B. Heywood of the British Antarctic survey, stated recently that, "If you drive a vehicle over lichen the track will be there for hundreds of years because everything is so slow moving."

Dr Heywood believes it is unrealistic to ask for Antarctica to be declared a wilderness area. "But we need firm international agreement that however the area is to be exploited it should be done with very careful management schemes."

Gareth Huw Davies

Sunday Times, 20 February 1983

Key Points: Physical Systems

● Natural environments are made up of physical systems which are active and ever changing. It is necessary to understand how they work before successful management can take place.

● Natural environments are important natural resources in their own right. They may not run out like oil, but they can be lost forever if human activity changes them too much.

● Some natural environments are more sensitive than others, but most are finely balanced. Economic exploitation should take this fact into account.

● All natural environments need careful management now if they are to become a permanent resource for future generations of people.

● The way of life in some countries is more closely bound to the characteristics of the natural environment than in others. Disturbing these environments may have long lasting social effects.

CHAPTER 6   SUPPLYING RESOURCES

Within the rocks of the earth's crust there are valuable resources of both minerals and fuels which have been mined and exploited for many centuries. Our demand for these resources is increasing with the growth of population and modern technology. The need to discover new resources becomes more pressing each year, but at the same time the need to conserve the resources we have becomes more vital. These resources are finite which means that once exploited they cannot, in most cases, be used again, unless they can be recycled, like scrap metal or paper. Recycled materials only supply a small proportion of our needs when compared to the new raw materials that we use.

In using and exploiting resources from the earth's crust we have not always been wise, or careful. Often the mining of the resources has been wasteful. Natural gas in oilfields has been 'flared off' or burnt, low quality ores have been neglected, or thrown on mine dumps — we cannot afford such wasteful practices any more. We must also look after the land in areas that are used for mining. Many mining landscapes bear the scars of years of careless development. Land has been left in a derelict and damaged state, unable to be used again for other purposes. Now the mining industry is expected to conserve the landscape and restore it so that earlier uses may be established again. Mining companies have important obligations to conserve both resources and land.

6.1 Mineral Resources

Rössing: uranium mining in Namibia

Use an atlas to find the position of Namibia in the continent of Africa. Figure 6.1 shows the location of the Rössing mine.

Country	Production (tonnes)
USA	16810
S. Africa (includes Namibia)	10225
Canada	7050
France	2634
Australia	1561
USSR	no data

Figure 6.2   Uranium ore production, 1980

Uranium ores have increased in importance since World War II. Uranium itself has two major uses: it is used in the manufacture of nuclear weapons, and as a fuel in nuclear power stations for the production of electricity. It has thus become a raw material of vital importance to all the major industrial countries of the world and also to many other countries. Production of uranium ore is concentrated in a few countries as Figure 6.2 shows. Together with its neighbour, South Africa, Namibia is responsible for about 20% of the world's uranium output.

Rössing uranium mine (Figure 6.3) is about 70 km from the Atlantic coast of Namibia. It is claimed by the company to be the largest open cast uranium mine in the world. Uranium was first discovered in the area as long ago as 1928. For many years little interest was shown in the ore deposit, partly because of its remote position in mountainous country, and partly because the demand for uranium ore was low. Full-scale exploration of the area began in 1966 and was difficult. The photograph of the present day site of the mine suggests that the area has very little rainfall, but in one rare desert thunderstorm, the entire exploration camp was washed away together with a Land Rover which was the only means of transport at the time!

Rio Tinto Zinc Ltd decided to go ahead with mining in 1973 and production began in 1976. A 20 year plan was prepared for the mining of the ore. Most of it will be obtained from an open pit with 15 m high benches,

Figure 6.1   Namibia and the Rössing mine

129

Figure 6.3   Rössing mine processing plant

or levels. At the end of 20 years the pit will be 3km long, 1km wide and 0.4km deep — try to imagine how large this pit would be in your own local area. All the mining plans are constantly updated so that at any one time enough ore is readily available to satisfy current demand. Usually about 1 million tonnes of ore are blasted every week and once blasted it is loaded by electric shovels into 150 tonne trucks. Operations of all of the trucks are radio controlled so that any delays are kept to a minimum. Because of the remote location of the plant, all servicing and repair of the trucks and heavy mining equipment is carried out at the mine.

Once the ore has been mined, it is delivered to a crushing plant where it is reduced to a size which can be handled in the processing plants, Figure 6.3. Here, a series of operations convert the ore into uranium oxide which is then shipped out from the plant.

Looking after the environment at Rössing

Look again at Figure 6.3 as a reminder of what the Rössing area is like. Much of the surrounding country is made up of low desert hills and mountains. The rainfall is so low that only a few scattered shrubs and poor grasses grow on the thin soil. In such an area, which is virtually uninhabited, screening of the operations is really unnecessary because of the vastness of the surrounding hills. In areas with a sizeable population, mining companies have to take much more care in attempting to conceal their operations.

In a large open-pit mine such as Rössing, dust in the air is a major problem. Even though water is in short supply, the roads and tracks in the mine are continually sprayed with it. Levels of dust in the air are

measured to assess whether or not it is necessary to provide some sort of respiratory protection for people working in the area. All equipment operated in the mine area is fitted with air conditioning equipment, so that it will work well in these difficult conditions.

Rössing produces something like 40 000 tonnes of solid waste each day from the processing plant and this is taken away for disposal. It is pumped, as a pulp, through a pipeline into a nearby valley. A dam has been built across the valley and the fine waste and water are stored behind the dam. Water from the dam is returned for reuse in some parts of the plant. Some water containing uranium (which, since it is radioactive, could be dangerous) seeps into the rocks. In the surrounding district a number of test wells have been dug and uranium levels are constantly checked to see that there is no danger of pollution.

In any plant dealing with radioactive material, such as uranium, health checks for the employees are absolutely essential. The uranium ore is very low grade and thus does not constitute a serious hazard; it is in the later stages of processing, however, that uranium contamination may be a problem. Employees in this section are checked every month to see if they have become contaminated.

Since Rössing mine was established in an area which was uninhabited, the mining company, together with the government authorities in Namibia, had to provide housing for its workers. Some employees lived in Swakopmund (about 65km away) but most of them needed to live much nearer the plant. In 1974 agreement was reached to build a completely new town at Arandis, 12 km from Rössing, Figure 6.5. Six hundred houses were built, together with a clinic, primary

Figure 6.4   Rössing mine, Namibia

Figure 6.5   Arandis township

school and shopping centre. As the town grew, certain changes had to be made. The layout of the town was altered to cope with the increasing number of cars, buses and lorries that used its roads. Pedestrian-only routes were built which gave direct access from the residential areas to the enlarged town centre. More shops, a town hall, a swimming pool, hospital and a recreational centre for all employees were built in the centre. Here are the views of some of the inhabitants:

'Arandis is developing fast and in a good way. The housing is super but one problem is the lack of public transport to Swakopmund . . . Arandis is a pretty town and people are trying hard to grow their gardens. The streets are very clean but there should be traffic cops because the place is growing fast. It is also a pity that the club and the town hall are so small for this community'.

'Many things are different here from the place where I came from — like the swimming pool, the club and the community centre. Also the way people live here and the way they communicate. I like Arandis very much.'

Living in a new town like Arandis is a new experience for nearly all of the workers at the mine. Imagine that you are a worker at the mine who had lived previously in a small village making a meagre living from farming.
Describe how your life has changed since you began to work at the Rössing mine, and the changes you would expect to find at Arandis over the next ten years. What further improvements to your life at Arandis would you like to see?

Mining in a developing country: is Rössing a success story?

Mining in developing countries is very often carried out by companies that have their headquarters in established industrial countries. Industrialised countries need raw materials to supply their factories and power stations and usually cannot find enough of the materials they require in their own country. Exploring and working ore deposits in developing countries is one way of securing new supplies, and companies

from developed nations are often given licences to work these deposits. The Rössing mine is owned by Rio Tinto Zinc, a multi-national company with operations in many parts of the world.

As well as opening up ore deposits and shipping out the treated products, foreign companies are expected to bring other positive benefits to the countries in which they operate. You have seen how Rössing co-operated in the building of a new town at Arandis to house workers at the mine, but the Rössing Corporation has to be judged on its entire record in Namibia. Questions that should be asked are, 'How much has it exploited the country?', 'To what extent has it made a genuine contribution to the development of Namibia?' and 'By how much has it brought about an improvement in the standard of living of Namibians?'

The following points were made in a speech by the Chief Executive of Rössing:
- Rio Tinto Zinc should serve the interests of its employees, its shareholders, the country in which it operates and the people of that country.
- Although Namibians do not make up all the labour force at the Rössing mine, training will enable more Namibians to occupy more of the jobs at the mine and fewer people will be brought in from outside the country.
- Equal pay is given for equal work and all employees are paid according to the grade of work they do, regardless of race.
- Arandis has been established as a modern town to house all married employees who wish to live near the mine.
- Medical aid, pension funds and insurance protection are provided for all employees.
- In 1980, Rössing paid out R40 million (R stands for South African Rand; £1 = R2.10) in wages and salaries to their employees. Another R56 million was spent on buying supplies and services from Namibian organisations, for example electricity and equipment for use at the mine. Rössing's expenditure in Namibia is equivalent to R100 per head for every man, woman and child.
- Rössing has established the Rössing Foundation in Namibia to improve educational standards throughout the country and to improve standards of living.

It has set up an Education Centre in the capital of Namibia (Windhoek) and is soon to establish a farm training centre.

Mining in a developing country, therefore, is not concerned only with extracting, processing, and shipping out the ore to the industrial countries of the world.

▶ I How successful do you think Rössing has been in developing Namibia rather than just exploiting its uranium ore? Use the points in the Chief Executive's speech to illustrate your answer.

2 What are the disadvantages for a country like Namibia in having foreign companies develop its mineral resources?

Ball clay in Dorset: mining in an Area of Outstanding Natural Beauty

Ball clay is one of the most important mineral resources of southern England. The map in Figure 6.6 shows that there are three main areas where it is worked: the Dorset Basin in east Dorset, the Bovey Basin in Devon, and the small Petrockstow Basin in north-west Devon. Ball clay is an important mineral resource because it is used in the manufacture of high quality pottery and porcelain. Figure 6.7 shows how much ball clay is sold at home and abroad.

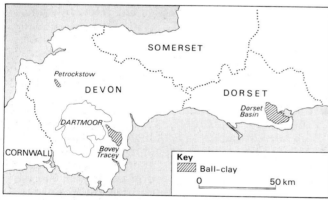

Figure 6.6   Ball clay areas in southern England

▶ Draw a graph to show:
   i Export sales of ball clay between 1962 and 1979.
   ii Total sales of ball clay (obtained by adding export sales to UK sales) between 1962 and 1979.
   iii Shade in the area between the export sales graph and the total sales graph. This shaded area will represent the home sales for the period.
Answer the following questions on the graphs.
   I What has happend to both home and export sales over the period 1962–1979?
   2 Has growth of production been steady or variable?
   3 When was growth in production at its steepest?
   4 What has happened to production since then?

The production of ball clay is important to the UK for two reasons. Firstly it is an important raw material for

Year	Sales	Exports
1962	455	247
1963	481	254
1964	538	288
1965	557	307
1966	608	334
1967	622	344
1968	631	363
1969	691	415
1970	732	434
1971	662	381
1972	672	380
1973	722	405
1974	779	462
1975	680	373
1976	670	375
1977	759	423
1978	737	410
1979	767	443

Figure 6.7   UK sales and exports of ball clay, 1962–79 ('000 tonnes)

our national pottery industry, and secondly it is an important export and brings foreign currency into the UK.

▶ The map giving the location of ball clay mines and pits in east Dorset, Figure 6.8, shows that there are seven underground mines and seven open pits. However, in 1981 only 25% of the production came from the mines while 75% came from the pits. Why do you think a much bigger percentage came from open-cast pits?

An Area of Outstanding Natural Beauty

Much of south-east Dorset is classed as an Area of Outstanding Natural Beauty (AONB). Such areas are chosen by the Countryside Commission for their attractive scenery and they usually have a range of wildlife and plants that may be in need of protection.

▶ Study the photograph of the heathlands of east Dorset, Figure 6.9. Why do you think that this area has been chosen as an Area of Outstanding Natural Beauty?

Much of this area of outstanding natural beauty is occupied by heathland. Heathland in Dorset is home for both rare plants and wildlife. One particular kind of heather is only found on the Dorset heath and amongst the rare wildlife are the sand lizard and the smooth snake, as well as the Dartford warbler, one of Britain's rarest birds.

As well as being an Area of Outstanding Natural Beauty, the eastern part of the Dorset heathland is bounded on the north by Poole Harbour with its wooded islands and on the east by the long sandy shore of Studland Bay. Both Poole Harbour and Studland Bay are part of the Heritage coast of Dorset, a very beautiful and attractive coastline that is now protected and looked after by Dorset County Council. Parts of the Area of Outstanding Natural Beauty have been planted with conifers, which can be seen on the photograph shown in Figure 6.9. In the west of this area there are army firing ranges on the heathlands.

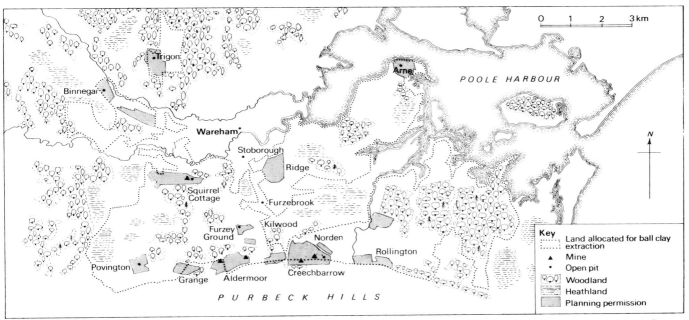

Figure 6.8   Ball clay in Dorset

Conflict: open cast pits in an Area of Outstanding Natural Beauty

Study the photograph of Povington Pit, Figure 6.9, and the map showing the distribution of pits, Figure 6.8.

▶ Do you think that Povington Pit spoils the view across the Dorset heathlands? Can you think of anything that might be done to improve the appearance of the pit? What can a mining company do after a part of the pit has been worked out to restore the landscape to its original state?

As well as the open-cast pits, processing works for the ball clay are located at Furzebrook, also in the Area of Outstanding Natural Beauty. These sheds and buildings are another intrusion into the landscape and near the buildings there is some degree of pollution from dust and noise. Lorries carrying ball clay from the pits to the processing plant are a source of nuisance and a danger on the narrow roads in the district.

As you might expect, there is a considerable degree of conflict between the mining companies who wish to expand ball clay working and those people who wish to conserve the wildlife, plants and scenic beauty of the AONB. Your view of the effect of the mining on the natural environment in the area can be assessed using the following table.

Figure 6.9   Povington Pit

Figure 6.10

Features of the Natural Environment	Features of Mining and Processing			Total Score
	Land Required for Mining	Transport (Lorries)	Processing Plant	
Landscape				
Drainage				
Soil				
Flora (plants)				
Fauna (wildlife)				
Quality of air				

▶ Copy out the table on page 133. For each of the mining and processing features, fill in the appropriate box if you think it affects the features of the environment listed on the left of the table. Use a scale of 0–5 (0 = no effect; 5 = much effect). Work out which aspect of the environment is likely to be most changed by the development of ball clay mining. Are all the changes adverse?

To be fair, it is important to set the environmental cost of mining ball clay against the benefits that it brings to the community in Dorset, and to the county as a whole. Amongst the benefits are:

● The mining company (ECC — English China Clays) contributes £1.5 million to the local economy in wages, salaries and services.
● It provides employment for 150 people in east Dorset and extra employment for contractors.
● Local industries use the clays. In 1978, 1000 people were employed in the pottery industry in nearby Poole.
● The pottery industry in Stoke-on-Trent provides jobs for nearly 60000 people and is particularly dependent on Dorset clay.
● Ball clay exports are an important earner of overseas currency.

Balancing the cost to the environment against benefits to the community is not easy, but it is a task that local planners constantly have to face. In 1975, the pit at Arne was the subject of a public inquiry. Conservation groups fought to prevent its development. Eventually a decision was given in favour of the mining company who were able to prove that the new mine would be in the national interest.

New proposals

The article from *The Swanage Times* for 23 April 1981, Figure 6.11, describes extensive new proposals for mining in the AONB.

▶ 1 Read the article and summarise the views of Mr Medley, Mr Moss and the ECC representative in Wareham.
2 What would you expect the views of the following people to be?
  i A local representative of the Nature Conservancy.
  ii A tourist visiting the area for a holiday.
  iii A householder living in the village of Stoborough, through which lorries carrying the ball clay pass.
3 What are your views on this set of new proposals? Do you think they should be allowed to go ahead? Justify your point of view in the form of a letter to be sent to the editor of *The Swanage Times*.

Figure 6.11

STORM OVER BIG MINING PLANS

A STORM has broken over proposals by the English China Clay Company to seek planning permission for excavations over a huge area of the Isle of Purbeck — and perhaps involving the demolition of one Corfe Castle farm and other buildings.

Nine applications for open cast ball clay mining have been made to Purbeck District Council, as planning authority, by E.C.C. Ball Clays Ltd., Wareham, and are for an area of about 380 acres. More than six million tonnes of clay are involved.

BROKEN ARC

Mr. P. J. Medley of Tarrants, Stoborough, is one local resident who has complained in writing already.

He refers to the "visual despoilation" of the area, which is designated as of "outstanding natural beauty."

Mr. Alan Moss of The Old Brewery, Wareham, says that the proposed workings form a kind of broken arc from Povington Heath in the west to Norden Farm, Corfe Castle in the east.

He understood from the farmer at Norden Farm, Mr. Michael Ramm, that the proposals ultimately included the demolition of Norden Farm and buildings —"and he is very concerned indeed about it."

The anticipated periods of extraction are from 7.3 years to 37 years. Mr. Moss said that some of the most lovely views and beauty spots in the Purbeck area would be affected.

Mr. Medley says "It is well known that this area has been designated as an area of outstanding natural beauty in which there are strict building controls and over which in recent years there has been considerable controversy in connection with oil and gas exploration.

ASSURANCES

"The effect of such a large area of open-cast mining on the appearance of the area is not hard to imagine.

"The visual despoliation is one aspect, reduction of amenity for the thousands of holidaymakers and visitors is another, and the effect on the income of those who rely on the tourist trade is yet another.

"Finally, the effect on the ecology, both during the work and after it is finished, is another aspect to be considered.

"I do not believe that the company's claim to back-fill and make good can be sustained. It would be nearly impossible to completely fill the holes they make."

He hoped public pressure would ensure any work was properly controlled and the site made good afterwards.

The director and general manager of E.C.C. Ball Clays Ltd., Wareham, Mr. Alan Williamson, said it was a prime concern of his company to ensure the countryside was damaged as little as was possible.

He said: "We have no intention of spoiling the countryside and do everything to make the least impact on the area.

"We have been mining in the area for the past 223 years. It is one of the basic industries of Purbeck started in the 1760s to supply clay originally for Josiah Wedgewood.

"These applications are nothing new. They are a continuation of our existing workings. We need to know where we can go in the long term in order to ensure continuity for the people we supply.

"Obviously we will be taking into account all the suggestions we receive."

Mesabi, Minnesota: the changing face of the iron mines

Locate the state of Minnesota on a map of the United States of America. Much of the state is underlain by old hard rocks that contain some of the most valuable ores in the country. Although iron ore was first discovered in 1850, the first iron ore shipments from the Mesabi range were not made until 1892.

The cross-section of the Mesabi Range, Figure 6.13, shows that once the glacial drift had been removed, the mining of the iron ore was a relatively simple task. The ore was sufficiently near the surface for open-cast methods to be used, and because the ore bodies were so huge, the open-cast pits are of enormous dimensions. Hull Rust mine, near Hibbing, is 4 km long, 1.6 km wide and over 100 m deep. (Imagine how this would compare with the open-cast pits in the ball clay country of Dorset!) The iron ore is taken by rail from the mines on the Mesabi range to the ports on the north shore of Lake Superior. From here it is taken by huge lake vessels known as whalebacks to the ports on Lake Michigan and Lake Erie where it is unloaded and railed to the blast furnaces in places such as Pittsburgh. Some is also smelted, at lakeside furnaces at Chicago (Gary) on Lake Michigan, or at Cleveland and Buffalo on Lake Erie.

▶ Using the figures, shown below, of iron ore shipments from the Mesabi Range, construct a simple bar graph to show how production has changed from 1901 – 1980. The figures are given for each decade.

	Million tonnes
1901 – 1910	193.5
1911 – 1920	332.9
1921 – 1930	331.9
1931 – 1940	230.9
1941 – 1950	598.2
1951 – 1960	567.5
1961 – 1970	487.2
1971 – 1980	509.6

Suggest a reason for the very high level of shipments in the period 1941 – 50.

Make a comment on the general pattern of change of iron ore shipments from 1901 to 1980.

Although production of ore has fallen since 1950, a very important change in the type of ore being produced and shipped has occurred. It can be seen from Figure 6.14 that, as shipments of natural iron ore began to decline in the years after 1955, so the production of taconite began to increase. As the better grades of iron ore began to run out, it was necessary to work the lower grade ores, that is those with less iron in them. Taconite is one of these ores. It was known for a long time, but it had never been mined because it was too hard, too dense and its iron content was too low. But, when one raw material begins to run out, another one has to replace it, even if it means developing a completely new way of dealing with the new raw material. Taconite must first be crushed to allow the iron minerals to be separated by magnets. These minerals are then rolled into pellets the size of marbles

Figure 6.12   Minnesota and the Mesabi Range

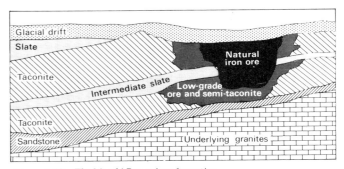

Figure 6.13   The Mesabi Range iron formation

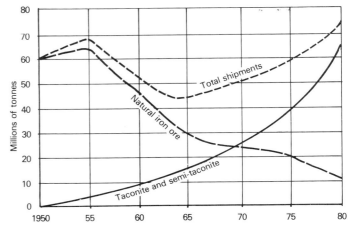

Figure 6.14   Shipment of iron ore 1950–80

135

and are heat hardened before being sent to the blast furnaces. Figure 6.15 shows the taconite processing plant at Mount Iron, St Louis County, Minnesota. Now that the high grade ore has almost run out, Minnesota has to compete with other areas in the world to supply the blast furnaces of the USA with iron ore. It will be a long time before taconite mining stops, but mining has ceased in many locations in this part of Minnesota.

When the mining ceases: mineland reclamation and development

Figure 6.16 shows all the districts of the Mesabi Range where mining has now ceased. Even with the enormous size of these open-cast pits, a time arrives when it is no longer worthwhile mining the remaining ore. Once mines are abandoned it is important that they are tidied up and do not remain unsightly. In the Mesabi Range mining areas there are a number of problems of reclamation, and they have been summarised in Figure 6.17.

Mining Feature	Problems	Treatment (Your suggestions)
Overburden stockpiles — waste material that had to be removed before mining could begin	No Soil; appear barren and invegetated; erode easily and debris dumped in streams and lakes; slumping	
Open pits — left after mining has ceased. May cover several km² and be several 100m deep	Steep slopes, often unfenced, very dangerous. Mining roads encourage cars and motor cycles into the old pit areas	
Lean ore stockpiles — dumps of low grade ore of low commercial value; often used by builders as fill or aggregate	Unsightly, liable to erode. Streams and lakes turn a deep red colour	
Tailings — ground rock and fine dust from ore processing, suspended in water behind large dams	On drying out, the dust is carried vast distances; it can act as a sandblast, damaging houses and cars	
Derelict structures — old crushing machinery, derelict sidings, loading platforms	Dangerous to people that trespass in the mine. Very unsightly	
Underground mines — shafts are sealed and surface buildings removed	Subsidence as the land begins to cave in	

Figure 6.17   Reclamation problems

Figure 6.15   The taconite plant at Mountain Iron, St Louis County, Minnesota

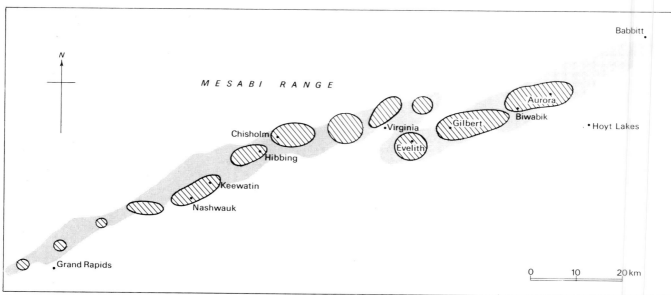

Figure 6.16   Clusters of exhausted mines

▶ 1 On a copy of Figure 6.17 complete the set of righthand boxes. To help you with this task refer to Figures 6.18, 6.19 and 6.20 which offer some possible solutions according to the nature of the problem:
Figure 6.18 Trout Lake — how to improve a stockpile.
Figure 6.19 Virginia Edge — how to improve a mine edge.
Figure 6.20 Ely Caved Ground — what to do in an area of subsidence.

2 Many tourists are now coming to see both working pits and abandoned ones in Minnesota. Imagine you are a tourist board official trying to encourage people to visit the area. How would you make it sound attractive, and what would you **not** tell prospective visitors in your brochure?

Summary Diagram

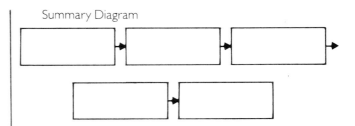

The above boxes show the stages of mining in an ore area like the Mesabi Range of Minnesota. Place the right words in each box, in the correct order.
Taconite mining, Rich ore mining, Tourist development, Ore body exploration, Mineland reclamation.

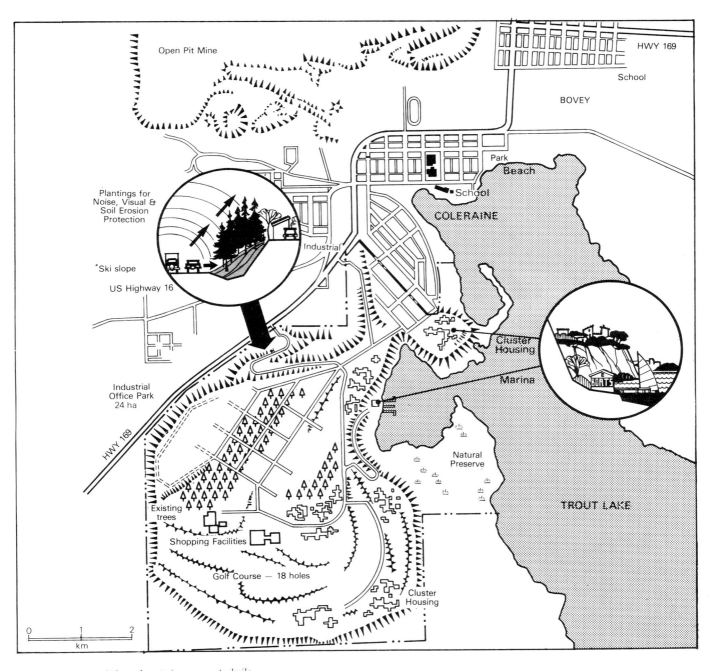

Figure 6.18   Trout Lake — how to improve a stockpile

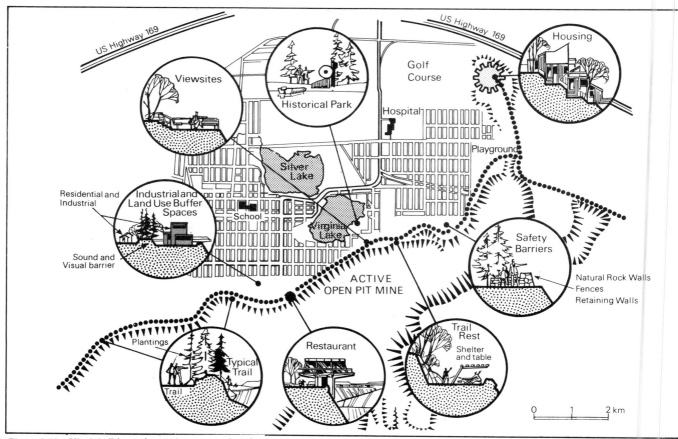

Figure 6.19   Virginia Edge — how to improve a mine edge

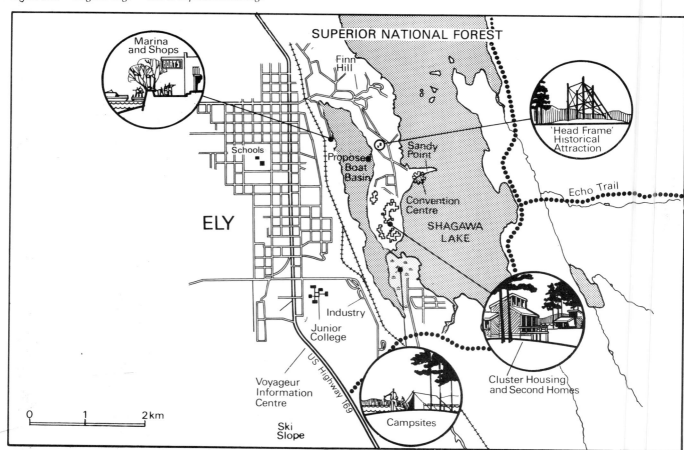

Figure 6.20   Ely Caved Ground — what to do in an area of subsidence

6.2 Energy Resources

Petroleum: fresh search for a declining resource

Production of petroleum now seems to be increasing more rapidly than the discovery of new reserves. As oil companies search new areas of the globe, and as existing supplies are used, new countries join the top ten of the world's oil producing states.

▶ Study the table given in Figure 6.21 and draw a suitable bar graph to illustrate the pattern of production between the ten countries. How many developed countries were in the top ten in 1965, and which ones had disappeared from the list by 1982? How many OPEC countries (Organisation of Petroleum Exporting Countries) are there in each column?

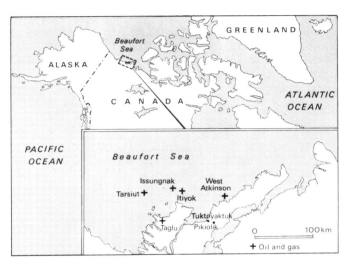

Figure 6.22   Oil exploration in the Beaufort Sea

1965		1984	
USA	321	USSR	613
USSR	186	USA	494
Venezuela	167	Saudi Arabia	229
Kuwait	92	Mexico	150
Saudi Arabia	75	UK	126
Iran	65	China	114
Iraq	49	Iran	109
Canada	32	Venezuela	97
Indonesia	23	Canada	73
Algeria	20	Indonesia	70
World total	1215	World total	2075

Figure 6.21   The top ten producers of oil, 1965 and 1984, million tonnes

In the 1960s and 1970s important finds of oil were made in the North Sea and the United Kingdom became the fifth highest world producer in 1982. In the 1980s the search for oil continues. Two areas now attracting attention from the oil companies are examined next.

Drilling for oil in the Beaufort Sea off Canada's Arctic coast

Oil is already being produced from the Prudhoe Bay fields of northern Alaska. It is pumped across Alaska along the cross-Alaskan pipeline to be shipped out from the ice-free terminus at Valdez on the south Alaskan coast.

The search for oil is still going on in Alaska, but it has now spread to the neighbouring part of Canada, not only onshore, but also in the Beaufort Sea, a part of the Arctic Ocean, Figure 6.22. This is one of the most difficult places in the world to drill for oil. Temperatures in the winter drop to −45°C, 'the sort of cold that rises through the feet if you stand still too long, that freezes eyebrows and beards in seconds'. Thick ice covers the Beaufort Sea for eight months of the year and workers have to wear face masks whenever they are working outside. Drivers have to leave their vehicles running 24 hours a day.

These severe conditions not only make life difficult for the workers, but the techniques of oil drilling have to be altered to cope with the intense cold. Even at inland sites like Pikiolik, new methods have to be used. Heat from the friction caused by drilling would cause the frozen ground to melt and make further drilling impossible. Special refrigeration equipment keeps the permafrost (permanently frozen ground) frozen and enables drilling to go ahead. Offshore drilling is even more hazardous. Itiyok is an artificial island, created by dredgers in the ice-free summers, which is made out of sand and gravel from the sea bed. Without artificial islands like Itiyok, further exploration in the shallow waters of the Beaufort Sea would not be possible. Itiyok will only last a year and when the drilling teams have gone, it will be abandoned to the waves.

Transporting the oil will be quite a problem too. If tankers are used they will have to be fitted with special ice-breaking equipment, and they will be loaded from offshore buoys. Pipelines are another possibility, but, before oil begins to flow in any quantity, the possible effects of its production on the environment and people of the area will have to be studied carefully. Much needs to be examined, such as the influence of

Figure 6.23   Innuit worker protects oil men from marauding bears

the installations on the movements of polar ice, on the beluga whale, on the permafrost terrain, and on the lifestyle of the Innuit, Dene and Metis people.

Canada needs the oil under the Beaufort Sea, because by 1990 Canada will need more oil than it is capable of producing from existing sources. Several thousand new jobs will be created as a result of the Arctic oil discoveries and up to 35 production platforms may be needed, some of which could be built in Britain.

The rush for oil in the South China Sea

A glance at the table of petroleum production for 1982 shows China to be an important world producer. It is likely that China's oil production over the next ten years could double to well over 200 million tonnes. China used to import oil from the Soviet Union, but is now already exporting oil to her neighbour, Japan. China, however, needs help from the western countries in order to develop her oil resources. Countries like the United States, Britain and France are capable of providing the technology to help the Chinese in their exploration. Although most of the Chinese oil is, at the moment, produced on the Chinese mainland, the main centre of interest now seems to be switching to the South China Sea.

The map Figure 6.24 shows the extent of oil-bearing sedimentary rocks in the South China Sea. Most of these rocks lie within the continental shelf, where water depths are usually less than 200 m. Geological surveying began in the south-west of the area in the 1960s and the first commercial oil was discovered in

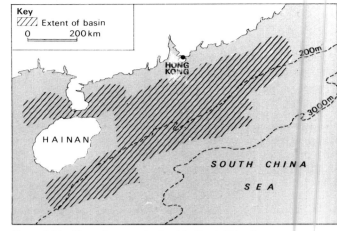

Figure 6.24   The sedimentary basin of the South China Sea

1977. By 1979, the Chinese were ready to co-operate with foreign oil companies. Figure 6.25 shows the sectors of the South China Sea that have been awarded to overseas companies for the purpose of exploration.

▶ Compare Figures 6.24 and 6.25. If working in shallow water and nearness to the Chinese mainland, or to Hainan Island, are considered to be important factors, which companies appear to have the choicest locations? What could make these locations completely unattractive? What experience particularly qualifies British oil companies for work in the South China Sea?

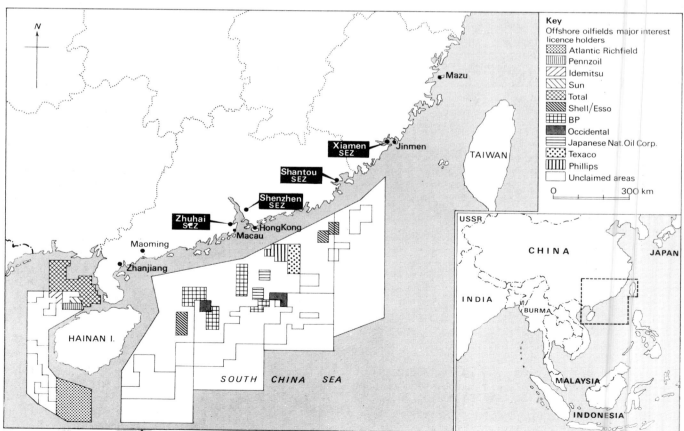

Figure 6.25   Oil concessions in the South China Sea

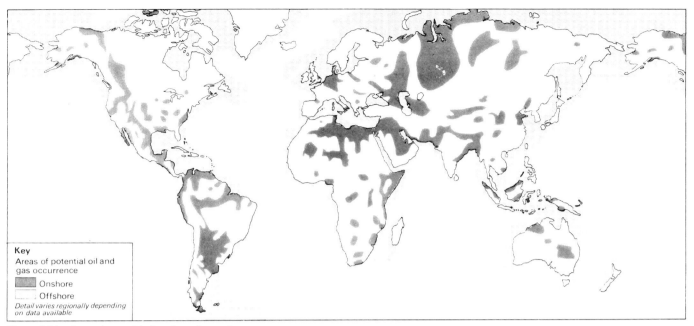

Figure 6.26   Areas of potential oil and gas discoveries

Scouring the world for petroleum

▶ Study the map of the potential oil and gas bearing areas of the world, Figure 6.26.

1 With the help of an atlas, find the position of the countries which occupied the leading ten positions in petroleum production in 1982.

2 Which other parts of the world (onshore) would appear to have potential for petroleum production?

3 Which countries, apart from Britain (North Sea) and China (South China Sea) have continental shelf areas that would be worthwhile exploring?

Coal's second coming

Britain's coal production has shown a decline from the peak years of the 1950s, when annual output was over 220 million tonnes, to present levels of production at just over 120 million tonnes. The reasons for this decline are in part explained by other energy sources such as oil and natural gas which took large shares of the energy market in the 1960s and 1970s. However, since oil prices have increased so much in the last dozen years, oil has become a less attractive source of fuel, and coal begins to look as if it might make a return and recover some of its lost market.

▶ Look closely at Figure 6.27. How has our total energy use changed from 1957 to 1982, and how have the contributions of different fuels changed? If you cannot see the changes just by looking at the figures, then draw a simple graph to show the changing relationships. What is particularly significant about the figures for 1982?

Recent exploration in areas near to existing coalfields proved the presence of very large reserves of coal at depth. Two very promising areas were discovered, one around Selby in Yorkshire, and another in the Vale of Belvoir in north-east Leicestershire.

Year	Total Energy Used (MTCE)	% Coal	% Oil	% Nat. Gas	% Other
1957	247	85	15		
1962	265	72	28		
1967	276	59	39	1	1
1972	302	40	46	12	2
1977	285	38	41	19	2
1982	295	40	36	22	2

(MTCE = million tonnes of coal equivalent)

Figure 6.27   Britain's energy use 1957–82

Selby: coalfield of the future

The National Coal Board claims that the Selby coalfield is a striking symbol of the re-birth of coal as a major energy source. Located in the county of North Yorkshire (Figure 6.28, page 142), the Selby coalfield has been proved to contain 2000 million tonnes of coal reserves. Of this total figure, 600 million tonnes are in a single seam known as the Barnsley seam, Figure 6.29. It has been decided to mine only 330 million tonnes in order to lessen the risk of surface subsidence.

When in full production, Selby will produce ten million tonnes of coal per year and provide employment for four thousand miners. All the coal will be taken in 'merry-go-round' trains from Gascoigne Wood to three of Britain's largest coal-fired power stations at Ferrybridge, Drax and Eggborough.

Protecting the environment in the Selby coalfield

Mining coal in a new coalfield is not just a question of sinking the shafts, installing the equipment and bringing up the coal. Mining tends to leave ugly scars on the landscape, as you have seen in the Mesabi Range and in Dorset's ball clay area. The National Coal Board has a responsibility to protect the landscape (Figure 6.30) where coal will be mined. Much of the land to the

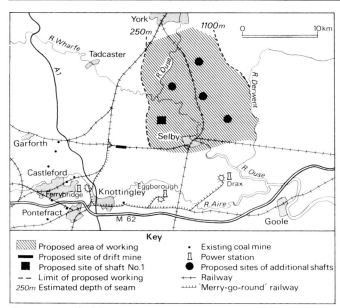

Figure 6.28   *The Selby coalfield*

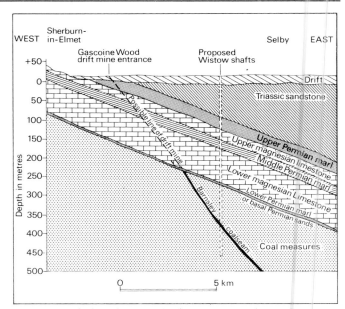

Figure 6.29   *Geological cross-section from west to east through Selby*

north of Selby is attractive, good quality agricultural land. Mining could affect the land in several ways.

Much of the land is low-lying and drained by the River Ouse, which itself is liable to flood particularly to the north and south of Selby. Flood prevention measures have already been taken to protect the low-lying land. If mining took place under the flood prone area, then subsidence could occur and the flood hazard would present an even greater threat. Even if subsidence was in the order of only one metre, further flood protection measures would have to be taken. Coal Board engineers, working with the Yorkshire River Authority, have produced a mining plan which will reduce subsidence to a minimum. Underneath Selby itself, a 'pillar' of coal will be left below the Abbey to prevent damage to its structure and this will be extended to underpin a large part of the town and the river bend.

Two areas of special environmental importance lie within the new coalfield's boundaries. Both Skipwith

Common and Wheldrake Ings are areas with wildlife and plant communities which need protection. Subsidence could affect both of these areas, which in any case, are low-lying. If the land subsided here, both plants and wildlife would suffer. Skipwith Common is near one of the mine shafts and dust, noise, fumes and arc lights at night affect the wildlife of the common.

People living in the area have also been concerned with the visual effect of the new mines and surface installations. Pit head gear can be ugly and although the height of the Selby towers is only 30 m (Figure 6.31), many of the local inhabitants consider that they spoil the landscape. However, since all the coal will be delivered to the surface at Gascoigne Wood, the other five mine shafts will not need railway sidings, any coal handling plant, or surface stockpiles. The nature of the coal in the Barnsley seam is such that very little waste material will be brought out and no surface 'washery' will be required for the coal.

Figure 6.30   *Farmland near Sherburn in Elmet, to the north of Selby*

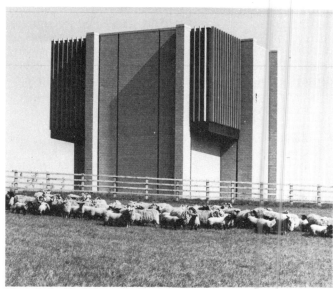

Figure 6.31   *The Wistow Pit, the 'Selby Towers'*

Housing the new miners

Nearly 4000 miners will be employed in the coalfield when it reaches peak production in 1987 or 1988. Of these, about 2500 are expected to live in the area, 400 will be locally recruited and the remainder will travel in from other parts of West Yorkshire from pits that have already been closed. Miners in other coalfields often live in villages where everybody is connected with mining and these villages tend to become 'closed communities'. People in the Selby area have been worried about the effects of new mining communities growing up. The map (Figure 6.32) shows how the problem may be solved. Homes for miners will be built in a number of different centres, such as Selby, Eggborough, Sherburn-in-Elmet and Riccall. Probably about 1000 miners will rent their homes, while another 1500 are expected to want to buy them.

▶ The development of the Selby coalfield will bring much change to the area. Some people will accept this change, others will not find it to their liking.

 1 Which groups of people already in the area do you think will welcome the coming of the mines? Give reasons for their particular attitudes towards the new mines.

 2 Which groups of people will not like the development of the coalfield? Give reasons why they would not be very keen on the new mines.

 3 If you lived in the Selby area, what would be your views on the new developments?

Nuclear power in France: progress with protest?

Plogoff wins its battle

Plogoff is a tiny village at the end of one of the three peninsulas that push out into the Atlantic at the western end of Brittany, see Figure 6.33. The village is close to a site that was chosen in 1974 for the construction of a nuclear power station with four pressurised water reactors (PWR).

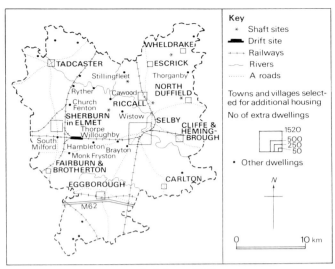

Figure 6.32   New housing at the Selby coalfield.

In a pressurised water reactor the heat given off by the nuclear reaction is taken up by water that is pumped through the reactor at high pressure to prevent it boiling. The hot pressurised water then circulates through a heat exchanger where water in a completely separate circuit is heated and turned to steam. The steam is used to drive turbines and generate electricity as in other types of power station.

In 1976 the state electricity concern Electricité de France attempted to survey a 90 ha site only 400 m from the village. The local people blocked all the access roads and forced the survey team to retreat. When the public inquiry opened in 1980 the mayors of the local villages refused to co-operate with the officials of the inquiry. Riot police were brought in to control the angry villagers and injuries and arrests were common. Everywhere graffiti proclaimed (as shown in the photograph) 'Plogoff n'est pas à vendre' – Plogoff isn't for sale.

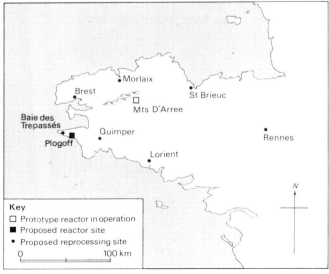

Figure 6.33   Nuclear sites in Brittany

(Plogoff — n'est pas à vendre)

The villagers were suspicious of nuclear power, distrusting its safety record. As well as the nuclear reactors, a reprocessing plant for nuclear materials was to be built at the nearby Baie des Trépassés. Villagers saw this as a threat to their local agricultural livelihood and feared marine pollution from the increased temperature of the local coastal waters. This would upset the traditional fishing carried out off the coast. This part of Brittany is particularly beautiful and the reactors and transmission lines were expected to ruin the spectacular and wild coastal scenery, Figure 6.34.

Figure 6.34 The Baie des Trépassés, Brittany

Nevertheless, despite all protests, the scheme was given due approval by the then President of France, Giscard d'Estaing. Local protesters did not give up: support for their cause was aroused throughout Brittany. Other sites in Brittany were also under study as possible locations for nuclear power stations, and Plogoff became famous throughout France for its defiance. If construction were to begin, more trouble could be expected.

In 1981, however, there was a presidential election in France and Francois Mitterand replaced Giscard d'Estaing as President. In the election campaign, Mitterand spoke of halting the nuclear power programme which he thought to be 'expensive and uncertain'. One of the first actions of the new President was to cancel the Plogoff project. The villagers were delighted, to say the least, and a new approach to the options for electricity generation in France seemed possible.

France's nuclear power programme

Study the graph of actual and future growth of electricity generation in France, Figure 6.35.

▶ 1 Which two graphs are almost running parallel with one another?
  2 What does this tell us about the future of nuclear power in France?
  3 What is likely to happen to conventional (oil and coal burning) power stations in France in the 1980s?
  4 What will happen to hydroelectric power production?

France has one of the most ambitious nuclear power programmes in the world. She has only small reserves of coal and has not been fortunate enough to discover any new resources like those at Selby. The country does not possess, as Britain does in the North Sea, extensive reserves of oil and is unlikely to discover any. Small natural gas fields exist, but they are now past their best. At the moment France relies heavily on imported oil, much of which comes from the Middle East. France turned to nuclear power as a matter of national security, allowing her a much greater degree of control over the national energy programme. France now has 30 nuclear reactors operating and 25 under construction.

▶ Study the map showing the distribution of nuclear power stations, Figure 6.36. Why do you think nearly all of the reactors are either on the main rivers, such as the Loire, the Rhone and the Garonne, or on the coast of France?

The programme for nuclear power announced in 1980 was for a vast increase in the nuclear power output in the country. By 1990, some 60 reactors at 20 sites were expected to be producing nearly 75% of France's electricity. When President Mitterand came to power in 1981 he cancelled the Plogoff project and development at five other sites was 'frozen' or suspended.

Opinion in France is divided over nuclear power. On the one hand there are those people who are worried about safety and are concerned about the effect that nuclear power generation could have on the local environment. People that lent support to President Mitterand in the election campaign felt betrayed

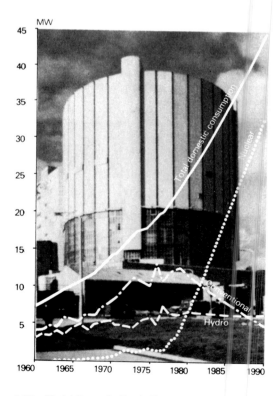

Figure 6.35 Electricity production in France

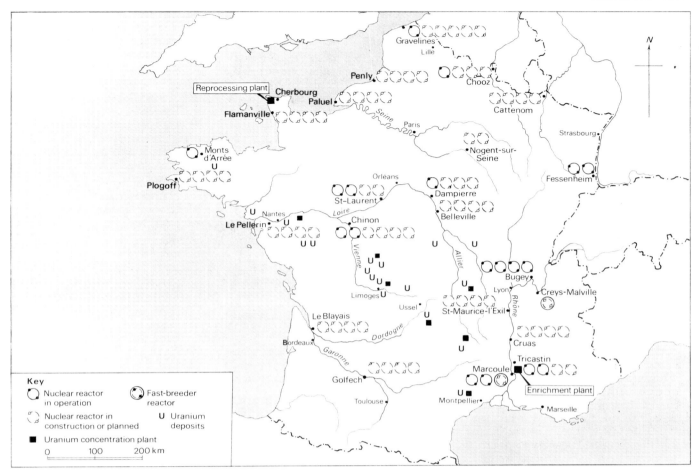

Figure 6.36   Nuclear power stations in France

when he only brought modest reductions to the nuclear programme for the 1980s. Violent protests have again occurred around the Golfech site on the Garonne river. The people of Golfech have seen the villagers of Plogoff win their battle and are equally anxious that the plans for their power station should be abandoned.

Those that support the nuclear power programme point to the fact that France has a huge technological lead in the nuclear industry and that it would be foolish to lose it. Energy independence is necessary in a world where oil prices are uncertain and oil supply problems are still likely to arise. The Government's position on nuclear power is somewhere in between. It has been prepared to reduce the nuclear power programme slightly, it has announced plans to increase coal production, and it has increased research into the development of new and renewable energy resources such as wave, solar and wind power.

▶ You have seen how opinion is divided over the nuclear power programme in France. Make a list of the main arguments for and against nuclear power. Which of these groups of arguments would you be prepared to support? Remember you must choose arguments that are best supported by the facts, so you should be asking such questions as 'Is nuclear power safe?' 'Is it cheaper than conventional (oil and coal burning) power?' Hold a class discussion on the subject, the Central Electricity Generating Board and Friends of the Earth are able to supply you with information covering opposing points of view.

Natural gas from Siberia

Apart from the Netherlands, and to a lesser extent West Germany and France, all of western Europe's major producers draw the majority of their gas from offshore wells on the continental shelf. Since the early 1980s, western Europe has begun to receive additional supplies of gas from the USSR.

Most of the vast reserves of natural gas in the USSR lie east of the Ural Mountains in Siberia. Already huge quantities of this gas are piped westwards across the Urals for consumption in European Russia, in centres such as Moscow and Leningrad. Soviet natural gas has been piped into Austria, Italy, West Germany and France for some time. Now a fresh deal has been signed between the USSR and several west European countries to bring huge quantities of gas from the new Urengoi field in the Yamal peninsula on the north coast of western Siberia. This has involved the laying of a new pipeline for nearly 5000 km from Urengoi to Uzhgorod on the Czechoslovak – Soviet border, Figure 6.37.

As well as receiving 10 500 million m³ of gas a year from the USSR, West German firms have supplied much of the equipment for the pipeline. This has included the pipe itself and the compressor stations that pump the gas from Siberia to western Europe. France and Italy are also set to receive considerable quantities of the gas.

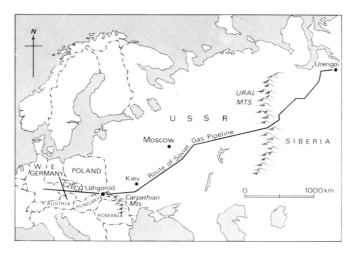

Figure 6.37   The route of the Siberian gas pipeline

Urengoi is said to be the largest natural gas resource in the world and by 1985 should produce nearly one-third of the USSR's output of 640 000 million m³. The pipeline runs through some of the most desolate country in the world, Figure 6.38. It has to pass through 120 km of permafrost, cross the Ural and Carpathian mountains, and negotiate 600 rivers, including the Ob, the Volga, the Don and the Dneiper. Normally pipelines in the permafrost are laid above the ground on stilts to prevent damage to the permafrost through heating. The Russians have buried the pipeline, but will cool the gas so that thawing of the permafrost will not occur.

President Reagan's government in the USA made serious attempts to halt the building of this pipeline. It was thought that western Europe would become too dependent on natural gas from the USSR and that the USSR would receive a steady supply of western currency payments for the gas. Valuable western technology would also become available to the USSR. When the deal was signed in November 1981, it was followed by an American ban on all firms supplying material for the pipeline. This ban meant that if firms supplied material and equipment for the pipeline they would lose contracts with the American government. The ban affected companies in West Germany, France and the United Kingdom, and European governments voiced their disapproval of the American action. Eventually it was lifted. However, some American companies, such as the one that was to have provided pipe-laying equipment, lost considerable sums of money from cancelled contracts.

The pipeline was completed in late 1983, and exports of gas were planned to begin in 1984. It is only one of six trans-continental gas pipelines built during the Soviet five-year plan up to 1985.

▶ Study atlas maps of the relief, vegetation and climate of the territory from the Urengoi site in Siberia to the Czechoslovak border. Write a summary of the environmental conditions encountered by the pipe layers, and suggest some of the difficulties of building a pipeline through such an area.

Figure 6.38   Building the Siberian gas pipeline

6.3 Renewable Energy Sources: Hope for the Future?

Power from the wind

Generating electrical power from the wind is seen as one way in which 'renewable' sources of energy might begin to replace fossil-fuels such as oil and coal. In the photograph, Figure 6.39, the first experimental 200 KW wind turbine installed by the CEGB at Carmarthen Bay is seen alongside a conventional coal-fired power station.

Carmarthen Bay is a lowland site. Wind turbines installed on exposed hill-tops could generate much more electricity because wind speeds are higher in such locations. In September 1983, a turbine was installed on Burgar Hill in the Orkney Islands. This is one of the windiest spots in Britain, where for 70% of the year, wind speeds exceed the 14 mph required to turn the rotor blades. A new turbine, with a rotor diameter of 60 m may be installed on Burgar Hill in the future. If similar turbines were to be installed on all the technically suitable hill top sites in Britain, the combined output would provide 7% of the UK's current electricity requirements.

▶ What would be the major objections to the installation of such turbines i) on commercial grounds, and ii) on environmental grounds?

One possibility in Britain is to establish wind turbines in offshore areas such as Cardigan Bay, or in parts of the North Sea. This is technically possible, but, at the moment, may be too expensive. Wind generated electricity is now seen as one of the most hopeful of all the renewable energy resources.

Some other sources of renewable energy

If all the power in the earth's tides was used to generate electricity, the world's present 'electricity demands could be met. Too much tidal power is lost in shallow seas and it is only in estuaries such as the Severn, which has the world's second highest tidal range, that tidal power schemes would be possible. The scheme would harness the high tide and release it through turbines. The latest scheme (shown on Figure 6.40) could save the equivalent of eight million tonnes of coal.

▶ Make a list of all the effects that the construction of such a barrage might have on the estuary environment. Draw two columns, one for effects that would benefit the area, and one for effects that would damage the environment.

Other means of generating energy from renewable sources include power generated from waves and geothermal power. The latter can be developed from underground sources which are hot enough to provide steam to drive turbines. All of these means have yet to be developed on a large scale.

Figure 6.39   The Carmarthen Bay wind turbine

▶ Conclude your work on supplying energy by investigating one alternative source of power generation and discovering a suitable location in Britain where it could be established. What effects would it have on the natural environment?

Figure 6.40   Tidal barrage in the Severn Estuary

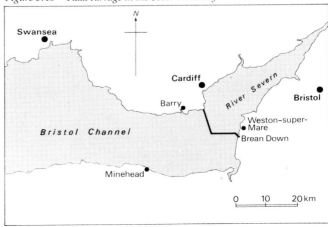

Key Points: Supplying Resources

● Discovering new resources is not enough by itself; it is important to conserve both existing and new supplies.

● Resource extraction can have important implications for both the natural and social environments in which people live.

● Developed countries are increasingly extending their search for new supplies of raw materials. The impact of this search is likely to be felt most in the less developed countries and in the more remote areas of the world.

● The transfer of resources, especially energy supplies, increases the dependence of different nations upon each other.

● Recycling finite resources, and continuing the search for renewable energy supplies seems to be the best way forward for the foreseeable future.

● Some forms of mineral extraction and energy generation are more controversial than others; political, economic and social influences all have to be taken into consideration.

Part IV
Living With
Natural Hazards

In Part IV your attention is turned towards the question of how the natural environment presents people with direct and difficult challenges. There are occasions when the natural environment is particularly difficult, if not impossible, to manage. These occasions are usually sudden and severe events and may disrupt human life on a considerable scale. Geographers have termed these events NATURAL HAZARDS.

In themselves, natural hazards are not disasters. They are a part of the working of the natural environment, but because they do not occur very often, people tend to turn their backs on them in the hope that they might 'go away'. It is this attitude that contributes to

the creation of disasters. As long as people remain in areas likely to experience natural hazards, they will suffer the consequences from time to time. But, it would be quite wrong to suggest that people should simply move to safer areas in order to avoid natural hazards. Not all people can afford to move, and many would not wish to do so. In any case, not all natural hazards are spectacular or unduly severe. They do not all make the headlines, and many are just localised inconveniences.

The challenge that remains for the foreseeable future is not how to conquer or run from natural hazards, but how to cope and live with them.

Working with the weather — an everyday hazard

Chapter 7   THE RESTLESS EARTH

7.1 It's Only Natural

Every week, either on the television or in the newspapers, we hear of people being killed or injured by some force of nature. Houses may be washed away in floods, or a volcanic eruption may destroy surrounding villages. Extreme events like these are called NATURAL HAZARDS. The word hazard implies that there is some risk involved in living in a particular area, but, of course, some areas are more hazardous than others. For example, people living on the side of active volcanoes are more at risk from lava flows than those living in London. Yet, different areas have different hazards, and people in London have had to live with the possibility of major flooding in the Thames Valley.

The natural world presents people with a number of hazards which they must either live with or try to overcome. Ninety per cent of natural disasters are of four types: floods (40%); tropical cyclones or hurricanes (20%); earthquakes (15%) and drought (15%). Of these, floods do most damage to property and tropical cyclones cause most deaths each year.

It is important to remember that natural hazards are only a problem if people cannot cope with them. For example, a heavy snowfall in parts of England might bring traffic to a standstill. Farmers might be unable to look after their animals and old people may die of cold. If the same amount of snow fell in Sweden, where people are used to bad winters, there would be little disruption.

▶ Figure 7.1 is a table showing some of the main natural hazards which can affect people. Copy the table into your notes and complete it by adding as many hazards as you can under each heading.

Physical Environment		Biological Environment	
Weather and Climate Hazards	Geological Hazards	Hazards Caused by Plants	Hazards Caused by Animals
Blizzard Tropical storm	Snow Avalanche Volcanic Eruption	Hay fever	Rabies Other diseases

Fig. 7.1   The natural hazards affecting people

Where are hazards found?

Natural hazards are an increasing problem in most parts of the world. There are several reasons for this. Firstly, there are more people living on the earth and this means that more land is occupied by human settlements. Therefore, more buildings and more properties are at risk. Secondly, the concentration of so many people in cities results in a much greater loss of life and property should a hazard occur.

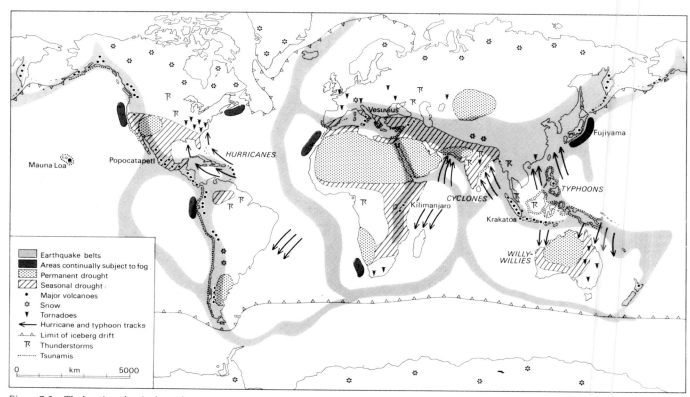

Figure 7.2   The location of major hazards

150

The map in Figure 7.2 shows the global distribution of the main hazards.

1 List the main areas affected by the following hazards:
    i volcanoes,
    ii tropical storms,
    iii earthquakes,
    iv drought.
    Use an atlas to help you name the countries affected.

2 Underline in red all the countries on your list that you consider to be developed countries, and use blue for those which you think are developing countries.

3 Which type of country (developed or developing) is most affected by hazards? Why?

4 Why do we consider the effect of natural hazards in places like Siberia or the Amazon Basin to be less severe than those in places like Bangladesh or Java?

People must choose

The total cost of the damage caused by natural hazards is rising rapidly and the loss of property is increasing, as is the death toll in the poorer nations. This is not because natural hazards are becoming more frequent, but because more people are now living in places where natural hazards occur. Figure 7.3 shows that around 30 major disasters occur each year, but that the number of deaths per year has risen alarmingly since 1967. In fact, the number of deaths is probably much higher, as the records of deaths in many developing countries are very inaccurate. The cost of repairing damage and of predicting when disasters will happen has now risen to about £30 billion per year. Many of the poorer countries rely on international aid to help them pay for emergency relief.

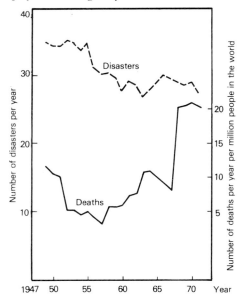

Figure 7.3   The number of deaths caused by natural disasters, 1948–1971

In the future it may be possible to predict when and where natural hazards are going to occur. It is already possible to give a few hours warning of events such as floods, storms, and earthquakes. Many problems arise because people refuse to accept that they are living in a hazardous area. In some cases the hazard may bring

advantages to an area as well as difficulties. For example, certain volcanic rocks eventually produce rich fertile soils which are ideal for farming.

In other places hazards occur so infrequently that people forget the danger. For example, the city of San Francisco (USA) is built in an earthquake zone. The last major earthquake was in 1906 and people have since forgotten the death and destruction it caused. Yet earthquakes occur in the San Francisco area every 50 or 60 years on average and one is expected soon. If an earthquake of the same size as that of 1906 was to occur today, 10 000 people would probably be killed. In addition, 40 000 would be injured and another 20 000 made homeless. The cost of repairing the damage would be in the region of £4 billion, which would result in higher taxes throughout the USA. Such a disaster would therefore affect every person in the United States in some way.

When people become aware of a hazard they have a number of choices open to them. Firstly, they can move away from the risk to a much safer place (MIGRATION). Secondly, they might manage to stop the disaster (PREVENTION). For example, dams could be built to stop flooding. Thirdly, attempts can be made to change the events (MODIFICATION), perhaps by trying to divert a lava flow around a town. Fourthly, they can stay and BEAR THE LOSS, either alone or with help from governments and friends. In most cases very little can be done to stop the destruction caused by natural hazards.

Figure 7.4 shows some of the choices which are available to a farmer who has lost his crops through drought.

1 Describe the 6 choices which are shown in the cartoon.

2 Which of these choices fall under each of the following headings:
    Migration   Prevention   Modification   Bearing the Loss

3 Choose one of the following hazards and draw your own picture to show the choices available to a person:
    Earthquake   Volcano   Flood   Plague of Locusts

Figure 7.4   The choices facing a farmer during a drought

Natural hazards in Derbyshire

People in Britain tend to think of natural hazards as events that occur in other parts of the world. All people, however, live with some sort of natural hazard which might affect them in some way. Take, for example the county of Derbyshire. If you look up its location on a suitable map you will see that it lies in the centre of England between a large number of major cities. Natural hazards are not everyday occurrences here, but some hazardous events have happened in the past. Between 1878 and 1978 the local newspaper in Derby reported a large number of events which caused some damage or danger, and these are listed in Figure 7.5.

Hazard	Number of Events 1878–1978
Snow	217
Flood	198
Thunder	115
Frost/ice	110
Gales	68
Fog	54
Landslip	39
Drought	24
Earth tremor	14

Figure 7.5   Natural hazards in Derbyshire

The figures show that heavy snow is the most common danger in Derbyshire, since it has fallen 217 times in 100 years, i.e. an average of 2.17 times each year. Not all parts of the county are affected by all the hazards; Figure 7.6 shows the general areas in which the individual hazards have occurred.

▶ 1 For each of the natural hazards in Figure 7.5 calculate how many times it is likely to occur each year. This figure is the hazard's RECURRENCE FREQUENCY.

2 From the maps, certain parts of Derbyshire seem to be more hazardous than others. Which areas appear to be most affected? You can work this out as follows:

  i On a piece of tracing paper construct a grid of 5mm squares large enough to cover one of the maps on Figure 7.6. Draw in the county boundary.

  ii Lay your grid over each of the maps in turn, and for each square award scores by adding up the recurrence frequency figures for each hazard found in it.

  iii Draw a second grid on plain paper, and again draw in the county boundary. On this new grid, work out a suitable colour key, and shade in the squares according to the total hazard value each one has scored.

3 Which parts of Derbyshire are the most and the least hazardous? Are the towns in relatively safe or relatively dangerous locations?

This exercise has shown the variations in natural hazards that can occur over a small area. Such information could be used to help planners cope with hazards. By calculating how often particular hazards are likely to occur, Derbyshire County Council is able to work out how much money needs to be set aside to relieve emergencies when they arise. Knowing where hazardous events are most likely to occur also allows the planning of matters such as where to keep snow-ploughs, and where to store salt to keep roads ice-free.

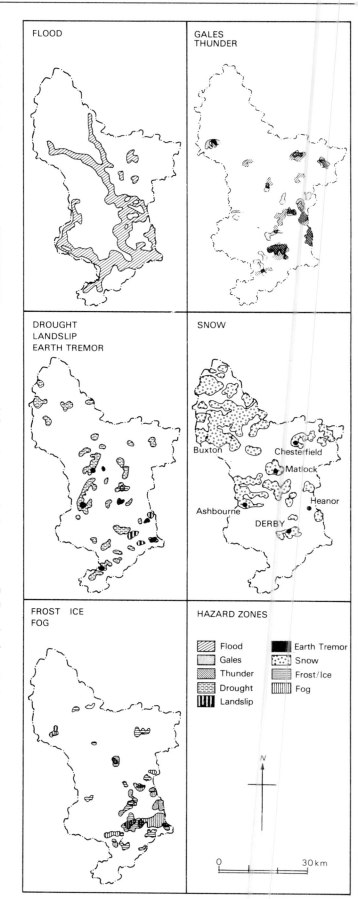

Figure 7.6   Derbyshire's natural hazards

7.2 Earth on Fire

On the morning of Monday, 27 August 1883, one of the largest volcanic eruptions ever seen on earth occurred on an island between Java and Sumatra. The island, called Krakatoa, was almost completely destroyed by a series of explosions which lasted for 19 hours. Flows of molten rock emptied the volcano which then collapsed, leaving just three small fragments of land where the island had once been. The largest of the explosions was heard 4700 km away at Alice Springs in Australia (see Figure 7.7). Krakatoa was such a major disaster that the effects of the eruption were felt worldwide. Three hundred towns and villages were destroyed in the surrounding islands. The sea formed huge waves, called tsunamis, which hit the shores of Java and Sumatra. These waves were up to 35 m high and were largely responsible for the huge death toll. The disaster is known to have killed 36000 people, but some scientists suggest that the death toll may have been as high as 100000. The effects of the shock waves were felt 8000 km away at Port Elizabeth in South Africa where ships in the harbour were rocked by the waves.

Tonnes of fine ash were blasted high into the air forming dust clouds which produced bright sunsets all over the world. Pumice, a light weight rock formed during volcanic eruptions, floated across the surrounding oceans for months, forming large spongy islands. The scale of destruction shocked the whole world as the details were made known by the newspapers. The islands that were the remnants of Kraka-

toa, Sertung, Rakata and Rakata Kecil, were left completely bare. None of the lush tropical rain-forest which had clothed the sides of the island before the eruption was left. In 1927, a new cone was formed during another eruption. It was given the name Anak Krakatoa, meaning 'child of Krakatoa'.

The eruption of Krakatoa is one of the most studied volcanic events. The sheer size of the explosions and the vastness of the area affected, go to show how dangerous volcanoes can be. They are one of the most severe natural hazards people have to face. The next section of this chapter examines the problems they create and what can be done to reduce the dangers they pose.

Volcanoes: hazard or blessing?

Volcanic eruptions can be spectacular. The noise and fire give the impression that the earth is being destroyed by some alien force! Eye witness reports have often spoken of 'the action of gods' or 'punishment of Mankind', and in some parts of the world volcanoes are worshipped and given sacrifices so that they will not become angry.

There is no doubt that volcanoes can be very destructive when they erupt. Some begin quietly, but others may start with a sudden massive explosion. Gas, steam, ash and lava are likely to be emitted from all

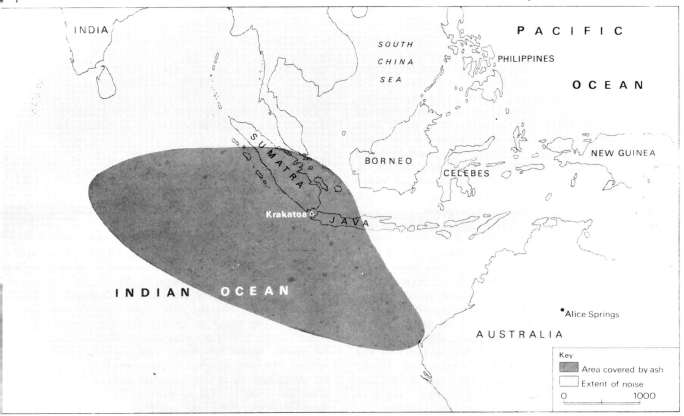

Figure 7.7   The area affected by the eruption of Krakatoa

Figure 7.8   Eruption of Heimaey, Iceland

volcanoes, but in very different quantities and with different effects. Apart from the risk of severe explosion, volcanoes present people with three main hazards.

Lava flows are the major hazard, burning and burying everything in their paths. Towns, villages and houses can be completely wiped out by a large lava flow. People are usually able to move out of the way, but the damage to property can be very great.

Showers of ash and volcanic bombs (pieces of solidifying lava) are also very hazardous. Hot ash can destroy and burn any vegetation that it covers. Water supplies may be polluted, and people's health can suffer through breathing in ash and poisonous fumes. If ash covers a town, its weight can cause the buildings to collapse. Ash flows also cause death because they can move at up to 150 km/h and catch people unaware. This is what happened at Herculaneum and Pompeii during the eruption of Mount Vesuvius in AD 79. These ancient towns have been well preserved under the cover of ash, and excavations have shown how rich and beautiful they were before the eruption.

A third major hazard are the large mudflows of wet rock and ash that can occur with little or no warning. Mudflows usually follow existing valleys, and if they block the valley severe flooding may also occur. The Mount St Helens eruption in the United States on 17 and 18 May 1980 produced a major mudflow. A mixture of rock, ice and soil swept down the western side of the volcano at about 75 m/s. It followed the North and South Fork Toutle valleys and filled them to a depth of 100 m. Everyone in its path was killed by the flow. The material blocked the North Fork Toutle valley and dammed the river. This led to further mudflows and flooding lower in the valley, which in turn destroyed farmhouses, farmland and bridges.

Volcanoes not only bring problems, however. The soils which form from the ash are often very fertile and in tropical areas where the soils are leached by heavy rain, a light fall of ash acts as a fertiliser and replaces many previously lost nutrients. Lava flows can form new land and volcanic activity may lead to the creation of valuable mineral deposits such as sulphur. Hot springs, which are associated with some volcanoes, provide hot water for bathing and heating. In some places volcanic steam is used to generate electricity, as at Wairakei in New Zealand. Finally, some volcanoes have become a popular tourist attraction. On Mount Etna in Sicily, and on Mount Fujiyama in Japan, cable cars have been built to take visitors close to the crater. Hotels and other services have also been provided to take advantage of tourist interest in volcanoes.

Is protection possible?

One of the major difficulties with volcanoes is that they are unpredictable. Each eruption is different and this makes it almost impossible to give exact warnings of when an eruption will occur. However, a careful watch is kept on volcanoes because it is quite common for there to be some change in the shape of the cone before an eruption. In the case of Mount St Helens a bulge developed on the side of the cone. Seismographs may also be used to detect the small earthquakes which occur before an eruption so that a warning may be given. Some eruptions can also be predicted by sound. On Hawaii it is not uncommon for eruptions to be preceded by a low-pitched humming noise. The islanders refer to this as 'hearing Pele', Pele being the goddess of the Hawaiian volcanoes.

Figure 7.9   Spraying lava with water on Heimaey

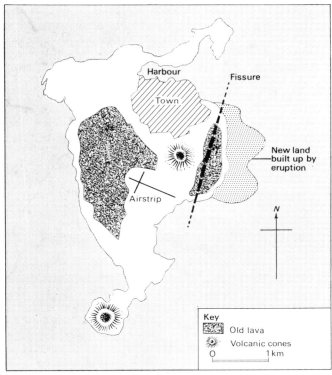

Figure 7.10   Heimaey and the fissure of 23 January 1973

Once a volcanic eruption has been predicted, or has begun, very little can be done to protect the people nearby. The only safe course of action is to evacuate the area until the eruption has finished. On 23 January 1973 the Island of Heimaey off the south coast of Iceland was awakened to the dangers of volcanic eruption.

At 01.50 a.m. the ground quietly split open to create a fissure which eventually reached a length of 1500 m. From this massive crack in the ground a curtain of lava was thrown up 100 m into the air. A small fishing port nearby, with a population of 6000 people, was threatened by lava flows and falls of ash and volcanic bombs, Figure 7.8. The main threat came from a lava flow which approached the harbour. Several attempts were made to stop the lava before it blocked the port. Jets of water were sprayed onto the lava, Figure 7.9, in order to cool its surface and to slow it down. It was hoped to form a lava wall which would divert the flow away from the harbour, but it was only a partial success. The lava was slowed down, but the force of the flow was too great for it to be stopped completely. Another plan involved diverting the flow by bombing the volcano's main crater, but this was considered to be too unpredictable and dangerous. Someone even suggested that the harbour should be left alone and if it became blocked then it would be cheaper and safer to build a new one rather than try to stop the lava. In the end the lava flow stopped before it reached the coast and the harbour was saved, Figure 7.10.

▶ Carry out an investigation into a major volcanic eruption of your choice, and describe its effects on the people living nearby. Some possible examples are:
Krakatoa (1883); Mount St Helens (1980); Vesuvius (AD 79); Paracutin (1943); Heimaey (1973).

Mount Etna erupts, 1983

The island of Sicily lies off the south-west coast of Italy and is dominated by the volcano of Mount Etna standing 3273 m high above the city of Catania. Throughout recorded history eruptions have been frequent, with 39 major ones since 1669 and five minor ones since 1973. Despite the apparent dangers, however, over one million people live on the slopes of the volcano; this figure represents one-quarter of the island's population. The attraction of the volcano lies mainly in the high fertility of the soils on its slopes — rich orchards, orange groves and vineyards clothe the southern and south-eastern slopes—and also in the money that can be made from the tourist industry. The high population density of the island (182 persons/ km^2) forces full use of the best land.

On 26 and 27 March 1983, several hundred small earthquakes were recorded on the volcano, together with one large one measuring 3.7 on the Richter Scale. On the morning of 28 March a 600 m fissure appeared at a height of 2400 m on the southern slopes. Lava started to pour from it at a rate of 130 m/h. The flow was 500 m wide, 10 – 15 m high and stretched for 2 km at the end of the first day. By 2 April, it was 4 km long.

By the end of April, 100 million tonnes of lava had caused widespread damage. One hotel, 3 restaurants, 25 houses, a ski lift and many hundreds of hectares of farmland had been destroyed at an estimated cost of £20 to £25 million. More serious, though, was the fact that the lava flow had started to approach the towns of Ragalna and Rocca, Figure 7.11.

The Sicilian authorities decided to attempt to divert the flow to save the towns. Three possible schemes were suggested. The first was to build a 10 m high wall over 1km long to divert the flow, but this was rejected because the engineers could not guarantee that the wall would not be swept aside by the force of the lava. The second scheme was to spray the lava with water to cool it and so slow it down, but a shortage of water prevented this plan from being tried. The third plan was to blast a hole in the wall of the lava channel near the fissure, and to construct an artificial canal to take the diverted lava to a different area of the mountainside. Although it cost £3 million, this last scheme was chosen. It took 100 men and five bulldozers over two weeks to complete the new 'canal', and on 15 May the explosion was carried out. Unfortunately it was only a partial success, for only 20% of the lava was diverted. Plans were made for a second explosion, but a slowing down of the lava's movement eventually meant that it was no longer necessary to take any action.

The 1983 eruption of Mount Etna saw one of the first major attempts to change the effects of a volcanic eruption. A smaller-scale attempt on Mount Kilauea in Hawaii in 1944 had failed, even though the United States Air Force bombed the lava flow. Despite the lessons learned on Etna most of the residents of this part of Sicily can still only respond in one way to eruptions and lava flows — move house, and bear the cost of any damage that is done.

▶ Different people see the effects of natural hazards in different ways. Put yourself in the position of each of the following people, and describe your feelings about the Etna eruption, the damage it caused and the proposed scheme for diverting the lava.

   i A hotel owner in Catania.
  ii The owner of a restaurant that has been destroyed.
 iii The mayor of the town of Ragalna.
 iv A resident of Palermo, another city on the island.
  v A farmer who owns an orange grove on the southern slopes of the volcano.
 vi A scientist with the United States Geological Survey working in the area around Mount Etna.
 vii A newspaper reader in London.
viii A member of the Italian government.

Which of the above people would suffer the most from having to 'move house and bear the cost of any damage done'. Give reasons for your answer.

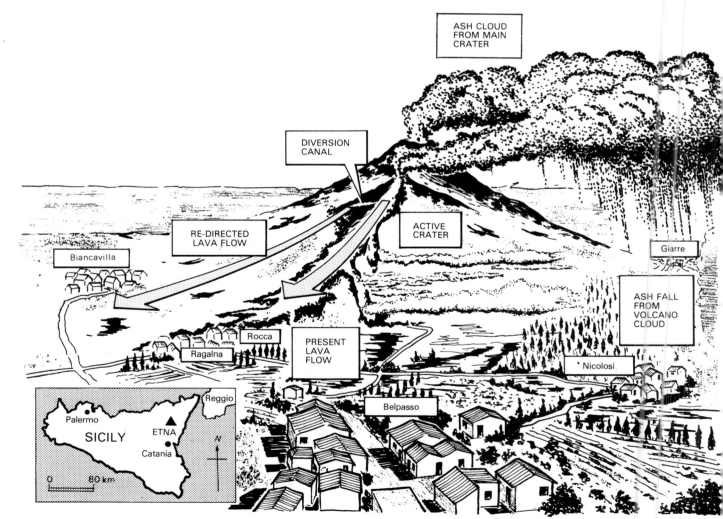

Figure 7.11   Mount Etna's eruption

7.3 The Trembling Earth

'And, behold, the veil of the temple was rent in twain from the top to the bottom; and the earth did quake, and the rocks rent.'
St Matthew ch. 27; v. 51

This quotation is one of several descriptions of earthquakes in the Bible, and it tells of the power involved.

Earthquakes occur whenever the crust of the earth moves. This movement can be very violent causing the land surface or the sea bed to shake and tremble. More often, though, movement is slight and it can hardly be felt at all by people in the area. We hear mainly about the violent earthquakes because they cause extensive damage and may result in a tragic loss of life. Minor earthquakes are more frequent and even affect the British Isles which are normally considered to be in a 'safe' area.

Earthquakes are the release of stress in the earth's crust. Stresses build up within the crust until the rocks begin to crack and move, usually along a geological FAULT. Movement of the rocks reduces the stress but sends a series of shock waves through earth. The point at which an earthquake starts is called the FOCUS and the point directly above this on the earth's surface is the EPICENTRE. Figure 7.12 shows the relationship between these two important points.

The instrument developed for recording earthquakes is called the SEISMOMETER and it is able to produce a continuous record of earth movements in the form of a graph, or trace. On a traditional seismometer, a heavy weight holds a pen steady while the rotating drum carrying the graph paper shakes when an earthquake occurs. Earthquake shock waves are of three types, known as P, S, and L waves. P and S waves can travel through the earth, but L waves can only travel through the rocks of the crust and they cause the worst damage. They also arrive last.

Earthquakes and their effects

Earthquakes are very difficult to measure and two aspects are commonly recorded. MAGNITUDE is a measure of the total amount of energy released during an earthquake. The scale used is the Richter Scale which ranges from 0–8.9; an earthquake of magnitude 3.0 has 30 times more energy than one of magnitude 2.0. The amount of damage caused by an earthquake is described using the modified Mercalli INTENSITY scale. Damage is assessed on a twelve point scale shown in Figure 7.13.

The devastation that can be caused by large earthquakes makes them a major natural hazard. Only a few of the earthquakes that occur each year make world headlines but these tend to cause a great loss of life and untold destruction. The most devastating earthquakes are not always the largest however, as deaths are most numerous if an earthquake hits a

densely populated area when most people are indoors. People are killed by buildings collapsing on them, or they are buried beneath debris.

The aftermath of an earthquake is made much worse by the frequent aftershocks which follow. This makes rescuing the victims an extremely dangerous occupation. Additional problems are caused by large numbers of homeless people who have to be found shelter, food, clothes and medical aid. Often more people die in the chaos and confusion that follows than in the earthquake itself.

Figure 7.12   The focus and epicentre of an earthquake

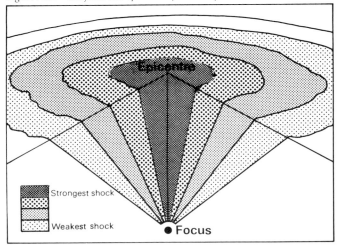

Figure 7.13   The Mercalli scale

I	Imperceptible	Detected only by instruments.
II	Very Weak	Detected by sensitive people at rest.
III	Weak	Loose objects may be disturbed slightly.
IV	Moderate	Rattling of doors and windows; some sleepers awake.
V	Fairly strong	Most sleepers awake; noticed out of doors; bells ring.
VI	Strong	Furniture overthrown; cracking of plaster.
VII	Very strong	Some damage to buildings.
VIII	Destructive	Walls crack; chimneys fall.
IX	Very Destructive	Severe damage; some buildings destroyed.
X	Devastating	Foundations, roads, pipes, etc. damaged.
XI	Catastrophic	Few buildings survive; fissures in ground.
XII	Major Catastrophe	Complete destruction; crumpling of ground.

In some cases earth tremors may trigger off major landslides that rush down steep hill and mountain slopes burying everything in their path. One such landslide of rock and snow was dislodged by an earthquake from the Nevados Huascaran peak in Peru in 1970. The rock and snow travelled at 280 km/h and completely buried the town of Yungay, killing 18 000 people in all.

If an earthquake occurs beneath the sea, the disturbance can dislodge rock and sediment and produce a rock slide under water. Offshore from Newfoundland, Canada, in 1929 telephone cables were broken by earth movements following an earthquake. In addition, large vertical shifts of the sea bed can produce enormous waves of water known as tsunami which can cause severe flooding in coastal areas. They are described in detail later in this chapter.

Earthquake control and prediction

One of the main reasons why little is being done to control and to provide protection against earthquakes, is that people are reluctant to believe that they will be affected. In many parts of the world people do not accept that earthquakes present real dangers to life and property. They do little to reduce the threat and continue to build in unstable areas. Even in countries where earthquakes are a major hazard, dangerous areas are used. In Tokyo, a steel mill and an earthquake disaster relief centre have been built on new land reclaimed from Tokyo Bay. This area is one of the worst affected in Japan, however, and is often struck by earthquakes and tsunamis!

Most of the research into the control of earthquakes and protection from them relies on accurate prediction. That is, being able to say when and where an earthquake is going to occur so that local people can be warned. The main countries involved in this work are the USA, Japan, China and the USSR, and a number of factors may help prediction in the future. The Japanese have found that small earthquakes, called microquakes, occur for several months before a major earthquake. Recording these microquakes is one way of giving an early warning so that people have time to take precautions before the main tremor occurs.

In the United States, research has shown that the ground close to the site of an earthquake begins to bulge upwards in the months before the 'quake. This may only be by a few centimetres, but it can be detected with very accurate measuring equipment. A continuous record is also being kept on some faults where earthquakes are common. It has been discovered that the amount of electrical current that can be passed from one side of the fault to the other increases just before an earthquake occurs. A further method of predicting a disaster is by measuring the amount of Argon gas found in the soil above a fault, for this also seems to significantly increase just before an earthquake.

Although it may be possible to predict the timing of an earthquake, it is far more difficult to know exactly **where** it will occur — and without some idea of this, it is impossible to predict its likely effects. While the main areas where earthquakes occur are well known

(Figure 7.2), the precise spot along a fault at which one may happen is difficult to work out. Recent work has shown, however, that there are often gaps, or windows, along faults where earthquakes have not yet occurred. These gaps may prove to be the site of future major earthquakes.

The control of earthquakes in the future may also become possible. It has been found that pumping water and oil down into faults can help reduce the size of earthquakes. The fluid lubricates the fault and allows the rocks to slip past each other more easily. Although this technique produces a number of small tremors, it prevents the large build up of stress which can cause a major earthquake. It also seems likely that the number of severe earthquakes can be reduced by using small, controlled nuclear explosions along the fault. This approach works in a similar way to using water and reduces the stresses that produce earthquakes.

Many of the deaths during earthquakes are caused through people being killed by the collapse of buildings. Figure 7.14 is a photograph of a town in Alaska showing the damage following an earthquake. It is possible to avoid this sort of destruction by building reinforced houses so that they can withstand earthquake shocks. The most sensible course of action is to avoid building in high risk areas, but people are unwilling to plan their lives around the dangers of earthquakes which may occur only once in a hundred years. Some people decide to accept the cost of rebuilding if an earthquake does happen. Insurance is available but only at a high price. In most countries where earthquakes are a major hazard, relief agencies are set up to deal with the after-effects of a large disaster. In the United States, for example, the Federal Disaster System provides relief and funds for rebuilding after earthquakes.

Figure 7.14   Damage after the Alaskan earthquake

1. Imagine that you are a reporter for a national newspaper. You have been sent to the scene of a major earthquake. Write an article describing the effects of the earthquake and how people are trying to cope with the disaster. Incude eye-witness accounts of the earthquake and your own sketches of the scene.

2. Figure 7.15 shows a list of suggested actions for when an earthquake occurs. Explain why each one is necessary.

The Italian earthquake, November 1980

On 23 November 1980, a large part of southern Italy suffered a very severe earthquake causing widespread damage to hundreds of mountain villages and to the city of Naples. The earthquake's intensity was measured at 6.8 on the Richter Scale, and 10 on the modified Mercalli Scale. The main tremor lasted for one minute and twenty seconds. The epicentre was shown later to be about 70 km east of Naples. Figure 7.16 shows the area that was affected.

Unofficial figures record that over 3000 people died as a result of the earthquake. Another 8000 people were injured and 480 000 people had their homes destroyed. Virtually all the buildings in many villages were made uninhabitable. A typical town affected was San Mango Sul Calore: 200 people out of a total population of 1665 died, and 800 houses were destroyed. In Naples, 20% of the buildings were lost or damaged, these being mainly in the old densely-populated central part of the city. Fortunately only 64 people died here, mainly from the collapse of one large multi-storey apartment block.

The earthquake was only one of many that have occurred in Italy in recent years, although it was one of the largest. The earthquake risk, together with the presence of volcanoes such as Mount Etna and Vesuvius, is the result of Italy's position on a very unstable part of the earth's crust. The country will continue to

Before the Quake

1. Prepare an earthquake kit: a sturdy container stocked with flashlights, a portable radio, candles, waterproof matches, a heavy duty portable lantern, a hand operated can opener, a tool kit, medicines, a week's supply of food and plastic bottles of water, a blanket, and a first aid kit.
2. Know how to turn off the water, gas, and electricity.
3. Prevent extensive damage to property. Keep beds away from windows. Keep heavy objects on low shelves. Water heaters should be securely bolted to the wall.

During an Earthquake

1. If you are at home during an earthquake, stay inside. Move away from windows, mirrors and shelves.
2. If you are outside, try to remain in the open, away from power cables or trees. If you are driving, pull into the side of the road until the shaking stops.
3. Most important, DO NOT PANIC — remain calm. It could mean the difference between life and death.

Afterwards

1. Attend to injuries. Do not move any seriously injured persons unless they are in immediate danger.
2. Check for fire and fire hazards. Inspect gas lines. Do not use matches or lighters. Before flushing toilets, make sure that sewer pipes are intact.
3. Check for and immediately clean up any spilled medicines, cleaning fluids or any harmful substances.
4. Check water and food supplies.
5. Do not use the telephone unless you have an extreme emergency. The radio will provide you with news.

Figure 7.15   Courses of action during earthquakes

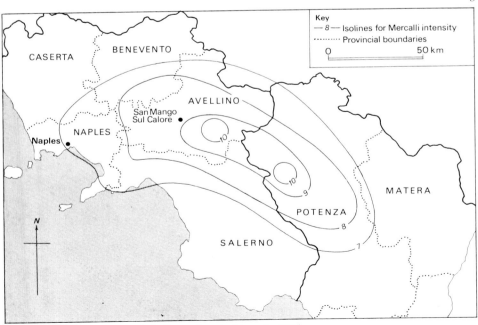

Figure 7.16   Area affected by the Italian earthquake, November 1980

Province	1976 Population ('000)	Persons/ km²	Number of Dead and Injured	Number of Homeless	% of Factories Damaged
Avellino	438	156	4500	119 000	82
Benevento	293	142	40	144 000	52
Caserta	729	276	150	3800	21
Matera	203	59	2	1100	15
Naples	2872	2453	1560	50 000	40
Potenza	414	63	725	26 000	70
Salerno	1003	204	4100	137 000	53

Figure 7.17   Effects of the Italian earthquake

be affected by the earthquake hazard and it is important that the people protect themselves against the worst side-effects. Many people died in the 1980 disaster because the country was badly prepared. It took many weeks for the relief workers to move in and to provide much-needed food and shelter for the victims. This poor organisation may have caused as many deaths as the original disaster.

▶ Study carefully the map in Figure 7.16 and the figures in the table Figure 7.17.
  1 On a copy of Figure 7.16, shade in the provinces according to the number of homeless people. A suitable key would be: More than 120000 — black; 100000 – 120000 —brown; 20000 – 99000 — green; less than 20000 — yellow.
  2 For each province calculate the number of homeless as a percentage of the population. Shade in a second copy of Figure 7.16 according to the following key:
  More than 25% — black; 10 – 25% — brown; 1 – 24% — green; less than 1% — yellow
  3 Which map shows the relationship between damage and nearness to the epicentre more clearly?

The Coalinga earthquake, 1983

The state of California in the United States lies on a major fault in the earth's crust known as the San Andreas Fault. Probably the most famous earthquake

of all time occurred here. The San Francisco earthquake of 1906 shook the whole state. It had a magnitude of 8.3 on the Richter scale and many people were killed. Despite living in an earthquake zone, however, Californians seem to have little real understanding of the danger they face. A recent survey showed that 96% of the people of San Francisco thought that they would experience an earthquake in their lifetime, but only 35% thought that the damage caused by it would be serious.

One of the most recent earthquakes in California occurred on Monday 2 May, 1983, at 4.42 in the afternoon. The epicentre was 8 km north-east of the small town of Coalinga (population 7000), in the San Joaquin valley. This earthquake had a magnitude of 6.5 on the Richter scale and it was felt in San Francisco, Monterey, Las Vegas and Los Angeles. It was the worst earthquake since one 12 years before which killed 70 people in a suburb of Los Angeles.

The Coalinga earthquake was caused by movement along the San Andreas Fault. Shock waves passed out from the focus and flattened about 150 buildings in the centre of Coalinga. No one died, but 45 people were hurt, 3 seriously. The injured were sent by ambulance and helicopter to hospitals in the nearby towns of Fresno and Monterey.

The disaster began with one major tremor which started a number of fires, Figure 7.18. This was fol-

Figure 7.18   The remains of a store in central Coalinga

lowed by 40 smaller aftershocks which continued for a number of hours. Some of these aftershocks reached 4.0 on the Richter Scale. The main danger came from collapsing buildings and many of the local residents slept in tents in their gardens rather than risk being crushed by their collapsing houses. In the worst affected areas people were evacuated and the police sealed off the town centre to prevent looting. One eye-witness described the scene like this, 'the buildings just collapsed like packs of cards. There was extreme panic. Dust was flying, bricks falling and it was total pandemonium.'

▶ Figure 7.19 is a map showing the town of Coalinga and the San Andreas Fault. Copy this map into your notes.

 1   Use an atlas and name the following towns and cities on your map: San Francisco, Monterey, Los Angeles, Las Vegas.

 2   How many kilometres away were the effects of the earthquake felt? Use the scale on the map.

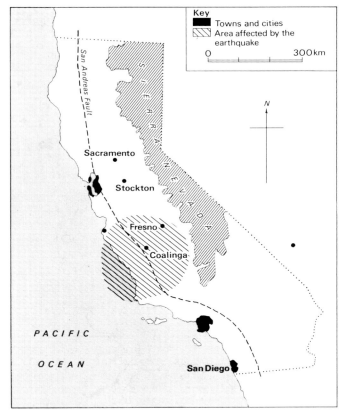

Figure 7.19   The Coalinga earthquake

7.4 Tsunamis: The Big Waves

Tsunamis are often incorrectly called tidal waves. It is wrong to call them this because they are not caused by changes in the tide at all. They are also more accurately described as a series of waves rather than one single wave. Tsunamis are extremely destructive and are a serious natural hazard but, fortunately, they are fairly rare. For example, tsunamis are experienced only once in every eight years on the coasts of the United States. They are most common in the Pacific Ocean basin and countries with a Pacific coastline are most at risk.

Tsunamis are formed when water is moved up and down (vertically displaced) by movements in the earth's crust. These movements may be caused by earthquakes shaking the sea-bed, by molten rock rising to the surface in a sub-marine volcanic eruption, or as a result of a major landslide on the ocean floor. The shock waves from any of these events may cause large waves on the surface of the sea.

Tsunamis differ from ordinary waves in a number of ways. They can travel quickly. In open water, tsunamis can move at 800 km/h whereas normal sea waves travel at less than 100 km/h. The wavelength of the tsunamis (i.e. the distance between wave crests) can be 160 km, compared to 100 – 300 m for normal waves. In addition, while tsunamis may have a wave height of only 1 m in deep water, their height is likely to increase to 20 m or more as they approach the coast.

The greatest damage occurs when tsunamis break onto the coast and the water surges across the land. The time between waves is usually between 15 minutes and one hour. At first there will be just a pronounced swell as the tsunami begins to approach. Then water is sucked away from the shore as the trough of the second wave occurs. Normally the third to the eighth waves are the largest and most destructive. Great loss of life may result from people being unaware that a tsunami consists of more than one wave. After the first wave people often flock to the shore to inspect the damage and they are then killed by the following waves.

Tsunamis are often the major cause of deaths when earthquakes occur near the coast or under the sea. The majority of people who died as a result of the 1964 Alaskan earthquake, died because of the tsunami which followed the shocks. They can be responsible for damage thousands of kilometres from the epicentre of the earthquake. In 1960, 61 people in Hawaii were killed by a tsunami which was caused by an earthquake in Chile. After only 15 hours the tsunami had crossed the Pacific and reached Hawaii.

Very little can be done to reduce the hazard and tsunamis are very difficult to predict, but once they have been detected coastal communities can be warned. The arrival of a large tsunami can be predicted to within 1.5 minutes for each hour of travel time. In the central Pacific there is a tsunami warning system which is operated from Honolulu in Hawaii. Scientists map the path of any tsunami and then issue frequent warnings to places which are most at risk.

Steps can then be taken to protect boats, buildings, harbours and roads which would otherwise be destroyed. Human lives may be saved, but the waves can have a disastrous effect on aquatic life including fish, shellfish and plants.

Japan 1983

Just after midday on Thursday 26 May 1983, the north-west coast of Japan was hit by a tsunami. It was caused by a severe earthquake measuring 7.7 on the Richter Scale, that had its epicentre off the coast of Akita prefecture (Figure 7.20). It was the largest earthquake to have affected Japan for 15 years and it produced a wave 3m high. The tremors of the main earthquake, and the numerous aftershocks were felt 480 km away in Tokyo.

The earthquake caused widespread damage to buildings and communications. 35000 houses were without electricity and the 'Bullet Train' service was stopped. Most of the casualties were the result of the tsunamis hitting the coast. There were three main waves and several smaller ones, and the sea remained rough for several hours. A wave alert was issued and the government declared a state of emergency.

The waves affected about 800 km of the coast of Honshu. Fishing boats were upturned and swept onto the pier (Figure 7.21). The docks were destroyed and cars were sucked out to sea by the receding water. The death toll was officially put at 30 but 69 others were missing, presumed dead. It was one of the worst natural disasters in Japan for many years.

▶ 1 An earthquake with its epicentre on the east coast of Japan has triggered off a tsunami which is heading towards Hawaii.
  i Imagine that you are in charge of the preparations on the islands to cope with this natural hazard.
  ii Using Figure 7.22, work out how long it will be before the tsunami reaches Hawaii.
  iii Draw up a series of plans describing what you would advise people to do. (An atlas map of Hawaii might help you.) Include plans for warnings, evacuations and perhaps prepare a statement to be read out on the radio and television.
2 Using the information in the text, write an imagined eye-witness account of the 1983 tsunami disaster in Japan.

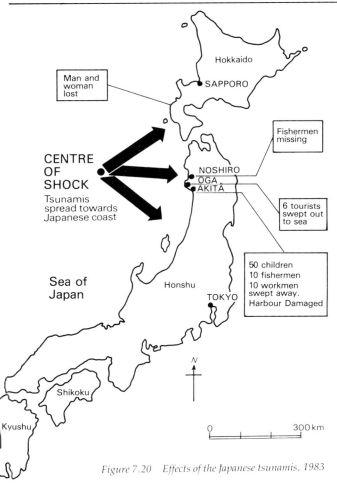

Figure 7.20   *Effects of the Japanese tsunamis, 1983*

Figure 7.21   *Boats stranded after the tsunamis in Japan*

Figure 7.22   *Tsunami warning system*

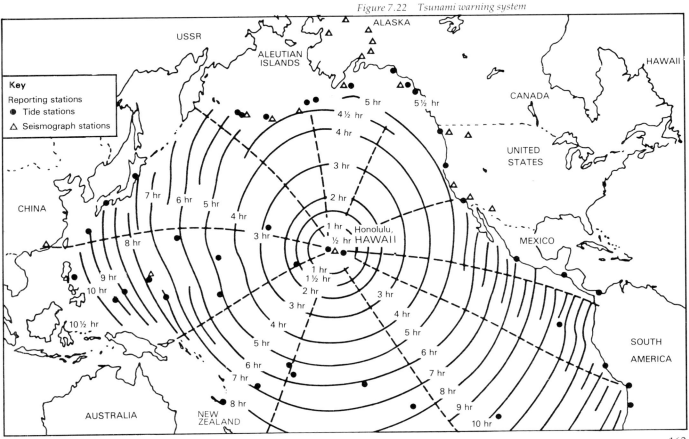

7.5 Firm Ground?

▶ You will need the following items: dry powdered clay; sand; gravel; a board; a brick; some water and a tray.

1   Pour some of the clay from a height of 30 cm onto a tray. Measure the angle of the slopes of the clay mound which forms. This angle is known as the ANGLE OF REST of dry clay. Do the same for the sand and gravel. How do the angles of rest of these three materials differ from each other?

2   Wet some of the clay, sand and gravel and repeat the experiment again. Does the water have any effect? What reasons can you give for your results?

3   Cover the board with a thin layer of dry clay. Place a brick on top. Gradually raise one end of the board until the brick begins to move. Measure the angle of slope of the board at this point. Wet the clay and try the experiment again. Try to explain your results.

4   Build a slope on the board using layers of your three materials. Shake the board. What happens to the slope? Now undermine the slope by removing material from the base. Shake the board again. What differences do you see? Why do these differences occur?

These experiments show something about how rock and soil on the earth's surface can move under the pull of gravity. This movement is known as MASS MOVEMENT. It is controlled by many factors such as the nature of the rock and soil themselves, the presence of water, the angle of slope and whether or not the slope has been undermined in some way. You will have seen the effects of all these factors in your experiments.

The speed of mass movements varies considerably. In some cases soil may move so slowly downhill that it is impossible to detect it with the naked eye. This process is called SOIL CREEP. Sometimes, however, very fast movement may occur. For example, rock avalanches in mountain areas may travel at 200 km/h, Figure 7.23.

Mass movements are triggered by changes in the nature of slopes. Most slopes look very stable but in fact they are changing all the time. Any change to the slope may cause it to become unstable and rock and soil may start to move downhill. These changes may result from a natural process such as erosion by rivers, or they may be due to human use of the slope. Some of the factors leading to mass movement are:

● Heavy rainfall or snowfall which increases the weight of the material on the slope.
● Seeping water which may cause the material to slide or flow more easily.
● Steepening of the slope by undermining at its base, e.g. by digging a road cutting.
● Earthquakes or explosions which may start the material moving.
● Natural weathering of the rocks (rock rotting).
● Removal of vegetation from slopes. This upsets the amount of water in the soil and also removes the roots which help bind the soil together.

Mass movements, particularly the faster ones, are a serious natural hazard causing a great amount of damage each year and loss of life. They may be due entirely to natural processes at work. In many cases, however, people have interfered in some way and have made the already bad effects of landslides worse. An example of a landslide due only to natural causes occurred in the Brazilian state of Paraná on 22 January 1967. It was a major landslide disaster following an electrical storm during which intense rain fell for 342 hours. The increased amount of water in the rock and soil of the slopes triggered off many hundreds of landslides. The flooding also undermined the slopes and made them more unstable. An area of 100 km^2 was affected by the landslide and the flooding. The amount of damage to property and industry was so great that it

Figure 7.23   The Hope slide, British Columbia

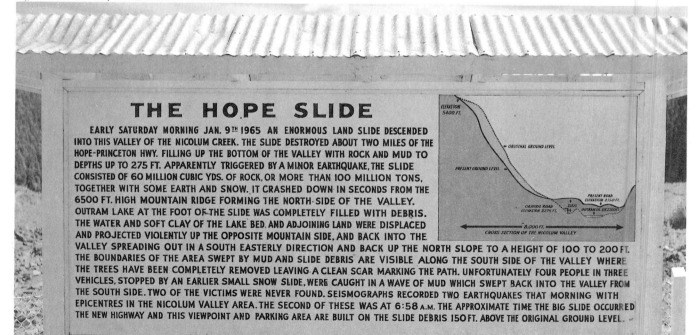

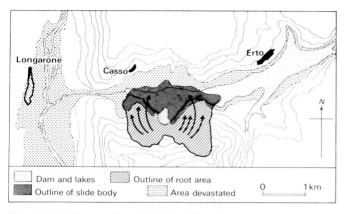

Figure 7.24   The area affected by the landslip at Longarone

was impossible to calculate the total figure. In addition, 1700 people were killed by avalanches of debris and mudflows.

People's activities can increase the chance of a landslide hazard. One such area where human activity was one of the main causes of a landslide disaster was at Longarone, a small town in northern Italy, Figure 7.24. The landslide came soon after the building, in 1960, of the nearby Vaiont Dam.

The dam was one of the highest in the world and yet it was built in an alpine valley where landslides had always been very common. Engineers kept a close watch on the slopes around the dam and the reservoir and measured the amount of movement using stakes driven into the ground. The average movement was 25 cm/week. In early October 1963 they began to realise that the speed of movement was increasing and that a large landslide was likely.

Unfortunately they realised too late that it was going to cause a movement of disastrous size. After heavy rain in late September and early October the landslide eventually occurred on 9 October. At 10.43 p.m. 300 million m³ of rock, soil and debris thundered down the mountainside at 95 k/h. The material filled the reservoir behind the dam and sent waves of water and mud 70 m high flowing down the valley. The slide and the flood only lasted for seven minutes in total, yet 2600 people were killed.

The big question asked after the disaster was why had the engineers not been able to give adequate warning so that people could have been evacuated. It is said that hardly any animals were killed by the landslide because, sensing the danger, they left the area on 1 October! Surely, if the animals were able to predict the disaster, engineers with the aid of machines and technical knowledge, should have been able to do so!

Prediction and prevention

In order to predict the effects of the landslide hazard it is necessary to:
● Identify areas where mass movements might occur.
● Modify slopes by engineering methods so as to prevent mass movements.
● Control and stop slow movements after they have started.

It is possible by careful research, to identify districts where landslides might occur and then to produce maps of areas where it is unsafe to build. Unfortunately it is almost impossible to prevent a large natural landslide from occurring, and only in the case of small or slow slides can the movement be stopped. To do this, the process which has caused the movement in the first place must be tackled. Where water is the root cause of the problem, drainage of the soil and rock should be started. If sliding starts to occur in rock which is difficult to drain, then it will be even harder to stop the movement. In this case either the angle of the slope can be reduced, or artificial barriers can be built to stop further movement downhill.

Engineers can reduce the risk of a disastrous landslide by using one or more of the following methods:
● The removal of unstable rock or soil.
● The use of low angle slopes in building any sort of cutting or embankment.
● Proper drainage of rock and soil.
● Building walls or other structures to hold back the debris.
● Using heavy bolts (called rock bolts) which are first placed into holes drilled in unstable rocks and then fastened into stable rock.
● Hardening the soil by freezing, heating or the use of cement.
● Blasting the rock and producing small controlled landslides before a large natural one occurs.

▶ Figure 7.25 shows a cliff section at Barton-on-Sea in Hampshire. Landslipping is particularly common along this stretch of coast.

1   Use an atlas to locate Barton-on-Sea, and draw a sketch map to show where it is.

2   Sandstones are permeable, i.e. they let water pass through them, while clays are impermeable. Label each of the rocks on Figure 7.25 as either permeable or impermeable, and draw a series of arrows to show the route that rainwater would take as it filters through from the ground surface.

3   Where would the water emerge?

4   For mass movements to occur, the rock and the soil must be lubricated. Try to explain why mass movements occur at Barton.

5   Make a list of the possible problems that landslipping may cause here, and try to suggest some solutions to stop it. Barton-on-Sea is a holiday resort with hotels built near the cliff top.

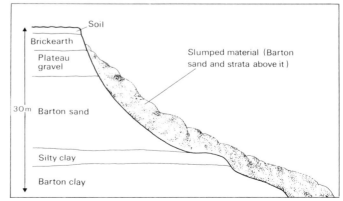

Figure 7.25   Cliff section at Barton-on-Sea

Avalanches in the Alps

An avalanche occurs when a large amount of snow and ice falls down the side of a mountain under the pull of gravity. The avalanche may consist mainly of wet snow sliding over the ground, carrying rock and soil with it. This is a GROUND AVALANCHE. In other cases dry snow may fall through the air as a cloud. This is known as a POWDER AVALANCHE.

Avalanches are probably the main natural hazard in the Alps. They occur on high mountains with open slopes, particularly in areas which have heavy snowfalls. The risk of a disaster is made much greater by the large number of people who either live in these areas or who visit them for winter sports. Avalanches can occur throughout the winter and spring months from November to June and when one does strike an area it can cause very serious destruction. People and animals may be killed or severely injured, buildings are likely to be destroyed and forests and farm land may be engulfed by snow and ice. Roads and railways are often blocked and if an avalanche leads to the damming of a river, then flooding may also occur.

One of the major problems with avalanches in the Alps is the large number which occur. Every winter, tens of thousands affect the mountain areas of Switzerland, Austria, and Italy, while the prediction of exactly when and where they are going to occur is almost impossible. They remain unpredictable despite the constant check made on the snowfields by the Avalanche Research Centre at Davos in Switzerland.

Figure 7.26 shows the four main types of avalanche. The first type is the Loose Snow Avalanche where snow and ice crystals start to move down a slope from a single point. The Slab Avalanche occurs when a whole wall of ice gives way and crashes into the valley. If the avalanche occurs on a wide, open slope then the snow and ice can fall freely as an Unconfined Avalanche. If the ice is concentrated in a gully on the mountainside a Confined Avalanche may take place.

All of these types will be accompanied by strong gusts of wind produced by the force of the falling ice.

Avalanches are usually triggered by a series of vibrations. Earth tremors such as those felt in an earthquake can easily dislodge large amounts of snow. Much smaller shocks may also start avalanches — even a tree falling, or the rumble of trains along their tracks. Once started, the moving mass of ice and snow grows quickly as more is collected further down slope.

One of the largest avalanches to affect Switzerland happened in February 1951. Blizzards and heavy snowfalls had affected the area around the village of Airolo for three weeks in January. The snowpack had built up steadily on the slopes above the village, and early in February, 200 people were evacuated because of the increasing danger from avalanches. Eventually the snow stopped and the villagers returned on 10 February. The next day there was a small avalanche on one side of the valley. People were again evacuated, although some ignored the warning and stayed in the village. Then, on 12 February an enormous avalanche of 500 000 tonnes of wet snow descended from the Vallaxia ravine on to the village below. Ten people were killed and 29 buildings were destroyed. This was only one of many avalanches in the Alps in the winter of 1950–51. During this time, 700 people were killed and 2500 buildings were destroyed.

Protection from avalanches

The most effective way to protect areas against avalanches is to make accumulated snow more stable. One simple way is to plant trees as they help to keep snow in place. Trees also slow down avalanches once they have started and good forest cover can reduce avalanche damage by 40–50%. Other methods which are used involve the building of cut-and-fill terraces, wooden snow rakes and snow bridges, Figure 7.27. All of these methods help to stop snow from moving down hill. Snow bridges, in particular, aim to break up the ice and snow as it slides and thus reduce the amount of destruction it causes.

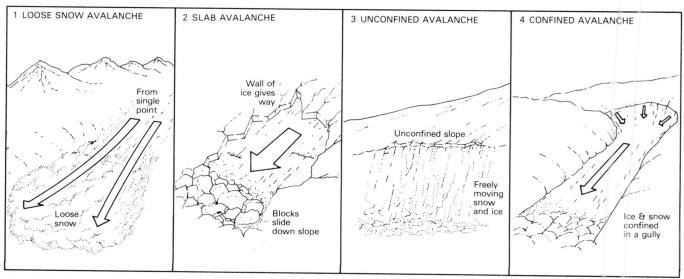

Figure 7.26   Four types of avalanche

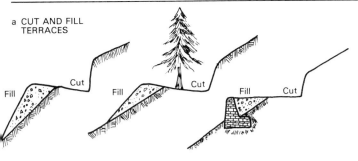

a CUT AND FILL TERRACES

Fill Cut Fill Cut Fill Cut

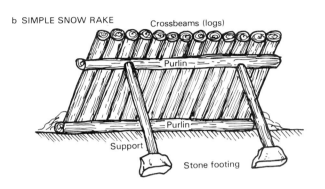

b SIMPLE SNOW RAKE

Crossbeams (logs)

Purlin

Purlin

Support

Stone footing

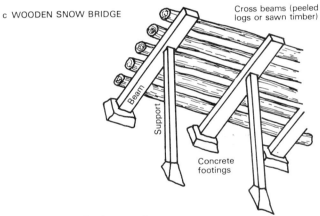

c WOODEN SNOW BRIDGE

Cross beams (peeled logs or sawn timber)

Beam

Support

Concrete footings

Figure 7.27   Avalanche protection

Complete prevention of avalanches is usually impossible, but it may be possible in many places to protect against the worst effects of those that do occur. Shelters may be built over roads in areas where avalanches are frequent. These have been used in the Gothard, Simplon and Grand St Bernard Passes in the Alps in an attempt to keep the roads open throughout the year. Diverting the flow of an avalanche is sometimes attempted. In some cases explosives are used to produce small controlled falls in order to prevent a large catastrophic avalanche later. However, explosives are a hazard themselves. The safest plan is to avoid areas at risk. The Swiss are also good at predicting avalanches. Predictions are part of a nation-wide plan for the evacuation of areas in danger and the forced closure of roads and railways if an avalanche is forecast. If a disaster does occur, skilled rescue teams, helicopters, electronic probes and the famous St Bernard dogs are all immediately available to rescue the unlucky victims.

▶ With the aid of diagrams, describe how avalanches occur. Attempt to explain the methods which can be used to help protect people from the worst effects of avalanches.

The Mam Tor landslip, Derbyshire

Overlooking the small Peak District village of Castleton in Derbyshire stands Mam Tor. This hill is very unstable and so many landslips have occurred there, that it is known as 'the shivering mountain'. The most recent landslip swept away the main road (A625) between Chapel-en-le-Frith and Castleton (Figure 7.29).

The mountain is made of thin beds of sandstones and shales known as the Mam Tor beds. These are slowly collapsing as the Edale Shales, which lie beneath them, are giving way. Small springs flow out at the base of Mam Tor and these are making the problem much worse by removing landslip material. Gradually the slope is steepened by this erosion and another mass of rock comes thundering down into the valley. During the last landslip, five million tonnes of broken clay, silt and shale fell from Mam Tor.

Figure 7.28   The Mam Tor landslip

The main issue now facing local planners concerns the replacement of the road lost in the landslip. Several options have been put forward. Figure 7.29 shows the original route at the base of Mam Tor and the surrounding area that will be affected by any new road scheme. Three possible routes are:

1 **Rebuilding the original road.** This road would follow the exact route of the original road at the foot of Mam Tor. It would cost £475 000 to rebuild. The main disadvantage is that this route would be in the line of future landslips.

2 **The limestone route.** This route is so named because it is built mainly on the limestone. It would leave the A625 road south of Treak Cliff Cavern and climb northwards along the edge of Treak Cliff on a shelf cut into the hillside. It would turn south at the Odin mine, clear of the landslip. From here, it would climb past the Blue John mine on a route running parallel to the original road in a cutting eight metres deep. The existing road would be rejoined west of the B6061 road to Sparrowpit. The cost would be £1.5 million.

3 **The Winnats Pass route.** This route leaves the existing A625 road approximately west of Castleton and follows the minor road past Speedwell Cavern to the Mam Tor road. The road at the top of the Pass would have to be completely realigned to provide a good link with the main road. The character of the Winnats Pass, a local beauty spot, would be changed. The cost would be £555 000.

▶ 1 On a copy of Figure 7.29 mark on the three proposed routes for the new road using the information in the text.

2 Draw up a list of the advantages and disadvantages of the three proposed routes.

3 Which route do you think the following people would favour?
  i The planners of the local county council.
  ii An environmental pressure group.
  iii The owner of Treak Cliff cavern.
Explain clearly the reasons for your answers.

Figure 7.29   Mam Tor and surrounding area

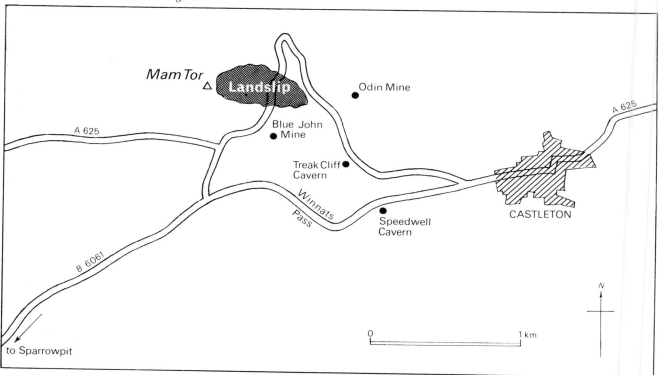

Key Points: The Restless Earth

- The dangers from natural hazards are becoming increasingly severe as the earth's population grows and people are forced to live in more vulnerable places.

- Natural hazards are largely unpredictable and there is no reliable way to prevent them.

- Protection against hazards depends upon the accurate prediction of when and where they will occur. This remains a difficult task.

- In some cases human activity can increase the chance of a natural hazard causing a disaster. This is especially true of landslides.

- Coping with natural hazards is hindered by people's apparent reluctance, or inability, to move to less hazardous areas.

- The problems caused by natural hazards are more severe in developing countries where less money is available to help cope with the after-effects of a disaster.

Chapter 8 CLIMATIC HAZARDS

8.1 Storms

At any one moment, 1600 storms are producing hazardous weather somewhere on the earth's surface. With howling winds, pouring rain and, in some, cases, thunder and lightning, storms are spectacular events. Admiral Beaufort, who devised the Beaufort Scale of Wind Force, described a storm as a wind blowing at about 30 m/s, or Force 11. On land, such a wind produces widespread damage to trees and buildings. Storms are therefore examples of natural hazards.

Storms affect people in many ways. High winds ruin crops and may be a hazard to transport, with high-sided lorries and buses being blown over on exposed stretches of road. Aircraft will have difficulty in landing and taking-off safely, and ships may capsize. Buildings might have their roofs and windows damaged. In addition to the direct effects of the wind, heavy rain can cause damage by battering crops or by causing severe flooding. Lightning is another hazard. It may start fires and in bad storms it may kill animals and human beings. The fire which destroyed part of the roof of York Minster in July 1984 was started by lightning.

There are several different types of storm. Some are very violent and last for several days, while others may be less fierce. Their effects may be widespread or highly localised, possibly confined to a narrow track across the land. In Britain we do not have many excessively severe storms, although as you will see later, they can cause a great many difficulties. In other parts of the world, such as the hurricane coast of the USA, storm damage is much more frequent.

Types of storm

Thunderstorms

The most common type of storm to cause damage in Britain is the thunderstorm. These are caused by very powerful up-currents of warm air which produce towering black clouds. Single thunderstorms affect relatively small areas of one or two square kilometres and bring lightning, thunder and heavy rain, often with hail.

Tornadoes

Tornadoes are very destructive weather systems which affect a narrower area than thunderstorms. They are formed over land by hot air rising rapidly and they possess enormous power. Above the ground there is normally a large swirling cloud which surrounds a calm centre. Strong winds spin violently around the centre and can cause a great deal of damage. Tornadoes are common on the Great Plains of the United States where they are a major natural hazard. They do occur in Britain in late summer and have been known to cause extensive damage to property. Figure 8.1 shows a photograph of a tornado which affected part of the state of Minnesota in June 1968. Notice the tube of cloud above the centre of the storm. This particular tornado killed nine people, injured fifteen others and caused $3 million worth of damage.

Figure 8.1   Tornado in Jasper, Minnesota

Tropical revolving storms

Tropical revolving storms are called by different names depending on where they occur. They are common near Japan where they are called TYPHOONS. In the Caribbean they are known as HURRICANES, in the Indian Ocean as CYCLONES, and in the north of Australia as WILLY-WILLIES. Unlike tornadoes they develop over the sea. Warm moist air rises to form large spinning systems several hundred kilometres across, with strong winds and thick clouds. The winds may reach 200 km/h and they have the power to destroy anything in their path. Tropical storms usually begin near the equator, and then move north or south along well defined routeways known as TRACKS. When they reach large areas of land they soon die away because the supply of energy from the condensation of the warm, moist air is cut off. Over small islands damage can be particularly severe because there is not enough land to cut off the supply of moisture from the ocean.

The effects of these storms can be catastrophic if they should strike a densely populated area which is not properly prepared. One of the greatest disasters of all time occurred in Bangladesh in November, 1970. A storm hit the coast of the country overnight and caused the high tide to rise to a level 7 m above normal. By morning, 225 000 people were dead, 280 000 cattle had been swept away and £40 million worth of ripening crops was destroyed. It was estimated that 85% of the families in the area had their homes severely damaged or destroyed by the cyclone. Six hundred thousand people were left homeless. The total cost of such a disaster is impossible to assess. For many months Bangladesh relied on outside relief agencies. The World Bank provided a loan of £115 million for rebuilding purposes.

What can be done?

Accurate forecasting is the key to preventing excessive storm damage and loss of life. Very little can be done to stop storms from occurring, although in some countries attempts have been made using CLOUD SEEDING. Clouds are 'seeded' with chemicals such as silver iodide sprayed from an aircraft. If all goes well, water droplets form around the chemical particles and later fall as rain. Cloud seeding can help to spread rainfall over a wider area and thus reduce the likelihood of a damaging downpour occurring in a small area. This work is still in its early stages, and as yet there are few examples of cloud seeding being used effectively for storm control.

Forecasting and issuing storm warnings is by far the most common policy. In Britain the Meteorological Office transmits regular shipping forecasts on the radio. If a storm is likely to develop near the British Isles, then gale or storm warnings are given. These reports include information on the position of the storm and on the direction and strength of the wind. In Australia the Bureau of Meteorology has set up a Tropical Cyclone Warning System with centres at Brisbane, Darwin and Perth. When a tropical cyclone

seems likely to occur the Bureau issues a 'Tropical Advisory' to tell the general public. If the tropical storm moves within 800 km of the Australian coast, then a flash warning is given on television, by radio and in the newspapers. A 'cyclone warning' indicates that the storm is very close and a final announcement is made when the danger has passed. This policy of keeping people informed is very valuable and helps to reduce the loss of life and damage caused by such storms.

Another common response to cyclones is to build storm proof buildings. Both the United States and the Australian authorities have tried to improve building designs. The main problems come from poor foundations and roofs which can easily be blown away. Improvements include firmer foundations, securing the frame of houses to the ground, and bolting on the roof.

In Bangladesh the government has built large banks of earth to stop tidal floods moving inland. The country now has a better forecasting and warning system to tell people of an approaching storm. There are also plans to evacuate people who live in the paths of approaching storms.

> 1 Name three types of storm which can cause damage.
> 2 List the main problems that severe storms can cause.
> 3 Give four examples of the ways in which countries can protect themselves against storms.

Storms at home

One of the main causes of storms over the British Isles is the passage of depressions. Depressions are areas of low atmospheric pressure which form along the PO-LAR FRONT. Warm air from the tropics meets cold air from polar regions at this front. A wave in the atmosphere may develop, and if it does, pressure will fall as the warm air rises up above the cold air. Eventually the depression becomes circular in shape as warm air wedges further into the cold to create a warm sector and a warm front. At the same time cold air moving southwards forms a cold front behind the warm sector, as Figure 8.2 shows.

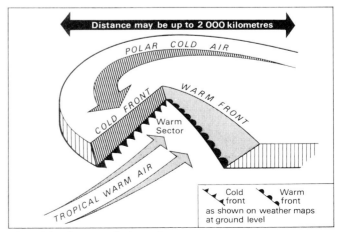

Figure 8.2   Structure of a depression

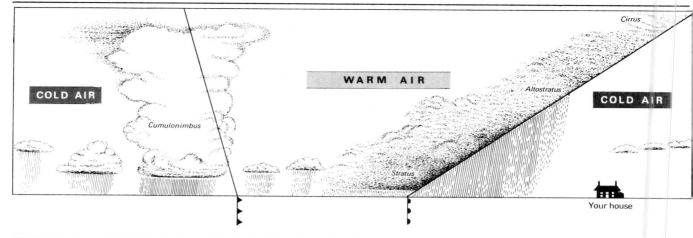

F	E	D	C	B	A
Wind moderates. Scattered shower clouds. Pressure rises.	At cold front: heavy rain often with hail and thunder; temperature falls; pressure begins to rise wind veers	Generally dull. Low stratus clouds with some drizzle.	At warm front: pressure steadies; temperature rises.	Pressure falls. Cloud layer thickens. Rain begins to fall	Weather fine. Wind light at first but increases in strength and backs. High cirrus cloud. Pressure begins to fall.

Figure 8.3   Weather through a depression

Depressions produce a particular pattern of weather. Figure 8.3 shows a cross-section through a typical depression together with the weather that will be experienced as it passes over an area.

▶ Using the information in Figure 8.3, describe the sequence of weather that would occur as a depression passed over your house. The depression in the diagram is moving from west to east.

In the year from August 1980 to July 1981, the Worthing area of West Sussex in southern England experienced four very deep depressions. These produced very severe storms which disrupted the normal life of people in the Worthing locality. During one day of stormy weather the rainfall was the highest ever recorded, with over 100 mm being measured in some places. Storms of this size are likely to occur only once in every 1000 years, but the local people were alerted to the dangers of flooding in the area.

Figure 8.4   Storm damage in the Horsham area, April 1981

The four storms

1 20–21 September, 1980

Heavy rain fell during the evening and night over the town of Worthing. The heaviest rainfall occurred between 7 p.m. and 11.30 p.m. and in Broadwater, a district in north-east Worthing, 112 mm was recorded. The storm was produced by a cold front associated with a depression in the Bay of Biscay.

The rainfall was concentrated over a very small area. Brighton, 16 km away, recorded only 7 mm of rain at the same time. The effects of this storm were not particularly severe because the ground was very dry after the summer. Some roads and 12 houses near Ferring, to the west, were flooded.

2 10–11 October, 1980

The second storm produced more widespread rain in Sussex. Worthing again suffered the highest rainfall totals with 133.3 mm being recorded. The storm lasted for 20 hours and was caused by a depression and its fronts moving across southern England towards France.

The effects of this storm were more severe because the ground was already very wet from the first storm. Flooding was extensive and more damage occurred. Several industrial premises in the Ferring district were flooded.

3 13–14 April, 1981

The third storm followed the same pattern as those in September and October. Heavy falls of rain occurred in Worthing (50 mm), and 90.9 mm fell in the Horsham area 30 km to the north. The depression responsible was centred over southern England and the rain continued for about 8½ hours. Many houses and roads in the Worthing and Horsham areas were once again flooded and transport was severely disrupted. The photograph in Figure 8.4 shows some of the effects of this storm.

4 1–2 June, 1981

Finally on 1 and 2 June 1981, a storm accompanied by thunder and lightning struck Worthing. It only lasted for 3½ hours but during this time 67.7 mm of rain fell at Findon, a few kilometres to the north of Worthing town centre. The rainfall was so intense that the automatic rain recorders in the area failed. Another cold front passing over the region caused this storm, which again produced bad flooding in many areas of West Sussex.

The effects of these storms proved to be very costly in terms of damage to roads and houses. Many people became aware of the flood hazard in the Worthing and Horsham areas, and drainage schemes along roads have since been improved. It is now hoped that these improvements will minimise the effects of heavy rainfall in future storms.

▶ 1 Figure 8.5 shows a map of the Sussex area. Make a copy of the map and, using an atlas, name and label the following places: Horsham, Worthing, Brighton, Bognor Regis.

2 Mark with a red cross the places which suffered the highest rainfall during each of the four storms.

3 Why were the effects of the later storms much worse than those of the first storm?

4 Draw a histogram to show the maximum total rainfall recorded for each of the four storms.

5 Figure 8.6 describes the effects of a storm in another part of England. What local issues were created by this storm?

Figure 8.5 Sussex

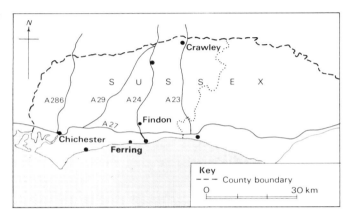

Figure 8.6 Storms — the local issues

Post mortem on big floods

THE flash floods which hit Fleet and Yateley last month have prompted councillors to call for urgent action to make sure it does not happen again.

New drainage schemes, tighter building regulations and education of the public on how to cope with flooding were some of the points raised at a post mortem debate by Hart Council.

A list has been compiled of areas which were swamped after a freak rain storm on July 23.

In Yateley alone 160 homes and shops were flooded. In some cases foul drains overflowed and sewage merged with the surface water.

Council staff helped many residents by disinfecting where sewage had overflowed, removing debris swept into gardens and collecting flood-damaged furnishings.

CONCERN

Discussing a report on the flooding Hart's health committee praised staff for their work on the night of the floods and the following day.

Coun. John Chadwick, the chairman, said: "This is an item about which there is a great deal of concern and will be continuing concern, but I think it should be discussed at length by the sewerage systems working party."

It would be wrong for the information in the report to cloud the issue of normal flooding, said Coun. John Stocks.

Coun. Alec Ecclestone thought some of the flooding could have been lessened if proper road sweeping had been done by Hampshire County Council.

"Every grid in Victoria Road was blocked by pine needles and cones. Once they were cleared the water went within 10 minutes," he said.

SHOCKED

Many points were brought up by the events of July 23, said Coun. Adrian Collett.

"The urgency is renewed for a number of drainage schemes to be done. Many people that evening said it was the third or fourth time they had been flooded and I doubt that we are taking enough action.

"It shocked me to see how many houses were built below road level. This is something we should look at in future with building regulations.

"Water was coming down in rivers from Blackbushe Airport and flooding the lower areas. Perhaps the water could be diverted with a storm culvert going round the back of Yateley to the River Blackwater."

Coun. Collett believed councillors should look at "the long-term possibility" of Hart having responsibility for highways as well as other surface water drainage, so that it would all come under one authority.

"We need to investigate ways of stopping the sewers overflowing and educate people not to lift the sewage manholes to drain away water from their gardens as this makes sewage flood into other people's houses on lower ground," he added.

SWAMPED

Coun. Charles Lynch said: "It is nothing new that people in Yateley are swamped — we cannot allow this to continue."

Coun. Stocks said that in many cases natural water courses had been changed by development.

Officials will now identify which areas had recurrent flooding problems and see which council had responsibility for them.

Tornadoes in the UK

Tornadoes are usually thought of as weather systems which are not found in the British Isles. Few British people would name tornadoes as a hazard to their way of life. However, they are in fact quite common. Four hundred tornadoes have occurred in Britain since 1960, i.e. about 60 each year. This is a small number compared with the United States where over 1000 tornadoes are reported each year. Yet, the tornadoes in Britain are extremely fierce and destructive.

The map in Figure 8.7 shows the distribution of tornadoes affecting Britain in 1974. In that year, 59 tornadoes were reported. Most tornadoes occur in July and August and form in the afternoons when the hot summer sun has heated the land sufficiently. In some cases, they are triggered by farmers burning stubble in their fields. Tornadoes formed in this way are given the name 'fire devils' and they have become more frequent as stubble burning has increased. Finally, tornadoes in Britain may also begin if depressions deepen with unusual rapidity.

Whatever their cause, all tornadoes have one thing in common — they destroy property in their path. One example occurred in Lincolnshire on 8 October, 1977. It moved along a line between Grantham and Newark and cut a 15 m wide path through the countryside. Over 60 houses and farms were demolished. Trees were broken by the strong winds and doors and walls were bent. A garden shed was carried 70 m above the tops of houses and a 35 seater bus weighing 5.6 tonnes was lifted off the ground!

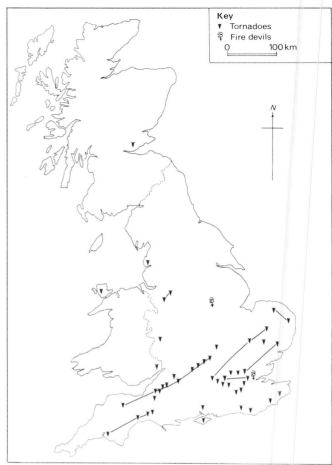

Figure 8.7   *The distribution of tornadoes and fire devils in the UK, 1974*

Figure 8.8   *Damage caused by the Chichester fire devil, September 1978*

When tornadoes pass over water they tend to suck it into the air forming a waterspout. In violent storms, small frogs, fish and other animals may be drawn into the cloud. They will eventually fall back to the ground in the rain. This effect probably explains the origin of the expression, 'raining cats and dogs'!

Fire devils can also cause great devastation. On 11 September 1978, one such storm swept through part of the Sussex countryside near Chichester. It was triggered by two stubble fires meeting. The ash and smoke clouds of the storm destroyed four farm buildings and caused over £100 000 damage. Figure 8.8 shows firemen putting out a blaze caused by the Chichester fire devil.

▶ Imagine that you have been warned that a tornado is going to hit your home town within the next six hours. Write an account of the preparations you made before the storm arrived and what happens to you during the tornado.

Typhoon Hope strikes Hong Kong

Hong Kong is a small territory on the south-east coast of China consisting of a large number of islands and part of the mainland. It is a major industrial and trading centre for much of South-east Asia. With a population of over four million in an area of 1018 km², it has one of the highest population densities in the world (3939/km²). Its location at 22°N 114°E means that it is in a region often affected by typhoons and these need to be prepared for and, if possible, predicted.

On 2 August 1979, a severe typhoon, code-named Hope, passed over the colony at a speed of up to 14 m/s. Windspeeds averaged 54 m/s with gusts of up to 68 m/s and between 1 p.m. and 4 p.m., the wind never fell below 45 m/s. Between 2 p.m. and 3 p.m., 82.1 mm of rain fell, and over the three days that Hong Kong was affected by the typhoon, 2874 mm of rain occurred. At one point during the peak of the storm, rain was falling at a rate of 251 mm/h — an enormous rate if you remember that London's rainfall is well under 1000 mm per year!

The effects of the storm were considerable. Twelve people were killed and 260 were injured, largely from the damage caused to buildings by the wind. In the harbour the water level rose over 3 m above normal as a result of the wind ponding up the sea, and 18 large ships were set adrift, causing much damage. The cost of the damage ran into many millions of pounds. Even so, the storm's impact was not as bad as it might have been. Several precautions had been taken:

● The storm had been tracked by weather observers for several days before reaching Hong Kong. Radar, satellite photographs, aircraft flights and weather reports from other islands had allowed its precise track to be predicted. Residents had been warned of its arrival and had boarded up buildings and taken other precautions.

● It passed over Hong Kong very rapidly and so the high wind speeds and intense rainfall were not experienced for too long.

● The peak of the storm coincided with low tide and so there was little flooding despite the storm surge it produced.

● Conditions were at their worst during daylight which helped the population to cope more easily with the problems they faced.

▶ With the aid of an atlas draw a sketch map to show the location of Hong Kong.
  1 Why would the impact of a typhoon be potentially much greater in Hong Kong than in most places along the south-east coast of China?
  2 Figure 8.9 shows a series of graphs of the weather conditions in Hong Kong during the passage of the typhoon.
    i When did the storm centre pass over Hong Kong?
    ii Describe the conditions experienced during the storm.
    iii Which aspect of the storm would be the most serious hazard for residents in Hong Kong?

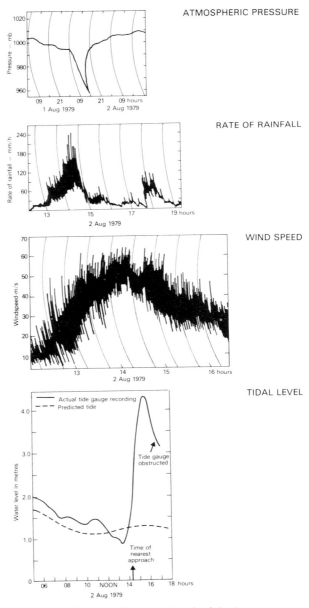

Figure 8.9   The effects of Typhoon Hope (local time) ·

8.2 The Variable Weather

We are all familiar with the unpredictability of the weather. In Britain, this variability has made it an important part of everyday conversation, and we expect large changes from day to day and even from hour to hour. Not all countries have such variable conditions, but even in places with more uniform climates, rapid changes can occur. Intense rainstorms in the desert can cause flooding and damage, and even in the apparently constant hot and wet tropical climates marked day to day changes are common. Figure 8.10 shows the daily weather pattern at San Juan in Puerto Rico over the period of July to October 1969 and the daily variations are very clear.

Year to year differences are also important. The hot, dry summers of 1976 and 1984 in Britain contrast greatly with the cool, wet summer of 1968, and the severe winters of 1962–63 and 1981–82 remain in many people's memories for a long time. Even looking at a longer time scale, over several decades or even centuries perhaps, extreme weather may be noted in comparison with other periods. For example, from the beginning of the 16th century to the end of the 18th century in Britain was a period of very cold winters and cool summers. It has been called the Little Ice Age.

Two key questions arise from these changes. They are: What effect does the variability of weather have upon people? and How can people best cope with the variability of the weather and save themselves from its worst effects?

▶ Look at the weather pattern shown in Figure 8.10.
  1 Add up the number of days on which:
     i   Rain fell.
     ii Rainfall was higher than 5 mm.
     iii Rainfall was higher than 15 mm.
  2 Show these figures as percentages of the total number of days in the diagram.

▶ 3 What effect might the variability of the weather have on:
     i Farmers in Puerto Rico.
     ii Office workers in the capital San Juan.
Figure 8.11 shows some of the years with extreme weather conditions in Britain since 1920.
  4 For each type of extreme weather, work out the average length of time between its occurrences.
  5 How many years had one or more extreme season over the period 1921–85?
  6 How often does it seem that we can expect 'bad' seasons and 'good' seasons?
  7 For each extreme type of season, calculate how many more times we can expect it to occur before the year AD 2000.
  8 For each type of extreme weather describe the effect it might have upon:
     arable farmers, clothes manufacturers, ice cream companies, building firms, holiday tour companies, water supply companies.

Poor Summers (Much cooler and wetter than the average)	Good Summers (Much warmer and drier than the average)	Severe Winters (Much colder and with more snow than average)
1927	1921	1940
1931	1933	1942
1936	1940	1947
1938	1955	1963
1944	1959	1979
1946	1975	1982
1954	1976	1985
1956	1983	
1957	1984	
1958		
1965		
1968		
1977		

Figure 8.11   Years with extreme weather conditions in Britain since 1920

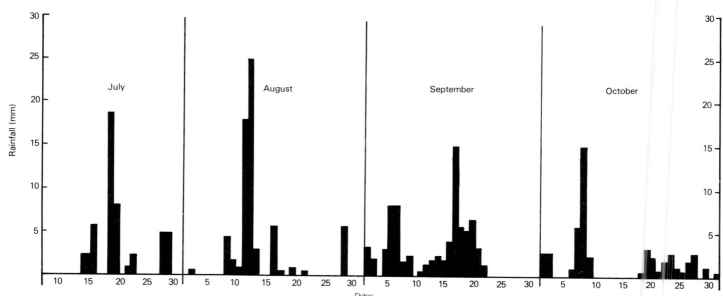

Figure 8.10   Rainfall in Puerto Rico, July to October

The causes

Many theories have been put forward to explain short-term variations in the weather. Daily changes can be explained simply by thinking of the normal processes of the atmosphere. In Britain, for example, depressions may pass over the country bringing rainy periods. On the other hand, high pressure anticyclones may last for several days bringing a spell of fine weather. Longer-term variations are less easily explained. Below are some possible suggestions.

Volcanic dust

When volcanoes erupt they throw large amounts of dust into the atmosphere. This dust reduces the amount of sunlight reaching the earth's surface and temperatures fall. Such a fall was recorded after the eruption of Mount Spurr in Alaska in 1953. The eruption of El Chichon (Mexico) in 1982 was held responsible for the cool, wet spring of 1983 in Great Britain.

Sunspots

These are features of the sun's surface that consist of cooler, darker patches. When there are many sunspots the heat received from the sun falls slightly. The number of sunspots varies from a high number to a low number and back to a high number every 11 years on average. This seems to fit in with an 11 year cycle in our weather on earth. Other cycles of 22, 44, and 88 years have been noticed. The good summers of 1975 and 1976 in western Europe occurred when there were few sunspots, while the harsher winters of the early 1980s happened when there were rather more.

Sea surface temperatures (S.S.T's)

The temperature of the sea surface can vary as a result of many influences. When it falls or rises by between 1 and 3°C in the Pacific Ocean, a complicated chain of events can cause the climate elsewhere in the world to vary. The droughts of 1983 in Australia and Southern Africa, and heavy storms in California (USA) could all be traced to a very high sea temperature in the central Pacific. But scientists do not yet understand the exact nature of the connection.

People

In the last two centuries people have influenced the weather in many ways. By filtering out sunlight, increased dust in the atmosphere and chemical pollution from industry may have caused temperatures to fall by 1°C. On the other hand, large amounts of carbon dioxide from the burning of coal and oil are thought to have increased the temperature of the atmosphere by 1°C. Much remains to be understood. The effect of clearing forests on the amount of oxygen in the atmosphere is not yet known, but it does seem certain that human activity will continue to have an important part to play in influencing the variability of the weather.

The effects

Variations in weather affect most of us in some way. Daily changes influence the clothing we wear, the food we eat, or our plans for spare time. Seasonal extremes might affect enjoyment of our summer holiday or the size of the winter gas bill. For many people, however, the changes can be more significant, and we shall look here at two examples – farming and the building industry.

Farming

Farming is very much affected by variations in weather. Severe storms damage crops, spells of unsuitable weather can prevent ploughing or harvesting, and late frosts can damage fruit and vegetables. Even ideal conditions for the crop may not help a farmer, for if all farmers produce large quantities of a particular crop they will have to store it before it can be sold!

The year 1983 illustrates very well the problems British farmers can face. The first few months of the year were cooler than usual and extremely wet. March and April had over twice as much rainfall as in an average year and this caused two problems. Cattle that had been kept indoors all winter could not be turned out into the fields and farmers had to spend large amounts of money on cattle feed. Those animals that were turned out damaged the grass by trampling it into the mud. Secondly, the wet soils meant that machinery could not be used on the fields and cereal crops and potatoes were not planted as early as usual. As a result there was a shortage of many types of vegetables in the autumn, and farmers lost money.

The summer was very different. July, August and September were hot and dry, with many days when temperatures rose above 32°C. Lack of water was now the problem, and irrigation had to be used. The farmers benefitted, however, from the early ripening of their crops which allowed prompt harvesting — providing they had managed to plant sufficiently early in the spring!

The building industry

Building is another industry that is greatly affected by the weather. Rainy days at any time of the year can stop all construction and in the winter months there may be many weeks when all work ceases. The number of 'lost days' varies from year to year, but leads on average to 3.5% of production being lost — 10 days per year. During severe winters building workers and companies lose a lot of time and money from stoppages, and 30000 to 50000 men are laid off each year for the winter months. In 1963, which included the bad winter of 1962–63, over 25% of building time was lost with 160000 workers laid off. In 1975, with its very mild winter months, only 1.5% of building time was lost.

Managing the weather

The variations in weather affect us very much, but what can we do to keep their impact to a low level? There are three possible ways of facing this challenge:

● Trying to change the weather to prevent damaging events.
● Trying to forecast the weather so that we can take action to protect ourselves.
● Protecting ourselves from the worst the weather can bring.

Changing the weather

People are still unable to alter the weather, even with modern technology. The working of the atmosphere is so complex, and its power so great, that human efforts make little impact on it. But some attempts have been made and one of the main lines of research has been cloud seeding. Triggering off the rain making process could be useful in very dry areas, or during very dry years. In the Ukraine (USSR), experiments over 3 million ha of land suggest that cloud seeding could produce 1% more rain in dry years, but many similar experiments in Australia show no great evidence of success. Only clouds already in existence can be 'persuaded' to give rain, and so cloudless areas cannot benefit. There is also a further risk. Rain being made to fall in one area might create a drought in another, or even add extra rain to already wet areas if unexpected winds blow up.

Attempts at reducing the seriousness of storms is another line of approach. The damage done by hailstorms can be very great and some European countries have taken steps to lessen their effects. In Italy, for example farmers have fired rockets containing gunpowder into clouds. The shock of the explosion breaks up the ice that makes hail. On a larger scale, attempts have been made in the Caribbean to reduce the force of hurricanes by again, cloud seeding. In August 1969, Hurricane Debbie was seeded as part of the United States 'Project Stormfury', and wind speeds dropped from 185 km/h to 155 km/h in six hours. Later experiments with other hurricanes seemed to have had little effect. Some Caribbean island governments have complained however, that while attempts to reduce the power of hurricanes might save lives, they may also reduce the rainfall that is so important to farming.

Predicting the weather

If we cannot change the weather, then we must try to predict it and take measures to avoid its worst effects. Figure 8.12 shows the ways in which weather forecasts can be helpful to different groups of people.

In each case, knowledge of the impending weather can mean that damage may be prevented and lives saved. Prediction of thunderstorms can cut the amount of damage by 20% because people can take measures to protect crops, buildings and themselves. Accurate forecasting of hurricane tracks would cut the cost of damage in the United States of America by 60% each year.

▶ Find out from your class:
  i how many people have seen, heard or read a weather forecast in the last week,
  ii the source of the weather forecast they used,
  iii how many make a point of seeing or listening to weather forecasts regularly,
  iv how many change or make plans according to what the forecast has to say,
  v how accurate they believe the forecasts to be.

Weather forecasting is a very difficult activity. Modern forecasts involve the use of thousands of thermometers, rain gauges and other more complicated pieces of equipment around the world. They also make use of satellites, computers and telecommunications. Figure 8.13 shows how forecasts in the United Kingdom are made by the Meteorological Office.

Stage 1

Information is collected about the present weather from many sources. i) Several hundred ground weather stations and weather ships at sea take readings every six hours of temperature, rainfall, air pressure, wind speed and direction, and many other aspects of the weather. These readings are transmitted to the Meteorological Office at Bracknell in England where they are stored in computers. ii) Radio-sonde balloons take instruments high into the atmosphere to make readings at different levels above the ground. The readings are sent back to earth by radio transmitter. iii) Geostationary weather satellites supply a lot of information. These satellites orbit at a fixed point above the surface of the earth. They take regular

Figure 8.12 The use of weather forecasts

Activity	Impact of Weather Variation	Use of Short-Term Forecasts (48 hours or less)	Use of Long-Term Forecasts (Up to one month)
Farming	2	Planning jobs each day e.g. frost protection	Timing sowing and harvesting
Air transport	2	Avoiding bad weather e.g. fog, thunderstorms	
Shipping	3	Route planning to avoid worst weather	Forecasting ice cover on seas and lakes
Road transport	3	Salting and gritting roads	Planning road repairs
Water resource management	4	Using dams and sluices to control flooding	Planning reservoir levels
General public	3	Choosing clothes, food leisure activities	Planning social and sports events or holidays

1 = Great Impact   6 = No Impact

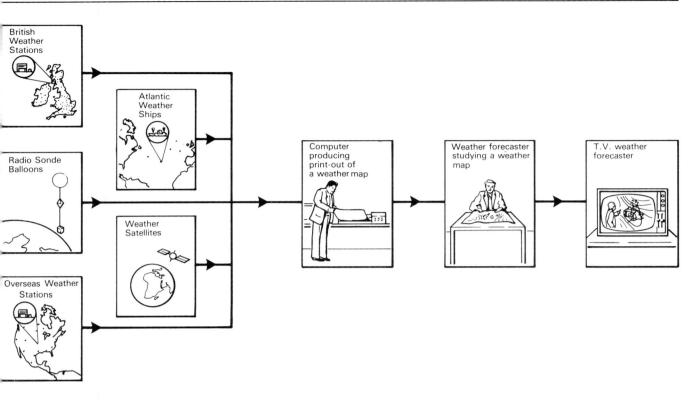

Figure 8.13   Information for weather forecasting

photographs of cloud movements, measure temperatures on the earth's surface and throughout the atmosphere and transmit the information back to earth. Today the whole surface of the earth is observed by a number of weather satellites positioned at 36 000 km above the equator. An example is the European satellite, Meteosat.   iv) International information. In 1950 the World Meteorological Organisation was set up by the United Nations, with its base in Geneva, to help countries exchange weather information. It is an important service because weather conditions in one country may move to neighbouring countries or have an effect upon the weather further away.

Stage 2
When the information has been collected, a complicated computer program constructs maps of the present weather around the world and then makes predictions of the weather situation a few hours ahead. To produce a weather map for the coming 24 hours takes 10^{10} mathematical calculations, so very powerful computers are needed. The predictions are based on knowledge of how the atmosphere works and changes.

Stage 3
A weather forecaster studies the present maps and predictions and, using his own skill and judgement, produces a forecast that can be published or broadcast on television and radio.

Two types of forecast are made. Short-term forecasts predict the weather for the next 48 hours or so, and are the type with which most of us are familiar. They are usually about 85% accurate. Long-term forecasts are less reliable, but give a general idea of the weather that might be expected over the next month or so.

As yet it is not possible for forecasts to be made for whole seasons or years, so the variability of weather on this scale is something we can do little to predict. All that can be done is to calculate how frequently extremes of weather might occur.

Learning to live with the weather

If we cannot control the weather, we must take steps to keep its less desirable effects to a minimum. There are many ways in which people have tried to do this, and here we can look at a few examples.

The general public
Perhaps the simplest way of avoiding the weather's variability is by living and working in buildings with heating and air conditioning. Rain and snow can largely be avoided and temperatures can be kept at the required level. Even when we have to go outside we can cope with extremes. Snowploughs, grit and salt can be used on the roads in icy weather, drains remove rainfall very rapidly, and by choosing suitable clothing we can survive most types of bad weather. Most countries have adapted their way of life and culture (food, clothing and buildings) to the short-term variations in climate they are likely to experience. Weather forecasts allow preparations to be made — and many people buy insurance against damage from extreme weather events.

Farming

Farmers are directly affected by variable weather. Climatic influences are very important to them, and the need to protect their crops and animals against extremes is usually urgent. Two familiar approaches are the use of irrigation to cope with dry weather, and drainage systems for very wet weather. Figure 8.14 shows how frequently irrigation is needed in different parts of England and Wales.

> 1 Which parts of England and Wales seem to need irrigation most often?
> 2 Which parts seem to need irrigation least?
> 3 Look at an atlas map of rainfall in Britain and then try to explain your answers to questions 1 and 2.

Frost is another serious problem for many farmers, particularly if it occurs unexpectedly at an unusual time of year. In England, frosts in June or July are not entirely unknown, and they can cause severe damage, especially to market garden crops. To cope with the frost hazard, farmers use a variety of methods:

● Smoke Pots. Oil burners can be placed in orchards or amongst crops to heat the air and prevent frost. They are expensive to run, cause pollution, and only raise the temperature by 1 or 2°C.
● Wind Machines. These are huge fans that keep the air moving and help cold and warm air to mix. Only one machine is needed for every 2–6 ha but they are expensive to run.
● Coverage. Row crops (e.g. strawberries) can be protected from frost by covering them with plastic cloches or covers, or with a mulch of straw or hay. In California, young lettuce plants are individually capped with paper cones if there is a risk of frost.

Storm damage, through heavy rain or hail, is more difficult to protect against. One storm in the Dutch province of Zeeland in June 1954 caused £330 000 of damage in 15 minutes through strong winds and hail! Insurance is the only real answer to such a problem, but the cost of insurance premiums may result in farmers simply risking the damage and accepting any loss it causes them.

> 1 Describe some of the ways in which *either* farmers *or* members of the general public are affected by variability of the weather. Explain the methods they can use to protect themselves from its worst effects.
> 2 As you saw earlier in this chapter, the county of Sussex, in England, experienced four storms in 1981 in which there was very high rainfall. It was calculated that the average interval between storms of this size was 1000 years.
> i Try to explain why four such storms could occur in only one year.
> ii Why could the weather forecasters not predict that such storms would occur until 72 hours before each one actually arrived?
> iii What steps could local farmers take to protect themselves against such storms?

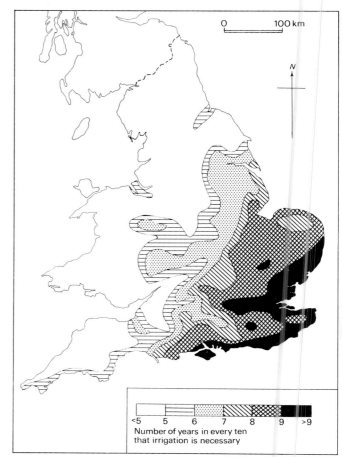

Figure 8.14   The need for irrigation in England and Wales

Heat drought and fire — Australia's variable climate

On Wednesday 16 February 1983, the worst drought in Australia this century caused the spread of huge bush fires in many parts of the states of Victoria and South Australia. These fires were caused by the extreme heat (over 40°C) setting fire to dry grass and trees. Sixty-eight people were killed, 2000 homes were destroyed and the equivalent of £167 million of damage was caused. Ten thousand people were involved in fighting the fires, the worst being around the towns of Cockatoo and Belgrave, near Melbourne, where 100 km/h winds fanned the flames and twenty-six people were killed. To help overcome the disaster the Australian government used troops as firefighters, and provided both care for the victims of the fire and temporary housing for those made homeless. Appeals to the public through television and radio raised the equivalent of over £1 million in three days.

By the middle of March the six-month drought was coming to an end — with floods. Worst affected were the dry interior parts of the country. At Alice Springs the Todd River flooded as a result of 150 mm of rain falling in 16 hours on 18 March. This quantity is 60% of the average annual rainfall in the area, and it caused the river to rise by 5 m. Roads and bridges were destroyed, sheep killed and all electricity to the town was cut off.

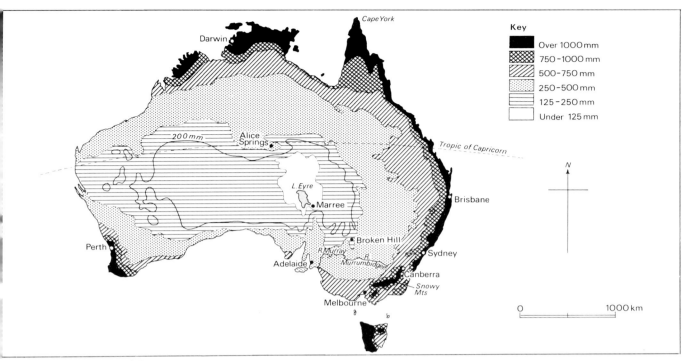

Figure 8.15   Australia's rainfall

Figure 8.17   Drought . . . and plenty – a reservoir near Broken Hill

Such variations of weather are not unusual in Australia. Figure 8.15 shows the average pattern of rainfall throughout the country. Very little of Australia receives more than 1000 mm of rainfall per year; 80% of Australia is said to be 'arid' or 'semi-arid' with less than 500 mm of rain. Added to these low figures, however, is the variability of rainfall from year to year. Figure 8.16 shows the rainfall pattern at Broken Hill, New South Wales, for the 20 years from 1954 to 1973.

The average rainfall for this period was 257 mm, but it varied from 83 mm to 481 mm. Variations such as this are very large, and where the average rainfall total is small anyway, variations on the low side can cause prolonged droughts. Australia has suffered drought somewhere in the continent in 32 out of the last 85 years. A serious drought occurs one year in every three and in this century, there were severe droughts in 1903, 1964–66 and 1982–83.

Year	Rainfall (mm)	Year	Rainfall (mm)
1954	279	1964	251
1955	446	1965	127
1956	376	1966	205
1957	164	1967	83
1958	323	1968	347
1959	137	1969	184
1960	230	1970	189
1961	251	1971	317
1962	319	1972	169
1963	258	1973	481

Figure 8.16   Rainfall at Broken Hill, New South Wales, 1954–1973

The effects of the droughts

Drought seriously affects Australia, for one million people live by farming in the dry areas. Fifty per cent of Australia's export income comes from farming. Crop failures, the death of sheep and cattle and the irrigation schemes cost the country $A40 million each year on average, and much more in severe years. The drought of 1964–66 cost $A1500 million and caused the loss of 20% of Australia's sheep and 30% of the country's wheat crop. The photographs in Figure 8.17 show the effect of drought on a reservoir near Broken Hill, N.S.W.

Surprisingly, drought can bring some benefits. Farmers in the areas not affected by drought may get a better price for their grain or livestock, while in the areas that are affected, the loss of sheep and cattle may allow the grass pastures to recover. Areas with regular problems also gain, for the government will provide money for irrigation schemes and send farming advisors to these areas. But, the real costs to many people remain high.

1 Plot a bar graph of the rainfall figures for Broken Hill.
2 Draw a horizontal line to show the average rainfall (257 mm).
3 How many years have received i) above average, and ii) below average rainfall over the 20-year period?
4 Assume that drought conditions exist at Broken Hill if the annual rainfall is less than 173 mm. How often has this occurred in the years 1954–73?

The data in Figure 8.18 shows figures for crop production and summer rainfall over a six-year period in South Australia. Plot the crop figures as lines and the rainfall figures as bars on the same graph. Describe the relationship between the two sets of data on the graph.

Summer Rainfall (mm) (October – March)	Wheat	Crop Production Barley	(million bushels) Hay
268	33	13	368
282	50	19	729
162	22	7	418
430	79	21	985
281	56	18	608
312	42	21	740

Figure 8.18   South Australia: rainfall and crop production for six summers

Overcoming the problems

A number of ways of overcoming the problems of drought have been tried in Australia, and in most areas several methods are used together. These are the major approaches:

Learning to live with it.

Many farmers simply accept that drought may strike and have adapted their farming methods to suit. Typical is farmer Bill Bauer who runs a large wheat and sheep farm in South Australia. Here drought occurs four years in every ten. By saving part of his income each year he can cope with up to two successive drought years. Since 1969 he has also been able to insure himself against losses from droughts. He also uses three farming methods to help:

- He keeps 15% of his land fallow each year. This conserves the moisture in the soil and means that there is always a part of his land where crops can be grown even in drought years.
- In each year he only plants seed after the rains have started. This means that if there is no rain he saves his seed until the following year.
- He uses a lot of machinery to allow seeding to take place very rapidly after the rains have come. This practice allows full use of the moisture as quickly as possible.

Providing drought aid

Most of the state governments provide aid when drought strikes. This help involves bringing in emergency water supplies by road or rail, or transporting livestock to better sources of water. Fodder may also be brought in. The overall cost of these funds is about $A1 per person per year throughout Australia.

Building irrigation schemes

Both the national and state governments of Australia have invested large amounts of money in providing irrigation schemes that can supply water to farmers even in drought years. Typical is the Snowy Mountains Scheme which takes water from the Snowy Mountains in the Great Dividing Range to the dry lands in the west. High rainfall (more than 1500 mm) in the mountains used to feed the rivers which flowed south and east, but, by building ten reservoirs (e.g. Lake Eucumbene) and many tunnels, the water is now transferred westward into the River Murray and River Murrumbidgee. From these rivers the water is used to irrigate large areas of arid land.

As with most countries, Australia has had to learn to live with drought, for it is simply a natural part of the continent's variable climate. By adopting suitable farming techniques, and by building irrigation schemes, the impact of drought can be lessened. As a developed country, Australia can afford the necessary technology. In developing countries advanced schemes can be built only with the help of foreign aid or loans. More often, the lack of ready money means that much needed schemes are simply not begun.

Key Points: Climatic Hazards

● The power of the atmosphere is so huge that there is little people can do to control its more extreme moments.

● Coping with climatic hazards very often means being able to pay for the damage they cause. The most vulnerable countries are those that can least afford to pay for repairs and rebuilding.

● Farming is the main sector of nations' economies at risk from pronounced changes in the weather. In less developed countries, where up to 70 per cent of the people may be involved in farming, the effects of unexpectedly harsh changes are particularly severe.

● Accurate forecasting and adequate emergency planning are the only two reliable ways at present of minimising climatic hazard disruption.

● Human activity may be the cause of long- and short-term variations in the climate and weather.

INDEX